Early Rangers of Glacier National Park

David R. Butler

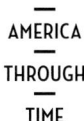

America Through Time
Fonthill Media Inc.
www.through-time.com

First published 2025
Copyright © David R. Butler 2025

ISBN 978-1-62545-158-3

All rights reserved. No part of this publication may be reproduced, stored in a retrieval system or transmitted in any form or by any means, electronic, mechanical, photocopying, recording or otherwise, without prior permission in writing from Fonthill Media Inc.

Typeset in 10pt on13pt Sabon
Printed and bound in England

Contents

Acknowledgments 4
Introduction 5

    1 Ranger Danger 9
    2 Rangers in the Pre-Park Period (1900–1910) 16
    3 The First Decade of Glacier Park Rangers 23
    4 Glacier Park Rangers of the 1920s and 1930s 39
    5 Glacier Park Ranger Stations Past and Present 51
    6 Glacier's Backcountry Patrol/Snowshoe Cabins 86

Endnotes 117
Bibliography 123

Acknowledgments

Historic photos used in this book come from a variety of sources. I have tried to be as specific as possible for each photo or image, and any errors in attribution are strictly my own. Sources include GNP, Glacier National Park; NPS, National Park Service; OHSL, Oregon Historical Society Library; USFS, United States Forest Service; and USGS, United States Geological Survey.

Thanks to Don Stolte for the use of the photos of the Arrow Lake Snowshoe Cabin, taken by his cousin, Jerry Stolte, and for sharing his remembrances of their trips to Arrow Lake and the snowshoe cabin.

Deep appreciation is offered to Leslie Lee, who allowed me to use photos and information about her grandfather, Ranger Norton Pearl. Her 1910s-era map of park ranger stations and backcountry/snowshoe cabins was also extremely helpful. The front cover photo of this book was graciously provided by Leslie Lee, and subsequently colorized by the publisher.

My thanks are extended to the good folks at Fonthill Media, the editorial and publishing team that worked with me in creating this book, especially Alan Sutton, Kena Longabaugh Smith, and Joshua Greenland. It is a pleasure to work with such professionals.

Finally, thanks as always to my family and friends. They accompanied me on many visits to Glacier National Park.

Introduction

Glacier National Park, in northwest Montana along the Canadian border with Alberta, was formed by an Act of Congress in May 1910. The area was near-wilderness, and through the 1920s no roads penetrated more than a few miles into the park from the surrounding areas. The only access from the west to east (or vice versa) side of the park was via the Great Northern Railway, connecting the new Park Headquarters in Belton (today's West Glacier) on the west with Glacier Park Station (today's East Glacier Park) on the east.

With the completion of U.S. Highway 2 in 1930, and the Going-to-the-Sun Road across the park from Apgar to St. Mary, the park became somewhat more accessible for park rangers and visitors alike. Nonetheless, through the 1930s, the park remained a distant destination, characterized by unpaved roads, vast areas of wilderness, and limited numbers of visitors. Rangers during this time continued the tradition of the previous decades, working year-round and conducting extensive patrols via foot or horseback in the summer, and by (primarily) snowshoe in the winter. Rangers were expected to patrol roughly 300 miles per month in their assigned territories, an average of 10 miles a day, rain/snow or shine, year-round.

Prior to the creation of Glacier Park in 1910, the area was administered by the U.S. Forest Service, who assigned forest rangers to patrol the area, primarily to watch out for and attempt to prevent poaching of fur-bearing animals. The rangers of this pre-park period dressed much like any western frontiersman of the time, identified as a forest ranger by a simple badge. Ranger uniforms did not come around until after the creation of Glacier National Park. The first authorized uniforms were received in the park in June 1911, and they looked very similar to military uniforms of the time. Ranger uniforms evolved over the years to become less military-like and recognizable as the familiar ranger uniforms of today.[1]

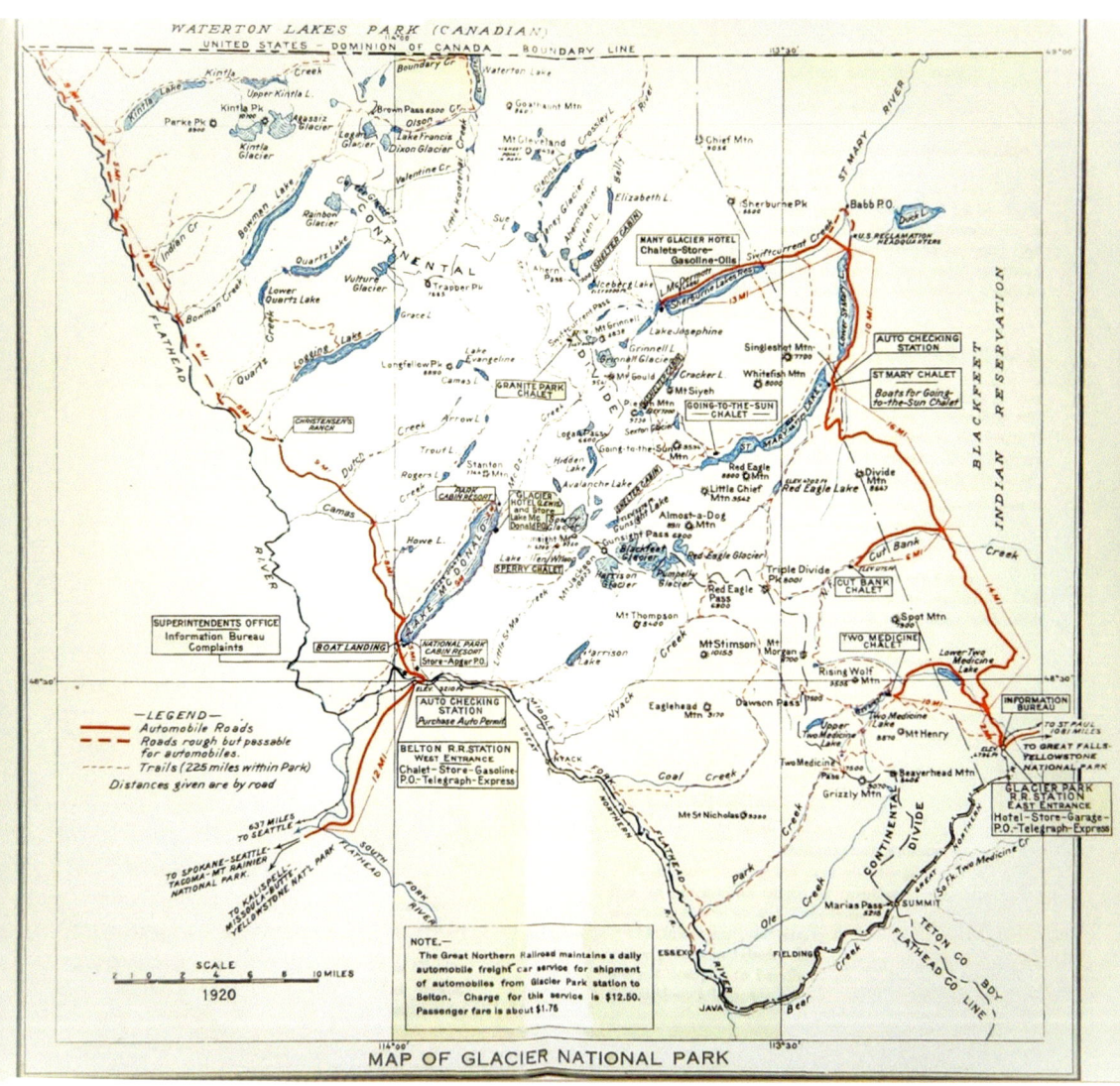

National Park Service Map of Glacier National Park in 1920, illustrating the limited number of roads in the pre-Park and early Park era. Belton (today's West Glacier) and Glacier Park (today's East Glacier) were connected only by the Great Northern Railway. No road existed between Lake McDonald on the west side of the Park and St. Mary on the east side, and the Inside North Fork Road east of the North Fork of the Flathead River was extremely crude and rough (conditions that exist to this day). (NPS)

Introduction

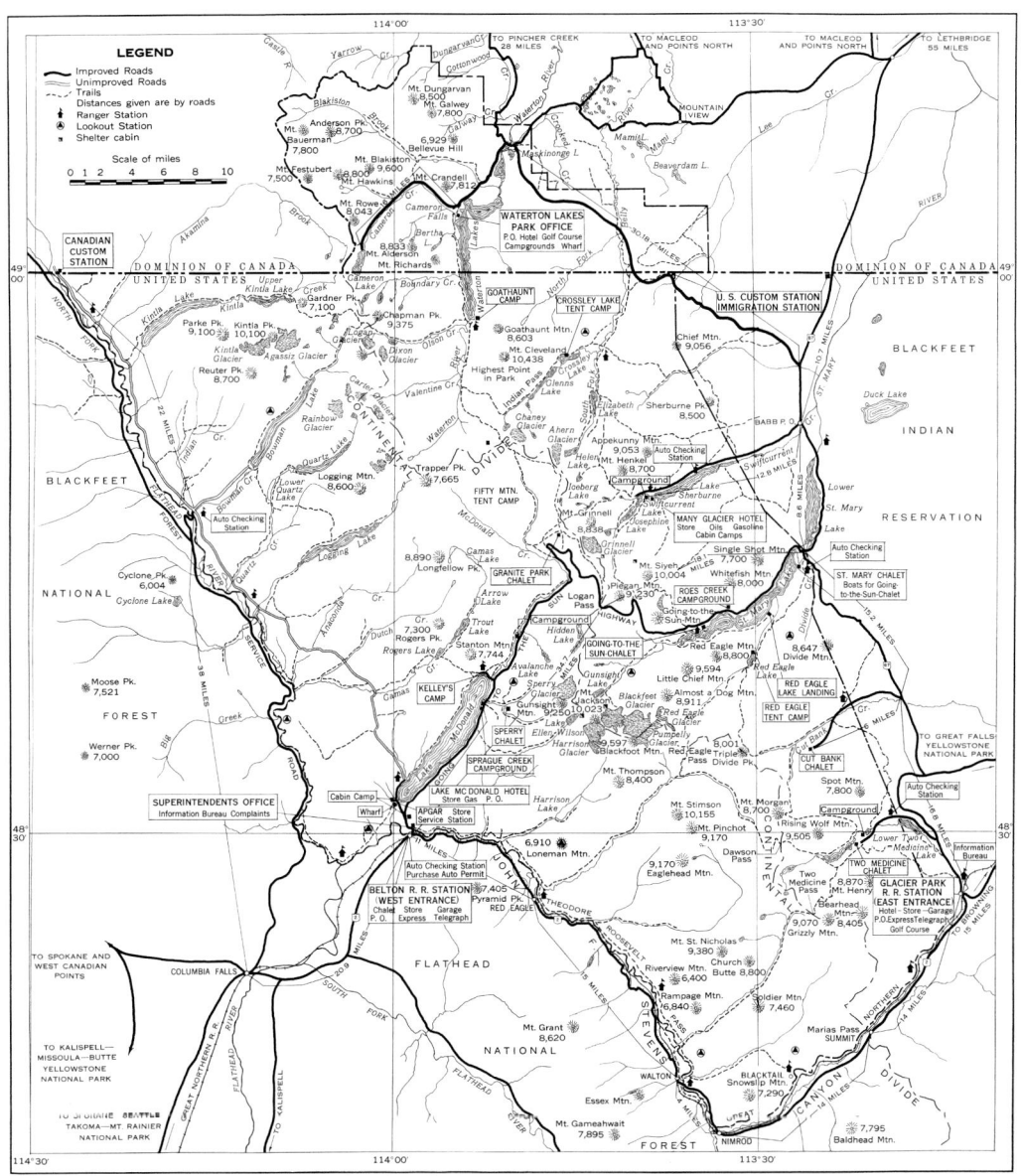

MAP OF WATERTON-GLACIER INTERNATIONAL PEACE PARK

National Park Service Map of Glacier National Park as the roads existed *circa* 1940. The Going-to-the-Sun Road connecting Apgar on Lake McDonald with St. Mary on the eastern Park boundary was completed and dedicated in 1933. The Chief Mountain International Highway, northwest of Babb, connecting Glacier National Park with Waterton Lakes National Park in Alberta, Canada, was completed in the summer of 1936. By this time, the Outside North Fork Road, west of the Park paralleling the North Fork of the Flathead River, was also complete to the Canadian border. (*NPS*)

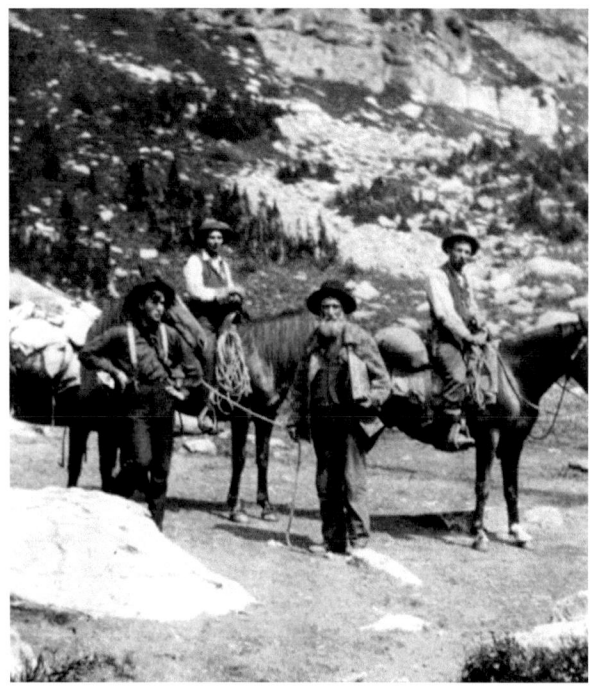

Early rangers in the Flathead Forest Reserve of the U.S. Forest Service, 1905, in what was to become Glacier National Park in May 1910. They did not yet have any form of standardized uniform. Shown here are two Forest Service rangers, Albert Reynolds (second from right) and Frank Liebig (far right) and their assistants. Both rangers are discussed in subsequent chapters. (*GNP, photographer unknown*)

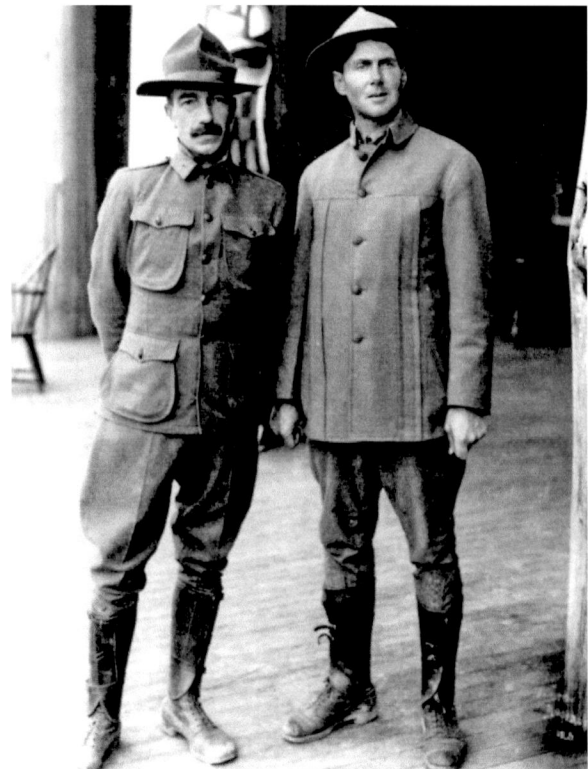

This photo compares the first authorized park ranger uniform in Glacier Park, *circa* 1911, on the man on the right, with a 1910 U.S. Army uniform worn by the man on the left. The two men are unidentified. (*Photographer unknown, GNP GLAC 9638*)

1
Ranger Danger

Up until approximately the start of World War II, park rangers patrolled Glacier Park year-round. Prior to park creation in 1910, rangers working for the U.S. Forest Service did the same thing. Regardless of the administrative framework and period within which a ranger worked (pre-Park, from Park creation until 1916 when the National Park Service (NPS) was created, and post-NPS creation), the job duties remained largely the same throughout the early 1900s to 1940. And those jobs were dangerous.

Early rangers had to patrol vast areas of the park, in the range of hundreds of square miles. Their duties consisted of watching for fires in the summer and poachers year-round but especially in the winter when animal furs and pelts were at their lushest. They assisted the occasional tourist, although early annual park visitation numbers were only in the tens of thousands until the completion of Going-to-the-Sun Road in 1933. They were involved in censusing various animal species, and in this period control (i.e. killing) of predators such as mountain lions, wolves, and coyotes was a primary duty. They put out feed for deer, elk, and mountain sheep herds (obviously a very different philosophy than today!) that were deemed "desirable" species. And as part of all these various duties, they patrolled their territories on foot, on horseback, on snowshoes, and on skis.

Among the potential dangers faced by early rangers were wild animals, extreme weather, sickness and injury, snow avalanches, cold fast-flowing waters, frozen rivers and lakes, fighting fires, encountering armed poachers, and isolation over long periods. A seemingly innocuous event on patrol could quickly and easily prove fatal.

Wild animals could and sometimes did prove dangerous to early rangers. Interestingly, few encounters with either black or grizzly bears are reported in ranger logbooks or reports; the same may be said for mountain lions or wolves. Rangers were more likely to be threatened by intransigent moose or elk refusing to yield the trail than by the animals with sharp teeth and claws. For example, while on patrol near Slide Lake near the northeast corner of Glacier Park, Ranger Channing Powell and his wife were charged and threatened by a bull elk. In December 1925, Ranger Clyde Fauley was charged and treed by a bull elk in the Muir Creek valley of southwestern Glacier Park. Ranger Ben Miller was treed by a displaced bull moose a mile below Bowman Lake. Ranger Hugh

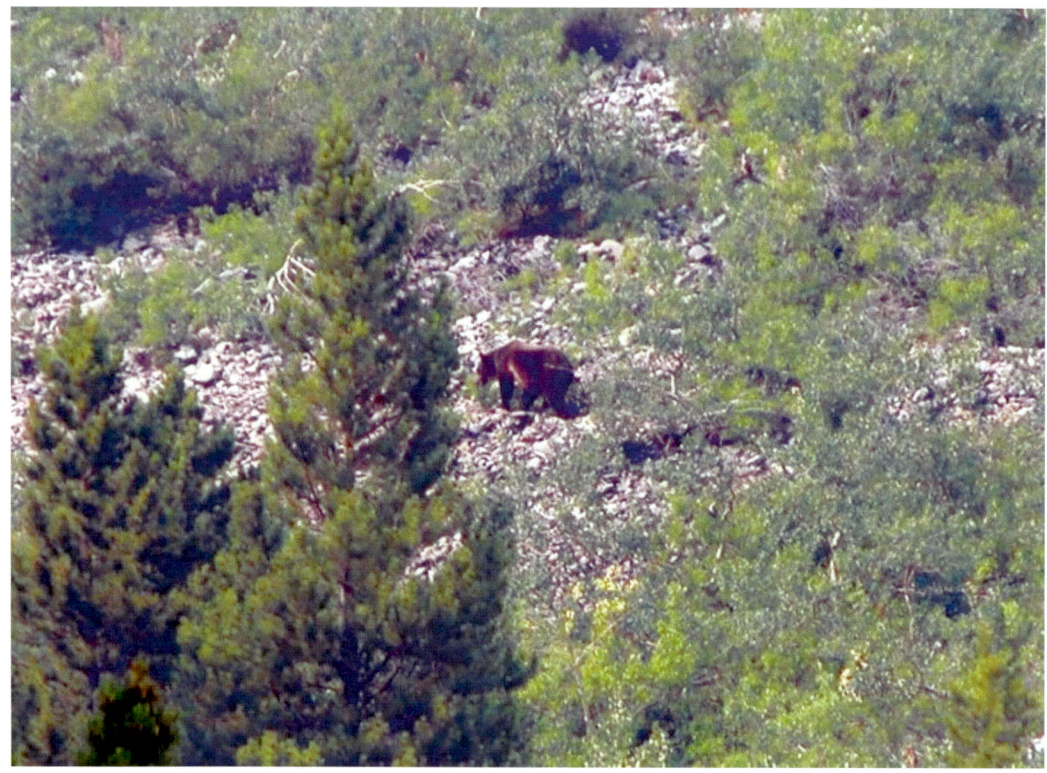

Dangerous animals were an ongoing background threat to early park rangers on patrol. Here, a grizzly bear crosses a snow-avalanche path in the Swiftcurrent valley on the northeast side of Glacier National Park. Photo taken July 28, 2003. (*Photo by author*)

Buchanan and his wife also encountered a pugnacious bull moose while riding on the trail through Rogers Meadow. The moose refused to yield the trail, causing the couple to wait half an hour for the moose to move on. In a perhaps unusual case, a mother ruffed grouse, in the act of protecting a clutch of eggs along the Coal Creek trail in the southern part of the park, flew up in the face of Ranger Miller's horse and caused the startled horse to rear and nearly displace the ranger onto the trail.[1, 2, 3, 4, 5]

Extreme cold was a danger to patrolling rangers every winter. One ranger, Joe Prince, died in January 1913 while snowshoeing from Cut Bank Ranger Station to St. Mary and the ranger station there. He was traveling with Superintendent James L. Galen, who insisted that Prince accompany him in spite of the extreme cold, and one other ranger (Norton Pearl, discussed in Chapter 3 of this book). Prince fell behind in order to adjust his snowshoe bindings, and eventually Galen and the other ranger noticed that Prince was no longer in sight. Backtracking, they found Prince's frozen body sitting on the ground against a tree. Some question exists whether Prince died of the cold or of a heart attack (he was seventy years old, an advanced age for a ranger!), but when the superintendent and accompanying ranger found Prince's body, it was already frozen solid, suggesting that the weather may indeed have been the cause.[6]

In addition to the cold of winter, deep snow challenged the winter patrols of early rangers. Snowshoes and skies were necessities, their usage depending upon the differing snow conditions and depth. Frequently, the snow became too deep and/or drifted for use by either snowshoes or skis. If such conditions happened while out on winter patrol, the results could prove fatal.[7]

Hand-in-hand with winter snow was the ever-present threat of snow avalanches in the steeper terrain areas of the park. Ranger Ben Miller, stationed at the Walton Ranger Station in the southernmost part of the park, nearly perished in a February 1933 snow avalanche:

> While snowshoeing on Scalplock Mountain in February I was caught in a snowslide, rolled unceremoniously down the slopes, and buried completely under a foot of snow. The snow was packed so hard that I could scarcely move a muscle; the pack on my back as well as the snowshoes tied securely to my feet aggravated the seriousness of my situation.
>
> Only after frantic tugging did I succeed in extricating myself from my pack and begin the tedious and tiring task of persistently hacking away the snow with a hand axe. During the night I heard dogs barking in the town of Walton, only two miles away, but

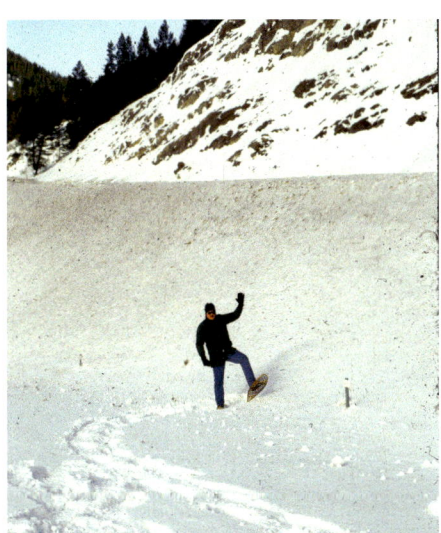
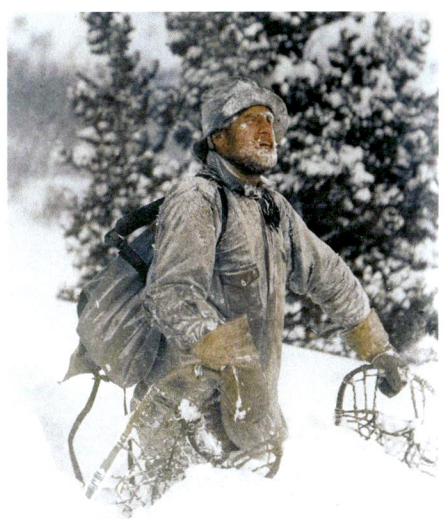

Above left: Early park rangers were expected to make year-round patrols of their districts, regardless of the weather and snow conditions. Snowshoes were an important part of the equipment used by these rangers, and they worked fine in tightly packed or shallow snow conditions. (*Photo of author in the Goat Lick Parking Lot on the southern end of Glacier Park, taken by Stephen J. Walsh, January 15, 1993*)

Above right: Unfortunately, when the snow became too deep or too soft, snowshoes were of little use to early park rangers. Here, Ranger Norton Pearl became "snowed up." Foot, especially heel, blisters were also common when snowshoeing, as was frostbite of the toes. (*Photographer unattributed, photo taken in February 1913. Photo courtesy of Leslie Lee, granddaughter of Norton Pearl*)

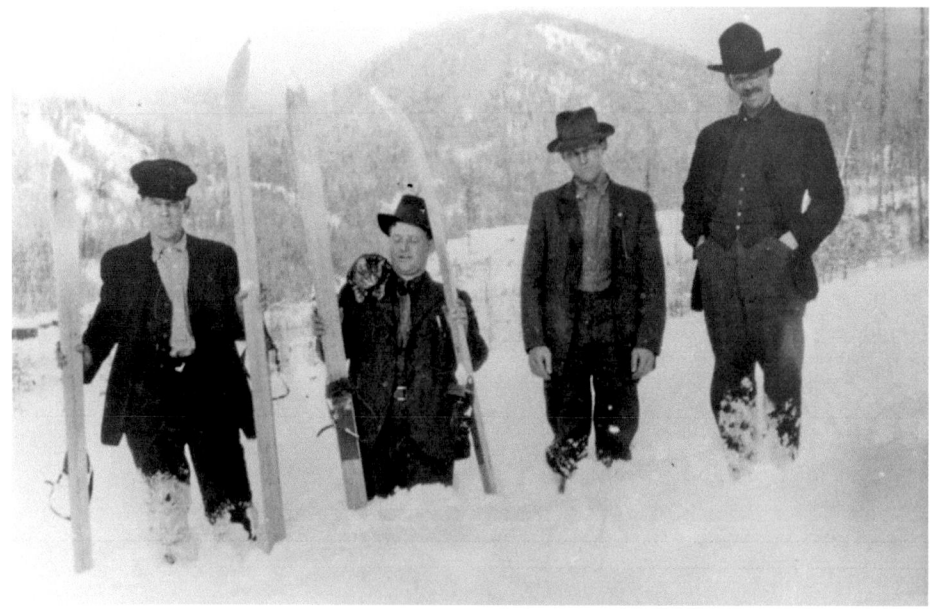

Four men in deep snow around Belton (West Glacier), *circa* 1920s. Two men hold old wooden skis rendered largely useless by the unpacked, deep, and loose snow. Third from right is Halvor Lee, Glacier Park ranger from 1926–1930. (*Photographer unknown, GNP GLAC HPF 9820*)

no one apparently heard my calls for help. Many a long hour passed before I could call myself free, for the slide occurred at 10:30 one morning and not until 11:30 of the next did I resume my journey.[8]

Ranger Miller's travails were not finished when he extricated himself from the avalanche deposit. He still had to hike back to the Walton Ranger Station. And disaster struck once again, as described in his own words:

The trail back to the station was so deep with snow that I had to walk on the frozen surface of the Flathead river. Twenty-four hours of burial should be full share of trouble for one man, but the ice broke and plunged me into the freezing water. Fortunately I was near the shore, and the water not deep. I crawled out and managed to cover in an hour the final two miles into the station.[9]

Ranger Miller was not the only ranger susceptible to falling through ice-covered waters. Ranger Clyde Fauley reported, in addition to frequently seeing elk broken through lake ice and drowned or frozen, that he had himself broken through the ice and received frigid dunking in both Harrison and Two Medicine Lakes.[10]

Amazingly, perhaps, no serious injuries were reported from episodes where rangers were involved in fighting forest fires, fording rivers, or encountering armed poachers. Nonetheless, these activities no doubt called for extreme caution, and for those rangers who were married, it engendered great anxiety in their spouses (although note the cautionary

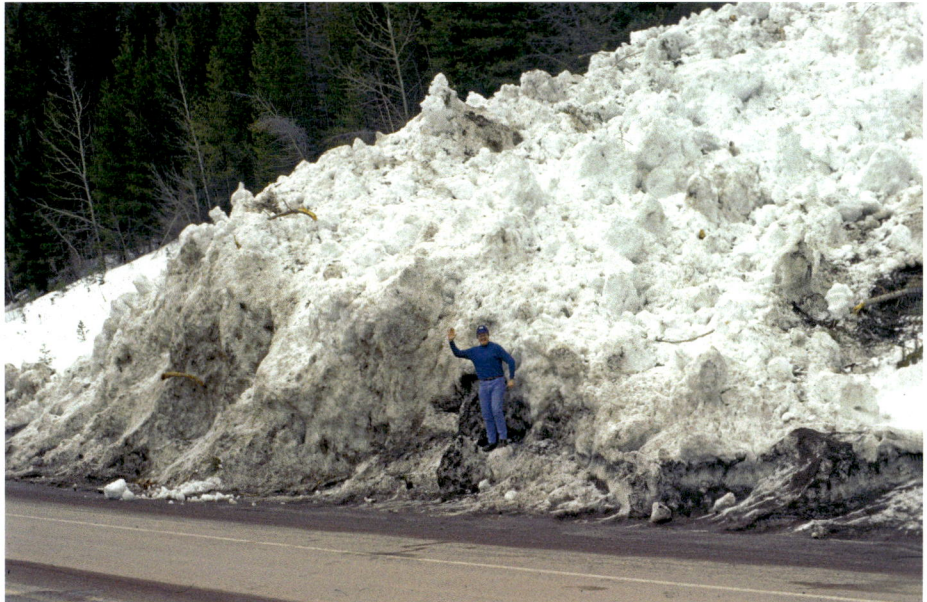

Snow avalanches posed a constant threat in the steep terrain of the park to patrolling rangers during winter and into early spring. This snow avalanche had blocked U.S. Highway 2 (in lower foreground) for a twenty-four-hour period in February 1995, until cleared by snowplows. (*Author photo, taken by Dr. Forrest Wilkerson, February 5, 1995*)

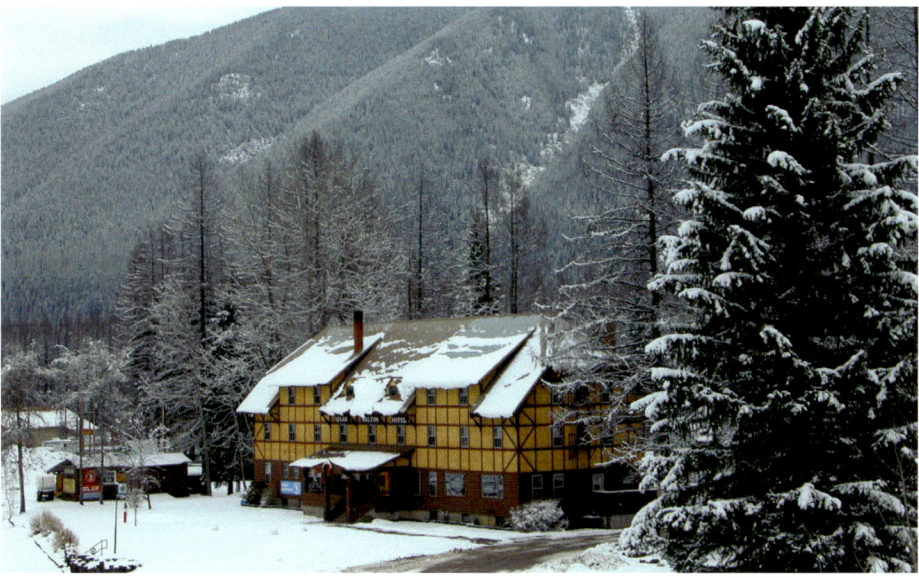

A view of Scalplock Mountain in southern Glacier National Park, behind the Izaak Walton Inn at Essex. A snow avalanche path descends from near the top of the mountain to near its base at right center. A patrolling park ranger was caught by a snow avalanche at this location in the winter of 1933, but luckily survived. (*Photo by author, taken March 17, 2005*)

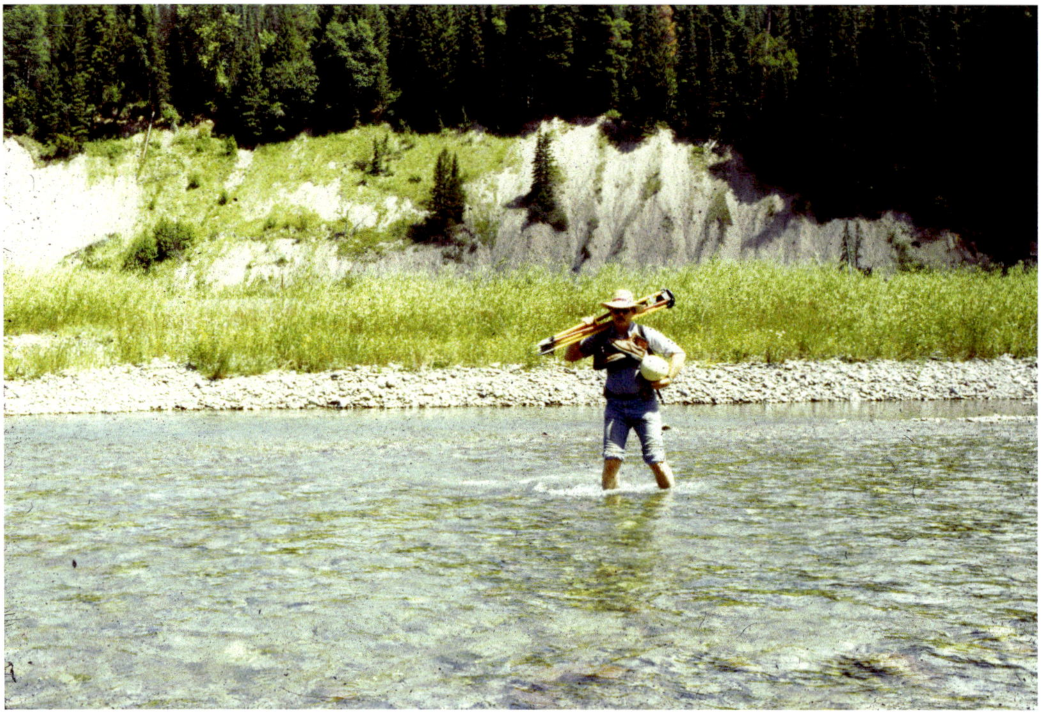

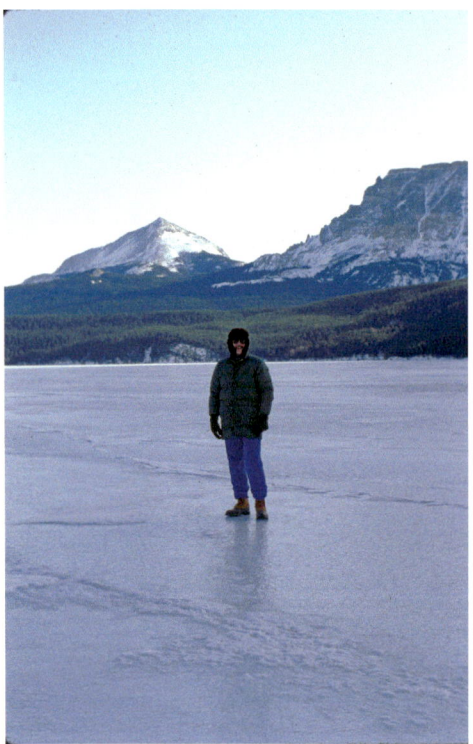

Above: Fording the cold glacial-fed rivers and streams of Glacier National Park posed a constant threat to patrolling rangers. A slip into the water could quickly lead to hypothermia and an inability to continue, possibly leading to death. Here, the author fords the Middle Fork of the Flathead River along the southwest boundary of Glacier National Park on July 17, 1988. (*Photo taken for author by Dr. George P. Malanson*)

Left: Frozen lakes, rivers, and streams posed a serious threat to patrolling rangers who would gingerly attempt to cross the frozen surfaces. Numerous accounts of rangers breaking through the ice to be plunged into the frigid waters underneath exist. Rangers also reported large animals such as elk were observed to have broken through lake ice and died. Here, the author is on the frozen surface of St. Mary Lake on the eastern side of Glacier National Park, near Rising Sun, below The Narrows. (*Photo for the author taken January 16, 1993, by Dr. Stephen J. Walsh*)

tale concerning Frank Liebig described in the next chapter). Springtime ice break-up on the Middle and North Fork of the Flathead Rivers also posed a danger to those caught unaware. Our friend Ranger Miller reported on an enormous ice jam caused by thawing on the North Fork, resulting in the loss of the pole bridge over the river by the Polebridge Ranger Station:

> The old bridge that spanned the north fork of the Flathead River in front of Bowman Ranger Station was destroyed in the evening of February 28 by a large ice jam. My wife and I were the only eye-witnesses to the destruction. Jumbled cakes of ice filled the river from bank to bank as far as the eye could see. First, the middle pier was swept away; the pier on the Park side followed; then the whole bridge sagged in the middle, listed, was caught on the crest of the onrushing flood of ice and water. With a crashing and splintering of timbers, the whole structure was swept away, having lasted only ten minutes after the first impact.[11]

Fortunately for Ranger and Mrs. Miller, they were not on the bridge at the time of the destruction of the bridge.

Injury was, nevertheless, a constant possibility for the year-round rangers. Probably the most serious injury in this period occurred during a late autumn/early winter patrol in the far northeastern region of Glacier Park. Ranger Elmer Ness, apparently a man of little embellishment, described his ordeal from November 1933 as reported by Chief Naturalist George Ruhle:

> On the fifteenth of November while crossing Gable Pass the writer slipped on a snow bank and slid into a rock with such force that a badly sprained hip was the result. Unable to walk without support of some kind, the writer crawled to the nearest timber, a half-mile away. Two small limber pines were cut and used for crutches. With this aid the remaining three miles were made to the station by the afternoon of the seventeenth. Built a fire and camped each night.[12]

Chief Naturalist Ruhle noted that Ness was wracked and emaciated beyond recognition by his wife upon dragging himself to the Belly River Ranger Station.

One other underrated factor affected park rangers during their year-round duties, especially those at the most isolated ranger stations—loneliness. As reported by historian Mark Hufstetler:

> In the winter of 1925–26, Kishenehn's ranger was a young man named William McAfee, a Texan who had relocated to Montana and settled on a homestead near Trail Creek. The winter isolation took its toll on McAfee, as did a failed relationship with someone he described only as "the kid." Things grew worse when the Park Service laid him off due to a lack of funds while still asking him to remain at the station for the winter until he could be recalled to duty. On January 13, 1926, McAfee wrote to a friend in Kalispell: "You know, take it all in all, there are many disadvantages to a job of this kind. You know what I mean. A fellow is shut out from the out side world too much and at times the lonesomeness is almost maddening. So I am thinking very much of quitting the Park Service for good." McAfee's depression apparently worsened in the weeks that followed, and on February 7 he stepped outside the Kishenehn station and shot himself in the head with his service revolver. Local ranchers discovered the suicide soon after and telephoned the news to park headquarters.[13]

2
Rangers in the Pre-Park Period (1900–1910)

Prior to the creation of Glacier National Park in May 1910, the park was patrolled by forest rangers in the employ of the U.S. Forest Service. These men were few and far between, patrolling vast areas year-round. A few of these men transitioned and became park rangers after the creation of the national park in 1910, and those rangers are examined in the next chapter. Here, I focus on three well-known forest rangers who did not become park rangers after May 1910.

Frank Geduhn

Frank Geduhn, German born, arrived in the Flathead valley in 1894 and was one of the first settlers in Apgar at the foot of Lake McDonald. Although originally settling at the foot of Lake McDonald, he soon moved to a homestead at the head of the lake on the western side of where McDonald Creek flows into the lake. Geduhn built several cabins for tourists, but also somehow found time to serve as a forest ranger in the late 1890s and early 1900s.[1]

Geduhn patrolled from Lake McDonald to Waterton Lake, on the west side of the mountains. He was particularly fond of the area around Logging Lake. Mt. Geduhn, located at the head of the Logging Lake valley, is named in his honor.

Geduhn also knew and worked with other west-side Forest Service rangers. In 1902 or 1903, Geduhn combined with rangers Frank Liebig and Fred Herrig to chase a band of Cree indigenous Canadians who were hunting moose up the North Fork back across the border into Canada.[2]

Rangers in the Pre-Park Period (1900–1910)

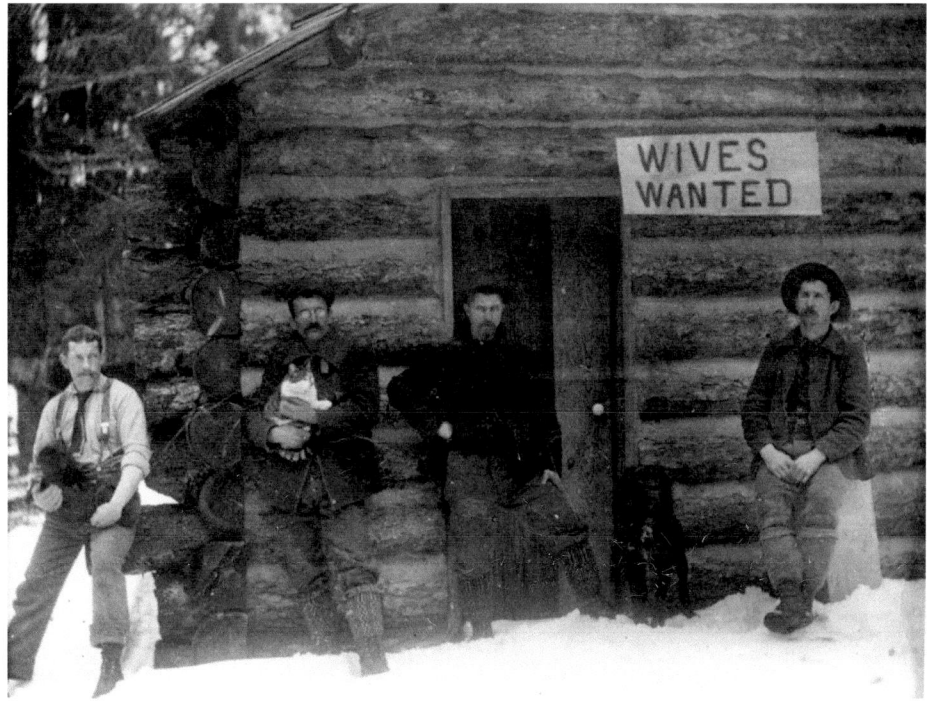

Frank Geduhn, early Forest Service ranger, on the west side of what would become Glacier National Park, second from left holding a cat, *circa* 1901. Left to right, the other men are Bill Daucks, Esli Apgar, and Harvey Dimon Apgar. Photo taken in Apgar, at the foot of Lake McDonald. (*Photographer unknown, GNP HPF 9871*)

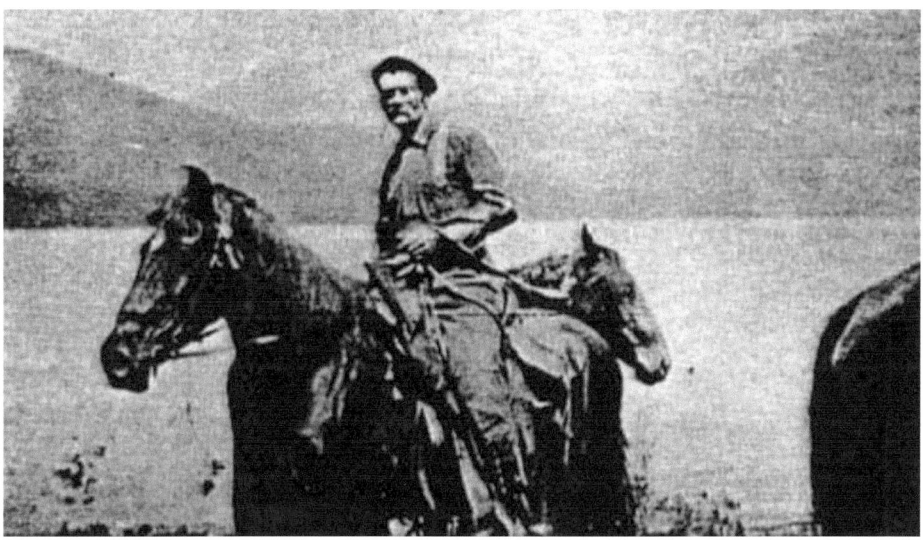

Frank Geduhn at the foot of Logging Lake on the west side of what would become Glacier National Park, *circa* 1907. (*GNP, photographer unattributed*)

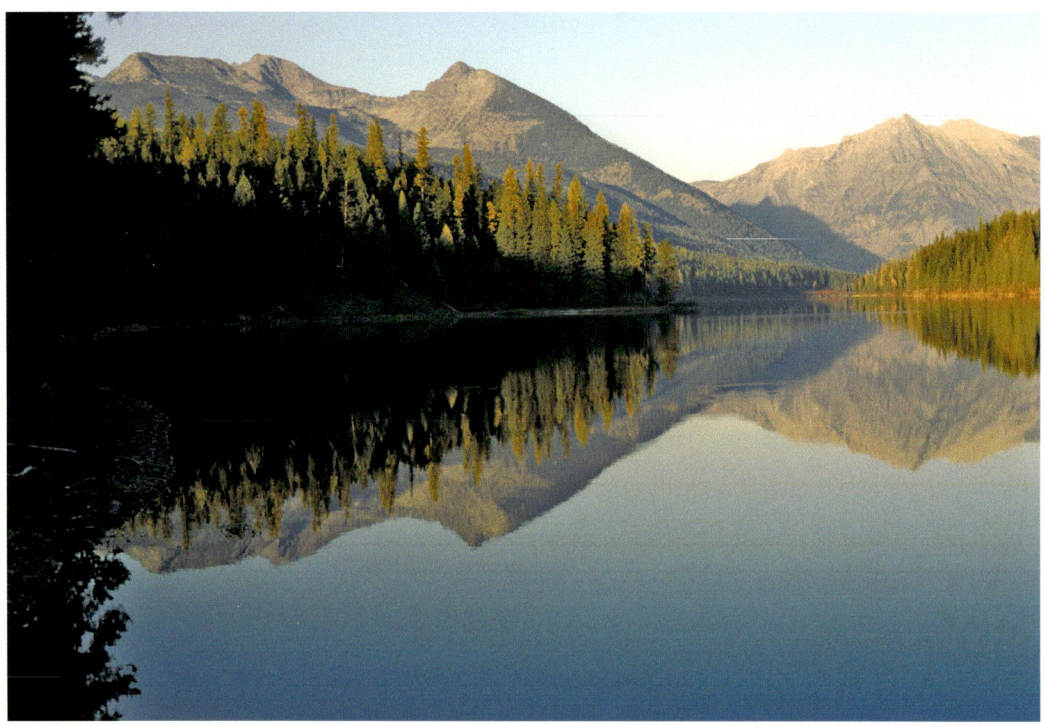

Logging Lake, and Mt. Geduhn at upper right, east of the Inside North Fork Road on what is now the west side of Glacier National Park. (*NPS, public domain photograph, photographer unattributed*)

Frank Liebig

Prior to the formation of Glacier National Park, the first and most prominent ranger was Frank Liebig, forest ranger for the Flathead Forest Reserve. Liebig's area of responsibility, which began with his appointment in 1902, covered roughly two-thirds of the acreage of today's park, from the Canadian border to south of St. Mary Lake, and from the North Fork of the Flathead River eastward to the western boundary of the Blackfeet Reservation. He lived in a cabin at the head of Lake McDonald, designated the Mount Stanton Ranger Station, roughly where the current Lake McDonald Ranger Station is located at the head of Lake McDonald.[3]

The winter of 1906–1907 was extremely cold with very heavy snow, making patrolling from his ranger station impossible for Liebig. He moved into Kalispell for the winter, close to the forest reserve headquarters, where he rented a house. Frank fell in love with Lulu May McMahon, the landlord's eldest daughter. Their romance blossomed, and they were married on June 6, 1907. After a honeymoon at the Belton Hotel, Frank and Lulu took up residence at the Mount Stanton Ranger Station.[4]

Lulu Liebig accompanied Frank on many of his patrols year-round. During forest fires, Lulu would serve as camp cook for the men (including Frank) fighting the fires.

Rangers in the Pre-Park Period (1900–1910)

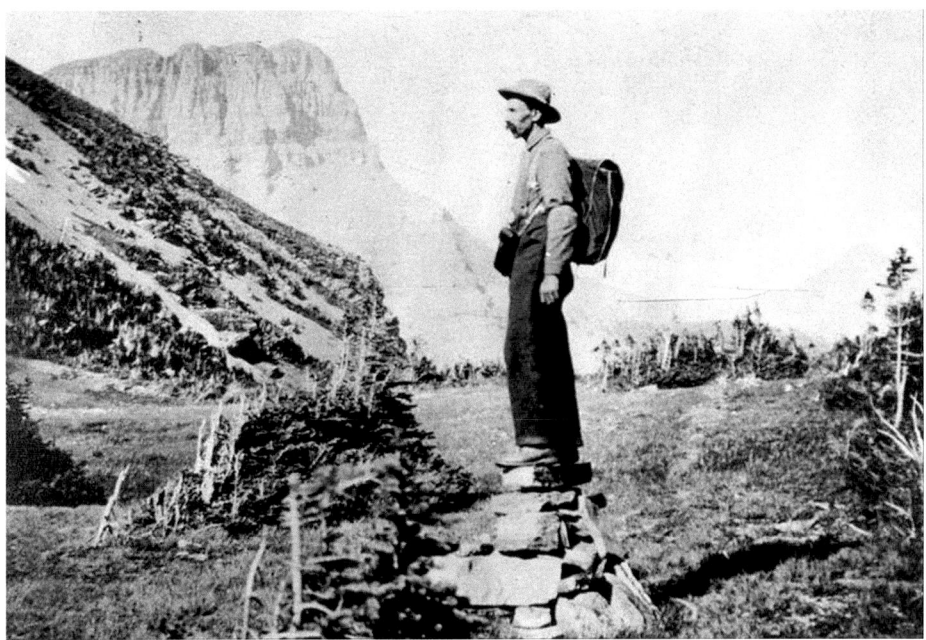

Frank Liebig on the Continental Divide at Swiftcurrent Pass, 1906. Liebig watched for fires from mountain tops and high mountain passes, essentially serving as both a forest ranger and as a firewatcher/fire lookout. (*GNP, photographer unknown*)

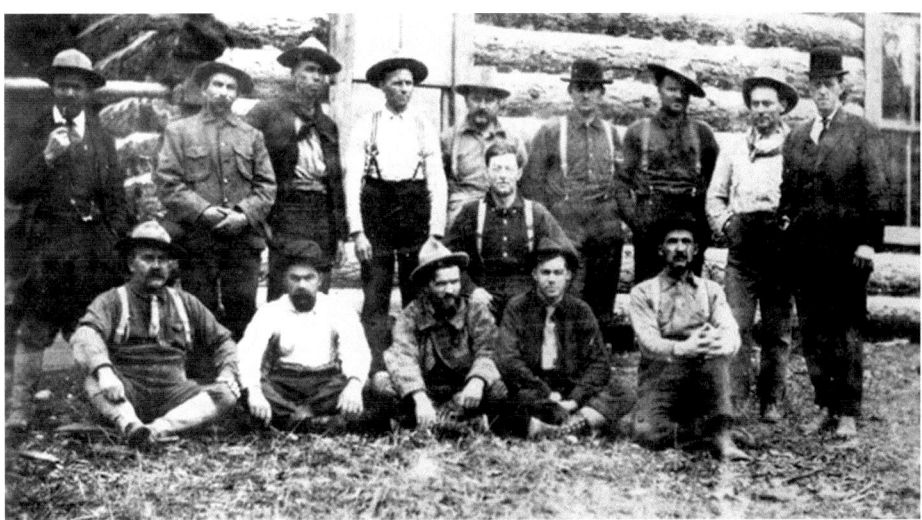

Gathering of U.S. Forest Service rangers in northwest Montana in April 1910. Frank Liebig is standing, second from left. Liebig would routinely climb Stanton Mountain adjacent to his ranger station/cabin on the northwest shore of Lake McDonald to search for smoke indicating a forest fire. Standing next to Liebig, third from left, is Joe Cosley, a famous park ranger in Glacier National Park after its formation in 1910. Cosley served from 1910 to 1914, when he was fired for trapping and poaching furs. (*USFS, photographer unattributed*)

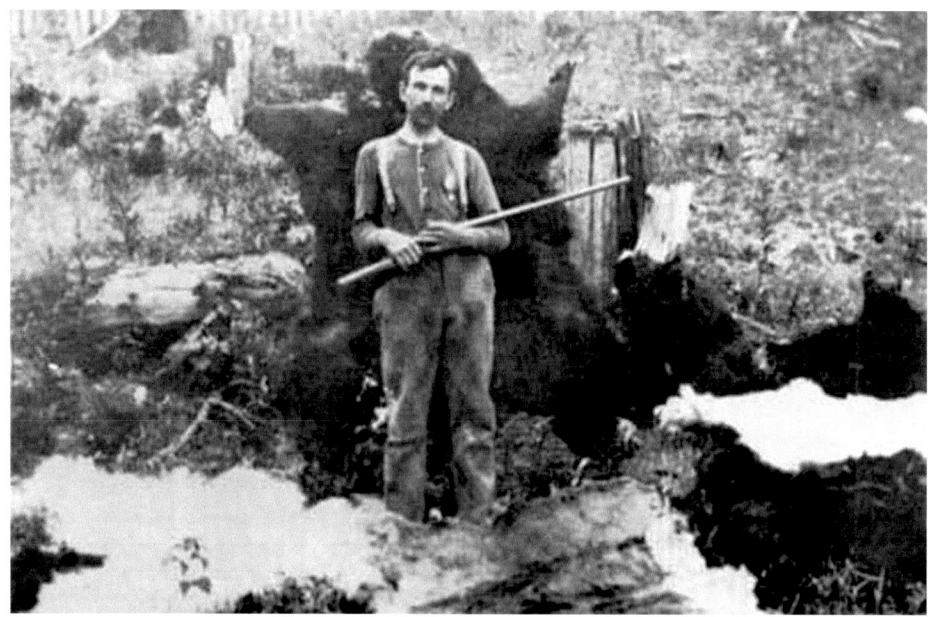

Frank Liebig and trophy furs at one of his cabins, *circa* 1900–1905. Early rangers were expected to hunt "varmints," including wolves, mountain lions, and bears. Liebig was assigned to guard what is essentially the northern two-thirds of present-day Glacier National Park. (*GNP GLAC 6288, photographer unknown*)

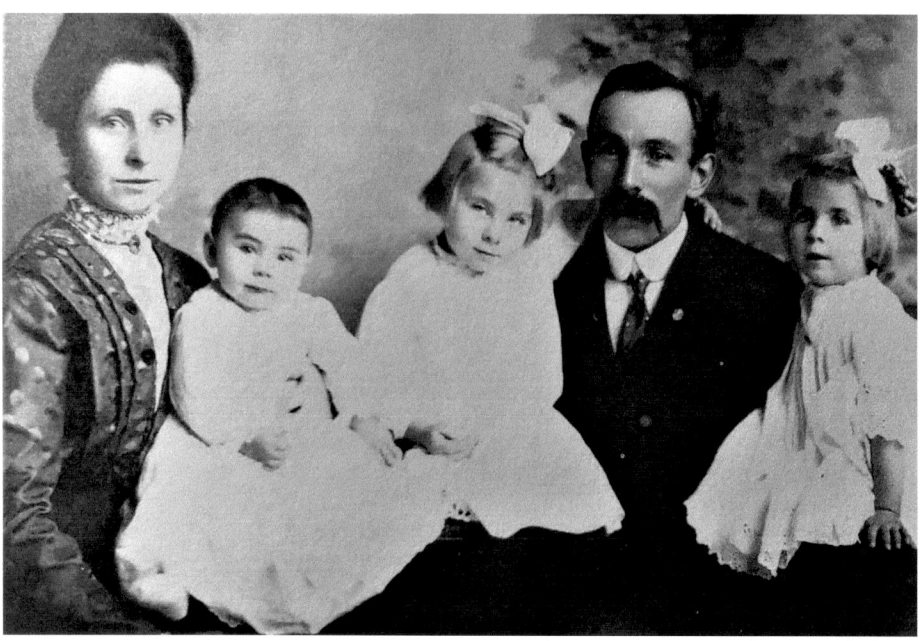

Frank Liebig and his wife Lulu Liebig, with their daughters (left to right) Margaret, Jean, and Frances, 1912 or 1913. (*GNP Archives, Liebig Collection, photographer unknown*)

Two children were born during this period of the Liebigs' residency at the head of Lake McDonald. The young family's life at the Mount Stanton Ranger Station continued until 1910, when Glacier became a national park. Several stories of Liebig's exploits in what became Glacier Park have been masterfully described by historian C. W. Guthrie in the books cited in this book's bibliography.[5]

Fred Herrig

Fred Herrig was born in the Alsace-Lorraine region on the French–German border in 1860 and came to America in 1875. A strong, strapping fellow, from 1893 to 1898 Herrig worked for Teddy Roosevelt's Elkhorn Ranch in North Dakota as a hunting guide. In 1898, Herrig was invited by Roosevelt to join his Rough Riders and Herrig thus embarked on a series of adventures with them during the Spanish-American War. With Roosevelt's subsequent backing, Herrig in 1900 secured the job of forest ranger (known as "range rider" in some circles) in the Upper North Fork district of the Flathead Forest Reserve. Stationed west of the North Fork of the Flathead River, Herrig's duties nonetheless frequently brought him across the river into the northwestern reaches of what is today Glacier National Park.[6]

Herrig's duties up the North Fork brought him into occasional contact with Frank Liebig, and the two became good friends after Liebig became a ranger in 1902. Frequently meeting on one side or the other of the North Fork of the Flathead, they worked together on issues such as poaching and forest fires. In October 1903, Herrig saved Liebig's life. Recall my comments from the previous chapter about wading the icy streams and rivers of Glacier Park. A forest fire was burning on the west side of the North Fork, and Fred Herrig came down to Big Prairie on the east side of the river where he met with Liebig. Liebig's horse had become lame in the journey to Big Prairie, so Liebig had to wade the North Fork to get to the fire west of the river, while Herrig had the luxury of riding his horse across. Sheet ice was floating down the North Fork as a result of recent very cold nights, and Liebig developed leg cramps in the icy water. He started attempting to drag himself to shore when Herrig rode to his rescue to drag him ashore safely. Liebig passed into unconsciousness, and Herrig had to vigorously rub Liebig's legs and body to restore circulation. Fortunately, Liebig recovered and about an hour later they headed to the fire to bring it under control. Soon thereafter, an administrative reorganization of the forest districts in the area sent Herrig west of the Whitefish Range, meaning his interactions with Liebig in the area to become Glacier Park largely came to an end. Herrig continued to serve in the Forest Service until his retirement in 1927.[7]

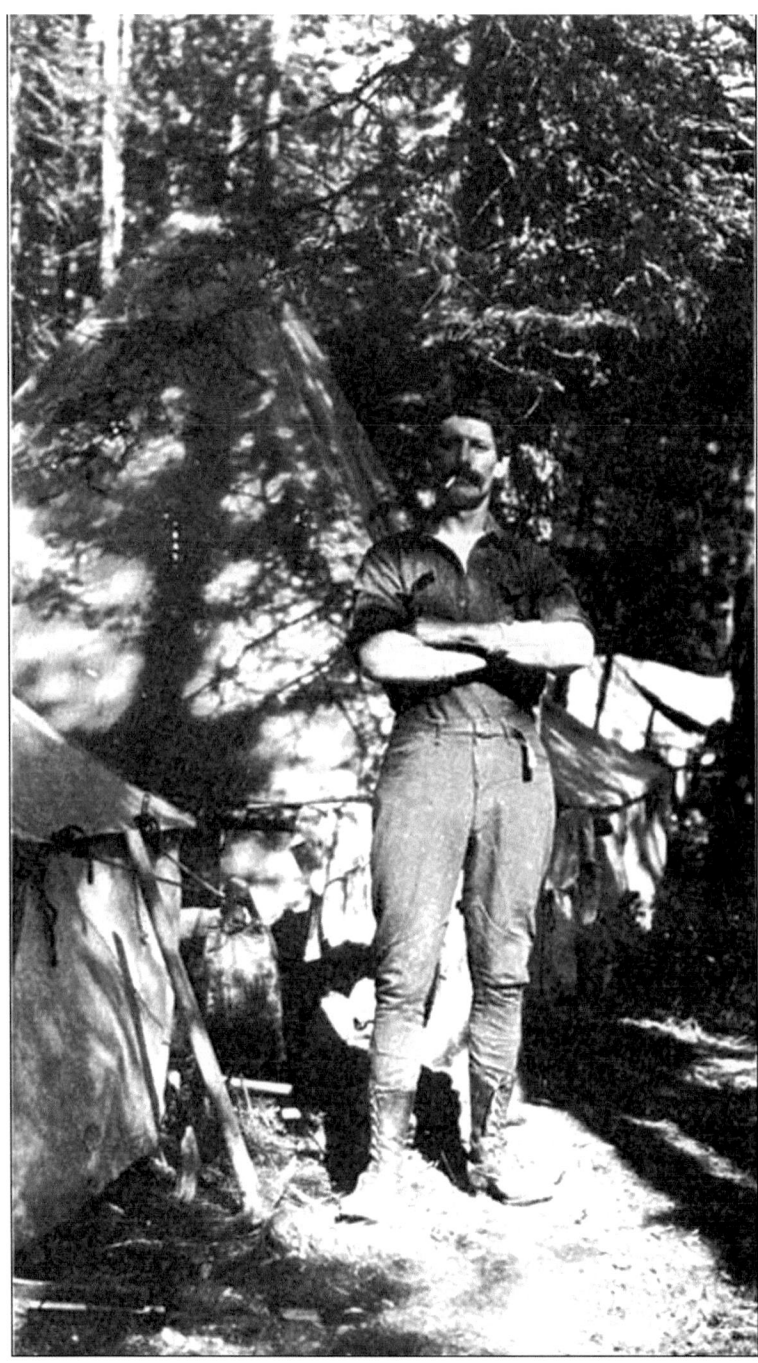

Forest Service Ranger Fred Herrig, who was stationed west of the North Fork of the Flathead River (today's northwestern boundary of Glacier National Park) but who crossed over the river occasionally to work with Frank Liebig in what became Glacier Park. (*NPS, undated, photographer unknown*)

3

The First Decade of Glacier Park Rangers

Glacier National Park was officially established by an Act of Congress on May 11, 1910. Upon park creation, employees of the Forest Service, such as Frank Liebig, no longer held positions in Glacier Park and were reassigned elsewhere. Nonetheless, a handful of early rangers made the transition from serving as a forest ranger to becoming a first-generation park ranger. Details as to why some people like Liebig were not given that opportunity while others were are shrouded in the mists of history. This chapter examines the earliest Park Rangers of Glacier National Park, a few of whom had served the area prior to the park's creation in 1910.

Albert "Death on the Trail" Reynolds

Albert Reynolds was hired as a forest ranger in the pre-park days, in 1901 (see the previous photograph of him with Frank Liebig). He guided U.S. Geological Survey geologist Bailey Willis around northern and central portions of what would become Glacier Park, and Willis's work laid the foundations for the first topographic map of the area. Reynolds looked like an Old Testament prophet straight out of Central Casting, but he was by no means feeble. His nickname, Death on the Trail (sometimes seen as hyphenated), was based on his legendary abilities to "eat up miles" while on snowshoes, and he was said to be able to climb like a mountain sheep.[1, 2, 3]

Reynolds was hired to be a park ranger in Glacier Park in 1910, and he was assigned to the Waterton valley area, at a now-gone station a few miles south of the present-day Goathaunt Ranger Station known as the Camp Creek Ranger Station. Reynolds patrolled throughout the area, and frequently hiked or snowshoed 17 miles northward across the border to visit his counterpart in Waterton Lakes National Park, Alberta (that park was founded in 1895), George "Kootenai" Brown. Brown and Reynolds became good friends, as they were of similar ages and interests. One of their favorite topics of discussion was finding a way to bind Waterton and Glacier together, i.e. their conversations were probably the initial precursors to the drive to establish the Waterton-Glacier International Peace Park, an effort that did not reach fruition until June 18, 1932.[4, 5, 6]

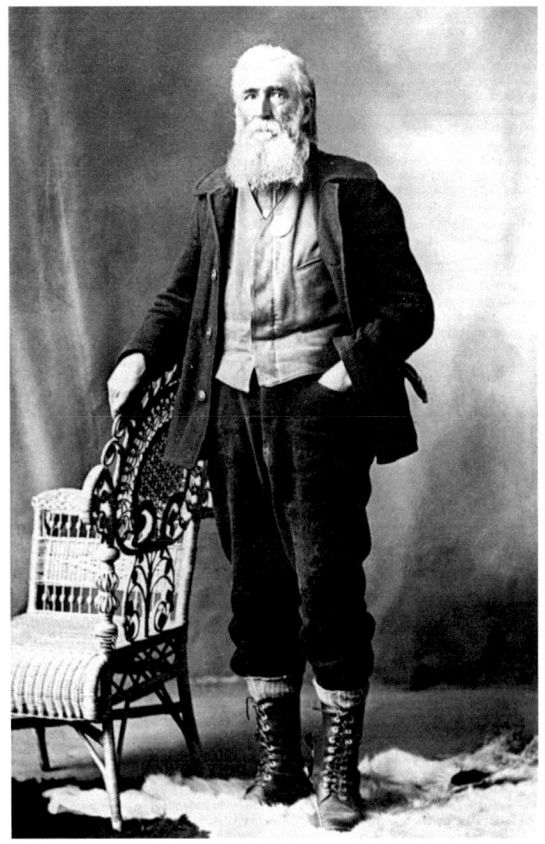

A formal-looking portrait of Albert "Death-on-the-Trail" Reynolds, early ranger who successfully transitioned from serving as a Forest Service ranger prior to 1910 to a Glacier Park Ranger from May 1910 until his death in February 1913. (GNP, *undated and unattributed photo*)

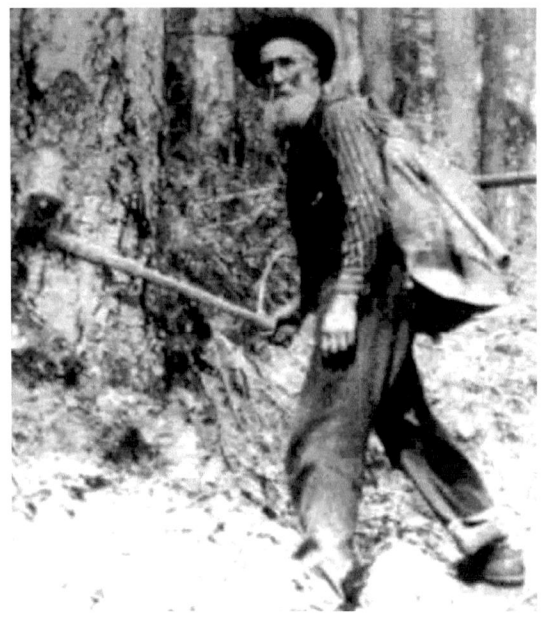

Undated photo of Albert Reynolds at work. (GNP *archives, photographer unknown*)

The First Decade of Glacier Park Rangers

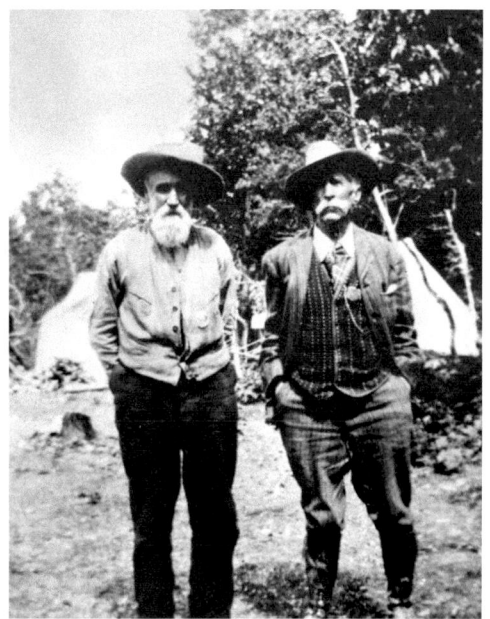

Albert Reynolds with his good friend Kootenai Brown of Waterton Lakes National Park, *circa* 1910. (*University of Calgary Libraries and Cultural Resources Digital Collections CU181036, photographer unknown*)

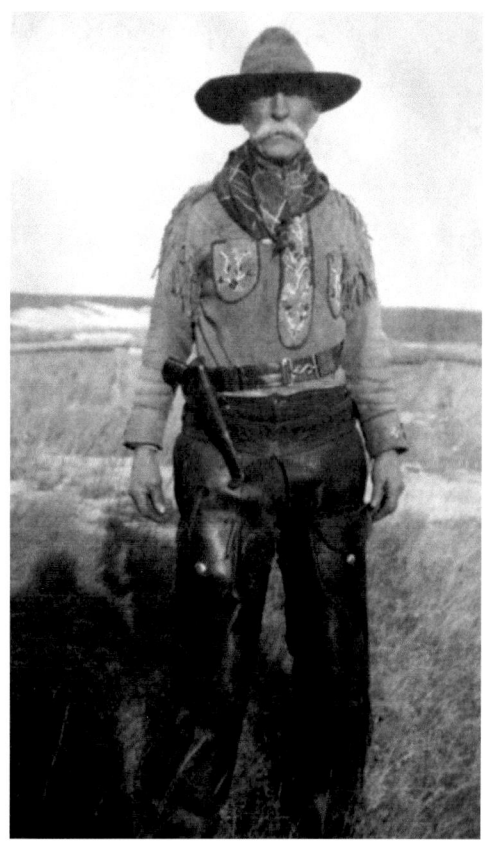

John George "Kootenai" Brown apparently had his long, shoulder-length haircut prior to this undated but likely *circa* 1900–1905 photograph being taken. (*Photographer unknown, Glenbow Library and Archives na-2539-19*)

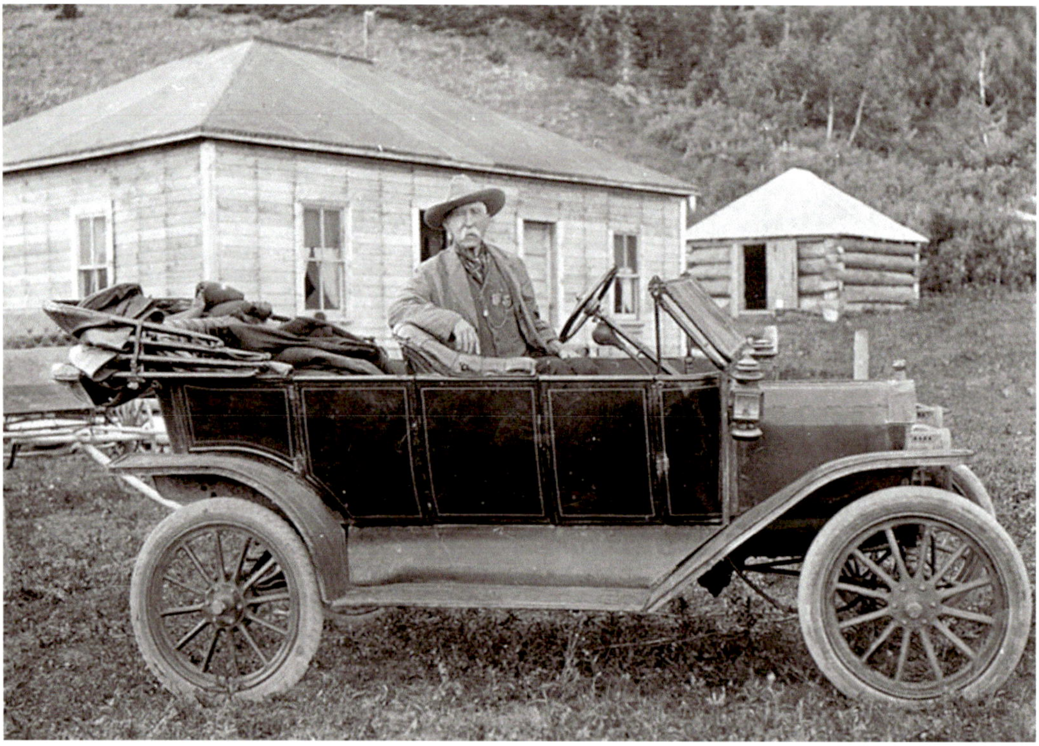

Early Rangers of Glacier National Park

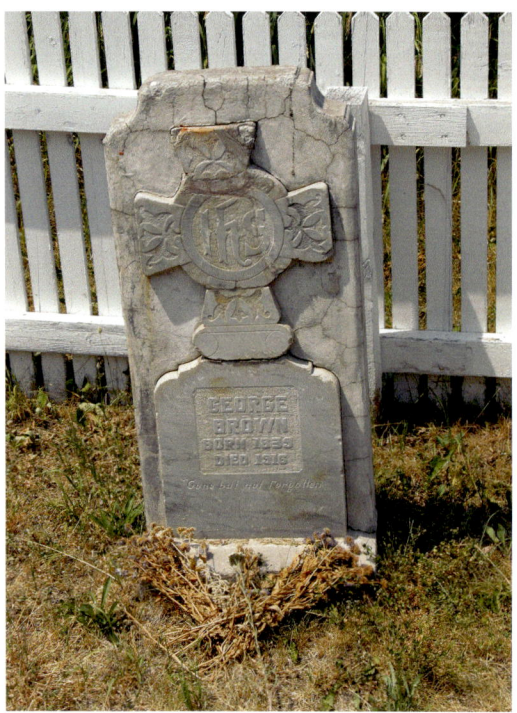

Above: Kootenai Brown in Waterton Lakes National Park in this undated, but likely *circa* 1910–1915, photo. (*NPS, photographer unknown*)

Left: Kootenai Brown's grave in Waterton Lakes National Park. (*Photo by author, photo taken July 28, 2003*)

The superintendent of Glacier Park wrote to Reynolds in late 1912 and increased the area he was to cover in his patrols, including in the depth of winter. Reynolds complained that the assignment was "a Patrol no man can make." Reynolds began suffering from frostbite (recall the dangers of snowshoeing and associated frostbite discussed in Chapter 1) as a result of his expanded patrols. In February 1913, Reynolds snowshoed to visit Kootenai Brown and arrived nearly frozen, severely frostbitten, and ill. The outside temperature was recorded by Brown at -32 Fahrenheit. Brown tended Reynolds overnight and subsequently transported him to Pincher Creek, Alberta, for medical assistance. Reynolds died there on February 8, 1913, at age sixty-five. Kootenai Brown outlived Reynolds by only a few years, dying in 1916. Brown was buried on the western shore of Lower Waterton Lake next to his wife. Brown's grave may be viewed by visitors on a short trail from the adjacent parking lot.[7, 8]

Norton Pearl

Norton Pearl first visited Glacier National Park in the park's first summer of existence, 1910. He was on holiday from his job as principal of a school in Butte, Montana. He visited the park, with a friend, from July 19 to August 15, 1910. His diary and photographs of that trip, and his subsequent time as an early park ranger, were preserved and transcribed by his granddaughter, Leslie Lee, in a marvelous, edited book published thirty years ago.[9]

By 1912, Pearl had become disenchanted with school board politics in Butte. He used some of his powerful Butte friends to secure him a park ranger job in Glacier Park. He arrived at the park to take up his ranger position on November 30, 1912, and would serve as a ranger for just over a year, until December 16, 1913, when he departed for his family home in Michigan.[10]

Pearl was assigned to the now-defunct Lower Two Medicine Ranger Station in the southeastern portion of Glacier Park. By early 1913, he had his station fully stocked with supplies for the winter, had become familiar with the few residents along the park boundary with the Blackfeet Reservation, and was ready to begin his massive patrol duties. His first extensive patrol was in January, accompanied on the first leg by Superintendent Galen, leaving Two Medicine on January 7. They snowshoed to the Cutbank Ranger Station where they met Ranger Joe Prince (Chapter 1). Pearl was to circumnavigate the northern part of the park, snowshoeing from Two Medicine up to Babb via Cut Bank and St. Mary Ranger Stations, from there to Babb and on to Waterton to visit with Waterton Ranger Kootenai Brown for any advice on how to get over Brown Pass to the North Fork of the Flathead valley. Pearl somehow found his way across the mountains in the North Fork valley (the route is not clearly stated in Pearl's diary), and down to Belton (West Glacier). After the freezing death of Park Ranger Joe Prince between Cutbank and St. Mary, Pearl and Superintendent Galen hauled his body to St. Mary. From there, Pearl continued through his first patrol solo.[11, 12]

Pearl began his second massive patrol accompanied by Ranger Cyrus Bellah to locate a new ranger station (actually just a backcountry patrol cabin) in the northeastern corner of the park on Lee Creek, leaving Glacier Park Station (East Glacier) on January 22, 1913. After riding the Great Northern from Glacier Park to Browning, the two rangers

Early Rangers of Glacier National Park

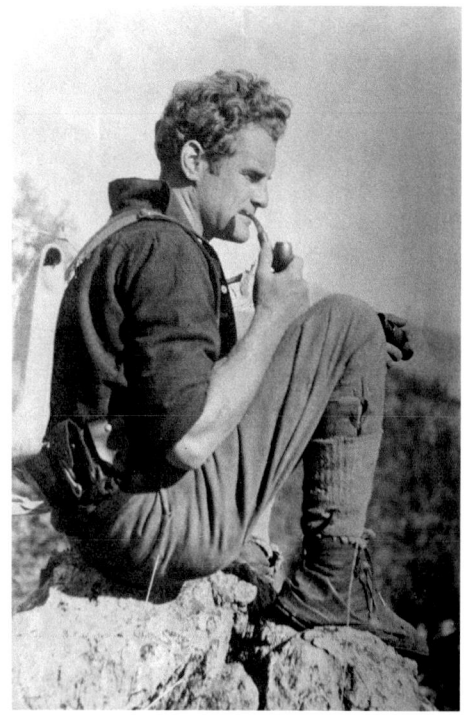

Left: Norton Pearl in Glacier National Park in 1910, which he visited as a tourist. He would become a park ranger there in November 1912. (*Norton Pearl photograph, photo courtesy of Leslie Lee, granddaughter of Norton Pearl*)

Below: Norton Pearl in a makeshift shelter during his summer, 1910, visit to Glacier National Park. (*Norton Pearl photograph, photo courtesy of Leslie Lee, granddaughter of Norton Pearl*)

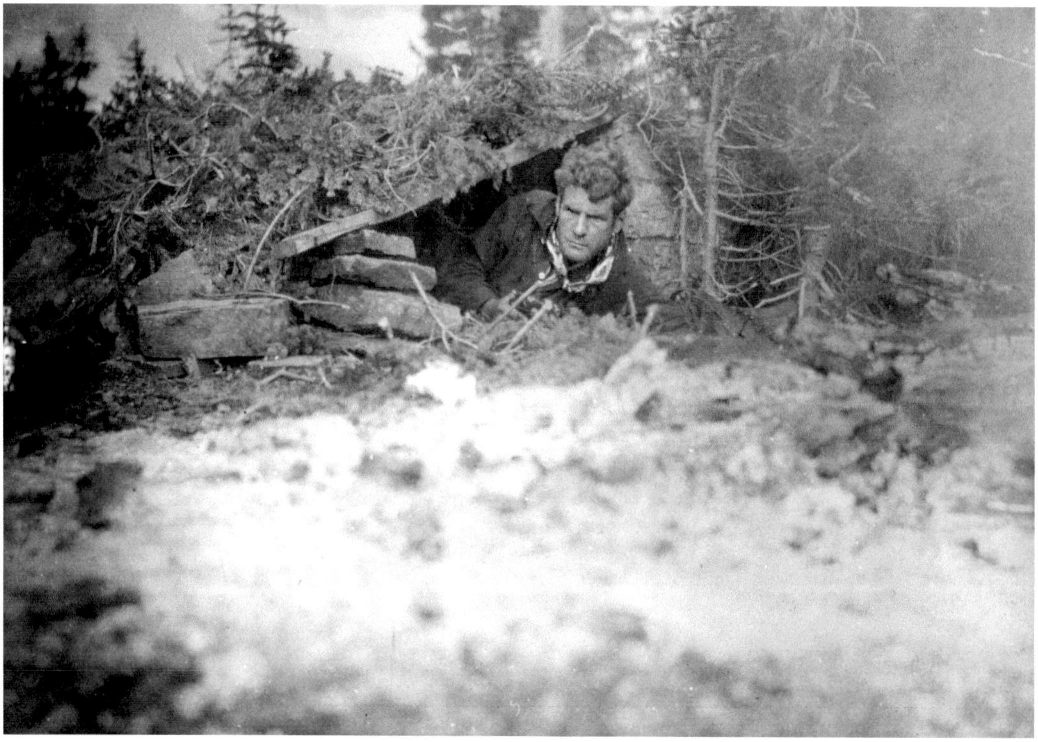

rode a stage to Babb. By February 7, they had arrived at the Belly River Ranger Station, home of Ranger Joe Cosley, but Cosley was not at home. The next morning, Pearl and Bellah parted company, and Pearl somehow found his way to Kootenai Brown's cabin in Waterton from the Belly River valley, without clear instructions as to how to do so! From there, and with Brown's advice, Pearl found his way to Kishehnen in the northwest corner of Glacier Park via South Kootenai Pass and Oil Creek, and thence down the North Fork valley back to Belton, arriving there on March 6. Pearl continued to carry out his ranger duties until he left the employ of the park on December 16, 1913.[13, 14]

Joe Cosley

Surely one of the most memorable characters in Glacier Park history was Ranger (and poacher!) Joe Cosley. Born of mixed parentage (a French-Canadian father and an Algonquin First Nation mother), Cosley came westward by age twenty-five and was a trapper who from the 1890s onward was familiar with the mountains of northwest Montana and western Alberta. He was hired in 1900 as a forest ranger for the Forest Service, and he was one of the first rangers who successfully (for a period of time) transitioned to be hired as a park ranger by Glacier Park in 1910. Then already known to be a poacher as well as a ranger, Cosley was nonetheless hired by new Park Superintendent Major William Logan under the philosophy that "it takes a poacher to catch a poacher."[15, 16]

Joe Cosley was a dramatic-looking individual who in his early days definitely looked the role of a mountain man. Once he became a ranger, he enjoyed the rounded hats now known as "Smokey Bear" hats, with his own unique addition to the underside of the brim. Upon his hiring by the superintendent of Glacier Park, Cosley soon became a fixture at the Belly River Ranger Station in the northernmost part of the park.

Cosley had an apparently well-earned reputation for being a ladies' man, and his reputation as such was widespread in southwestern Alberta and northwest Montana. He not only named a lake near the Belly River Ranger Station after himself, but also named several lakes in the Belly and Mokowanis River drainages after his favorite lady friends. These lakes include Sue Lake at the head of the Mokowanis valley, but also Helen and Elizabeth Lakes in the headwaters of the Belly River.[17]

Given the location of the Belly River Ranger Station, it is logical that Cosley knew both Albert "Death on the Trail" Reynolds in the Waterton River valley to the west, and Kootenai Brown in adjacent Waterton Lakes National Park. Cosley and Brown particularly seemed to be good acquaintances, and Cosley even wrote a well-written pamphlet about how he had come to meet Kootenai Brown for the first time in the 1890s.[18]

Cosley's poaching, carried out as a park ranger, eventually got him fired in 1914 under a different superintendent than had hired him. After his dismissal, Cosley volunteered for the Canadian Army in World War One. Serving honorably, Cosley returned to his personal cabins in the Belly River region where he once again took up his poaching/trapping lifestyle. We shall return to this aspect of Cosley's non-ranger life in the next chapter.[19]

Early Rangers of Glacier National Park

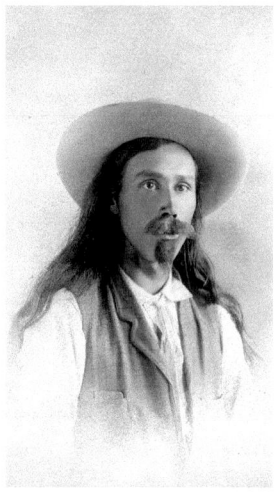 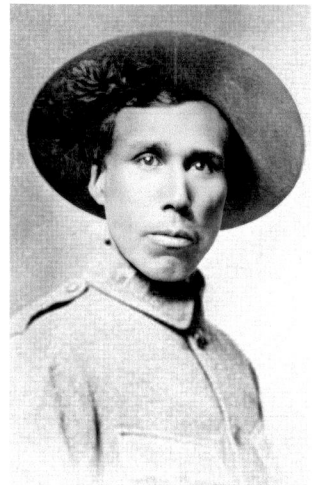 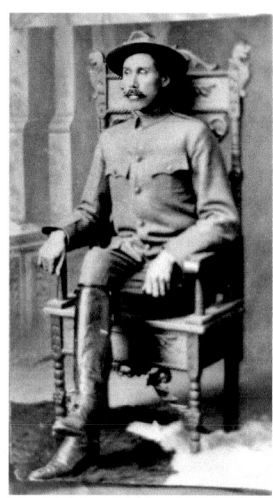

Above left: A photograph of a young Joe Cosley from his pre-rangering days. (*Undated and unattributed photo, NPS*)

Above middle: Joe Cosley portrait featuring him in a modified Glacier Park ranger uniform, 1910. Cosley was one of the first men appointed as a park ranger by Superintendent Logan after the park was established in May 1910. Note how he had painted (red) roses on the underside of the hat brim. (*Photo unattributed, NPS*)

Above right: A formal portrait of Joe Cosley in his ranger uniform, 1912. (*Photographer unattributed, NPS*)

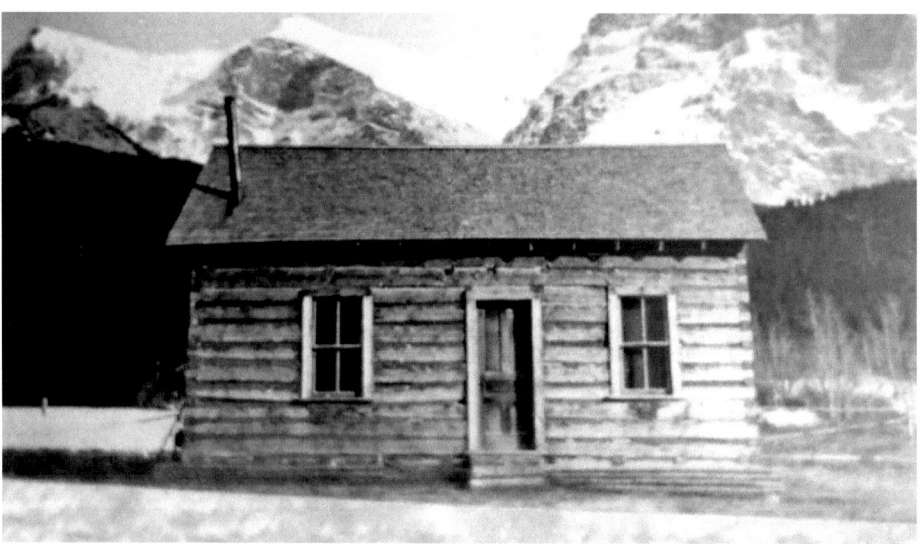

The original Belly River Ranger Station, built in 1908 or 1909 by Joe Cosley as his living quarters. The building still exists at the modern Belly River Ranger Station as a compound barn. (*Photo undated, photo by Kurt Wilson, from Early Columbia Falls History Facebook page*)

The First Decade of Glacier Park Rangers

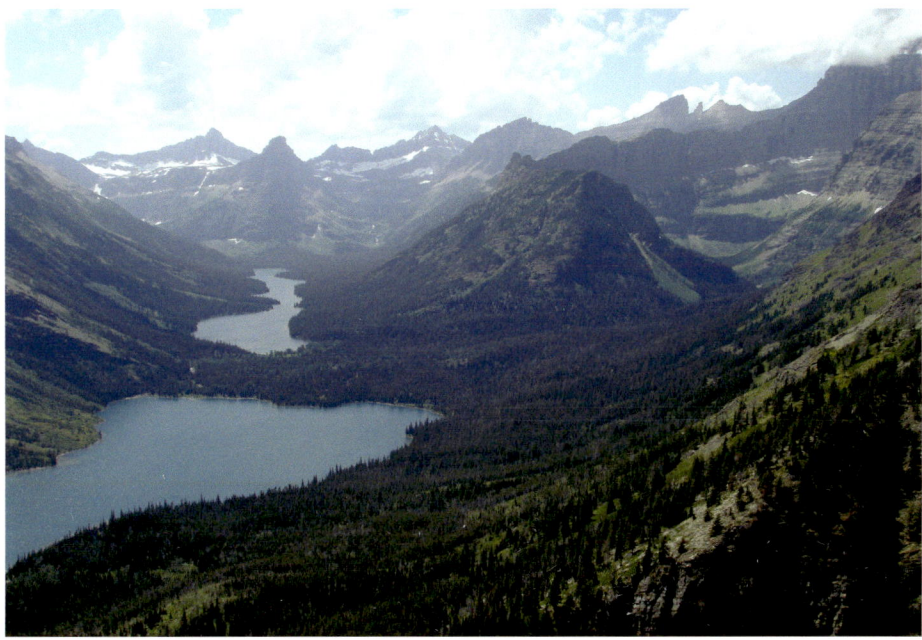

A view up the Mokowanis River valley in Glacier National Park, looking from the shoulder of Bear Mountain. The lake at lower left is Cosley Lake, named by Joe Cosley after himself, with Glenns Lake up the valley. (*Photo by Dr. Jon J. Kedrowski, taken July 25, 2009*)

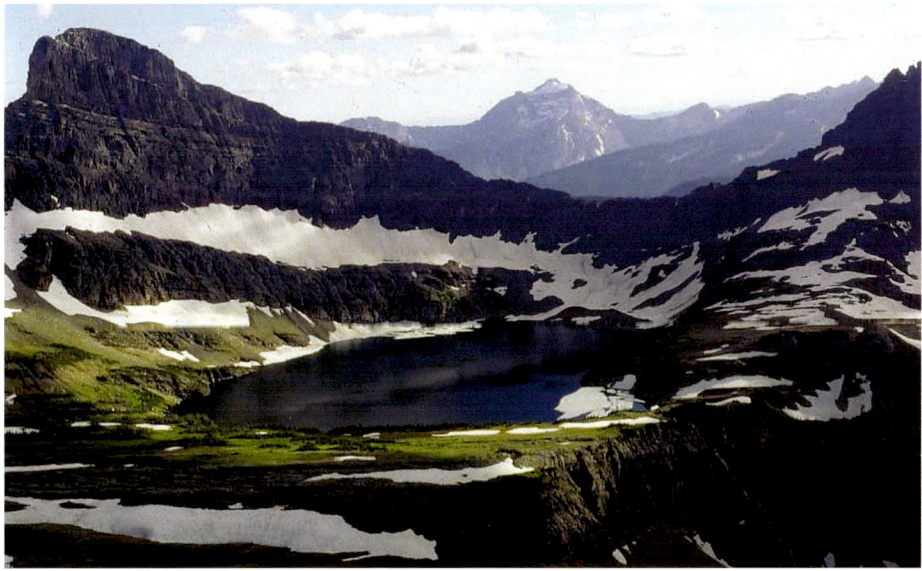

Sue Lake, at the head of the Mokowanis River valley. The lake was named by Joe Cosley for Sue Henkel, a flame of his who lived in Babb just east of Glacier Park on the Blackfeet Reservation. The Henkel family still resides in the area. (*Photo by author, photo taken August 9, 1995*)

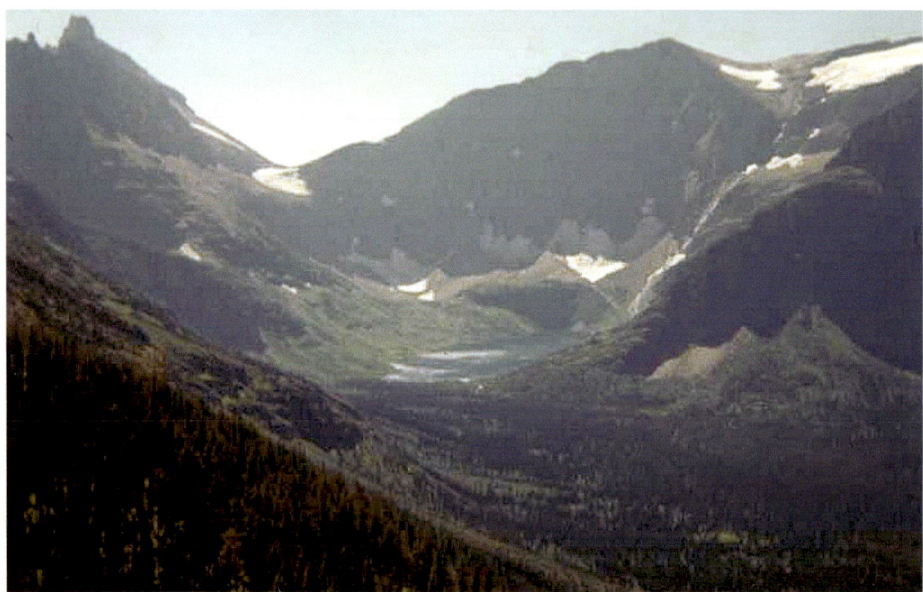

Ahern Pass is the low point on the mountain ridge at upper left center. Below and to the right is Helen Lake, named by Cosley after at least one of two of his girlfriends with the name Helen. Cosley used Ahern Pass as a route from the Belly River valley, in which Helen Lake forms the headwaters, over into the headwaters of the McDonald Creek valley on the west side of the park. (*Photo by author, photo taken in August, 1973*)

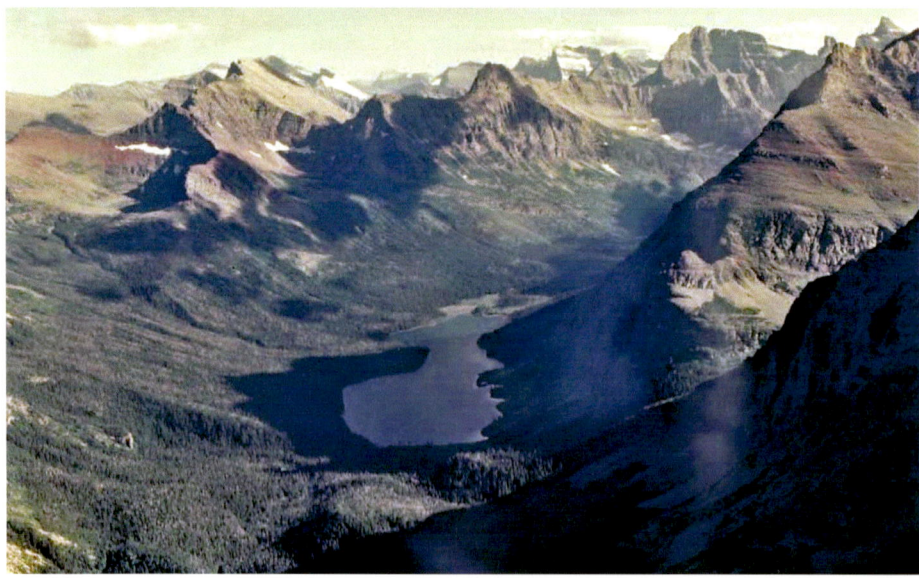

A view looking up the Belly River valley. Elizabeth Lake is in the center of the photo, Helen Lake is out of sight beyond it up-valley, behind the middle mountain. Elizabeth Lake was named by Joe Cosley for his primary girlfriend in the area, Elizabeth Webster of Mountain View, Alberta. (*Photo by author, photo taken August 9, 1995*)

Dan Doody

Dan Doody was a frontiersman, settler, and trapper who in the early 1900s had a homestead near Harrison Creek, on the east side of the Middle Fork of the Flathead River. In some ways, he was the southern Glacier Park counterpart to the northern Joe Cosley. Due to Dan's local knowledge and tracking abilities, he was among the first group of park rangers hired in 1910 by Park Superintendent William Logan, in spite of being well known not only for his tracking but also for his poaching abilities. Doody lived in a cabin on his homestead with his common-law wife, Josephine, a notorious figure in her own right known widely as a bootlegger and nicknamed "The Bootleg Lady of Glacier Park." The cabin and land became a non-federal "inholding" surrounded by Glacier Park when the park was created in 1910.[20]

In addition to his work as a ranger, Dan Doody became well known in the area as an outdoorsman guide with a wealth of knowledge about the local area, and his reputation attracted big game hunters, including James J. Hill, president of the Great Northern Railway, which passed nearby and across the river from the Doody homestead. Hill in fact had the railroad build a siding stop for the Doody homestead to facilitate his visits across the river.[21]

Dan Doody was annually reappointed as a park ranger until his termination for unstated reasons (but probably because of his on-going poaching activities) on March 15, 1916. The Doodys continued, however, to live in their "inholding" enclave within the young national park, and Mt. Doody near Coal Creek in southern Glacier Park is named after them. Dan Doody passed away from a heart attack in 1921. Josephine

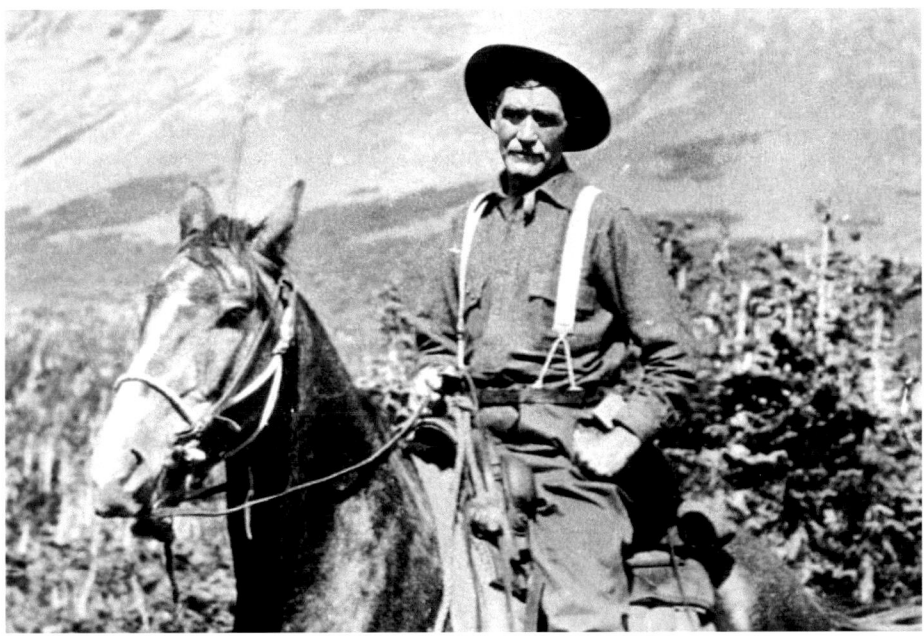

Ranger Dan Doody on patrol in Glacier Park. Doody was among the group of six men named the first rangers of the park. (*GNP Archives, photo undated and unattributed*)

Early Rangers of Glacier National Park

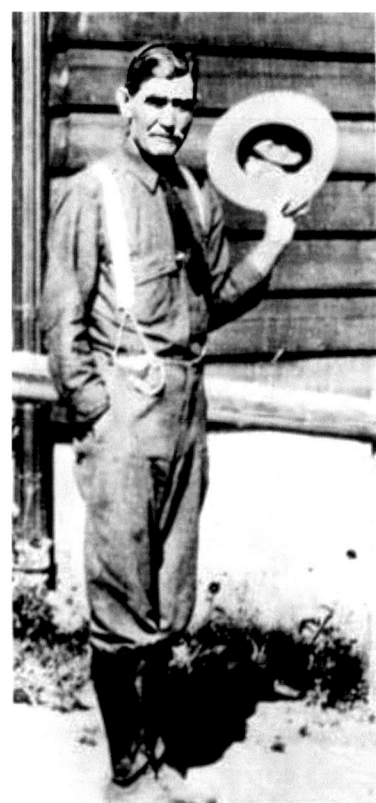

Left: Ranger Dan Doody in his park ranger uniform, 1915. (*Photo unattributed, GNP GLAC HPF 9463*)

Below: Early rangers were expected to "hunt varmints" in order to protect what were deemed "desirable" animals, including deer, elk, moose, bighorn sheep, and mountain goats. Here, Ranger Dan Doody and his Airedale dog stand next to a number of "varmint" furs at the Doody homestead. (*Undated and unattributed photo, GNP archives*)

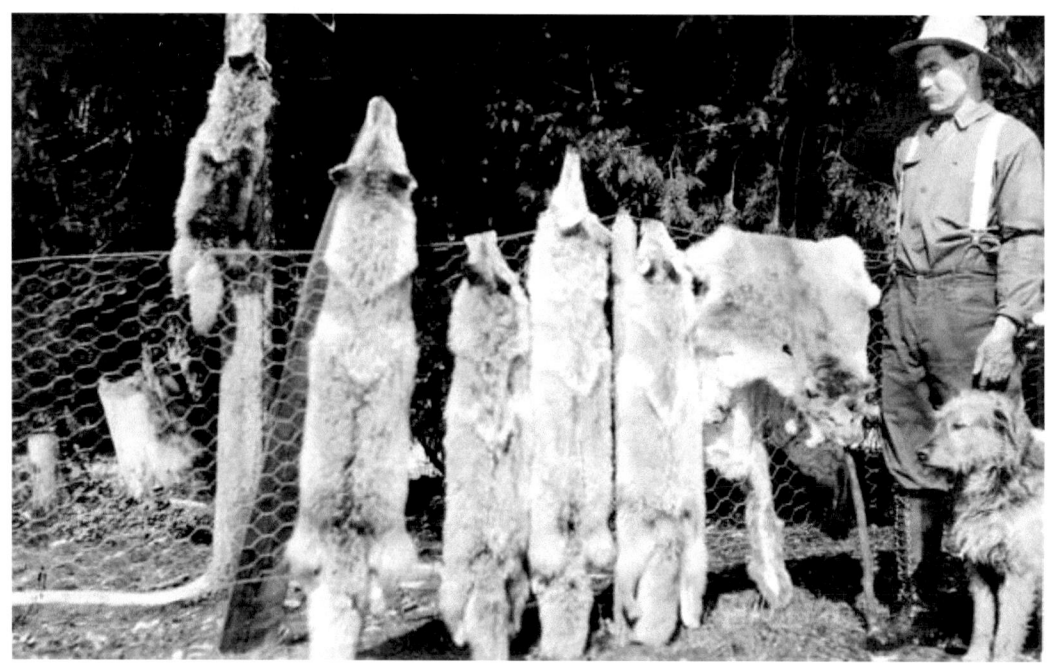

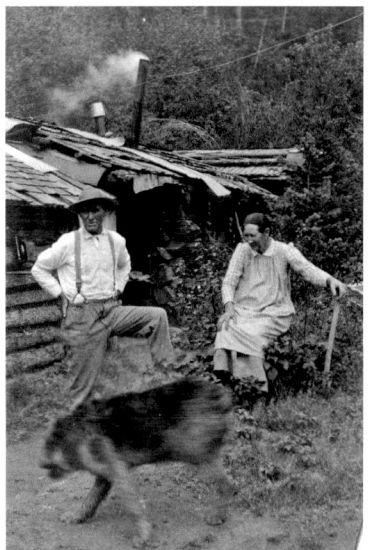

Dan Doody and his wife, Josephine Doody, in front of their cabin near Nyack along the Middle Fork of the Flathead River, in Glacier National Park, *circa* 1910–1915. Their cabin was the first one built along the southern boundary of the park south of Lake McDonald. (*Photographer unattributed, GNP archives*)

continued to live within the park until 1931, when she moved across the river to a cabin near the new U.S. Highway 2. The Doody homestead continued as a private land inholding within the park, however, until purchased and donated to the park in 2012.[22]

Chauncey "Chance" Beebe

Chauncey E. "Chance" Beebe was among the first three homesteaders on the west side of the North Fork of the Flathead River in 1908. Only twenty years old at the time, Chance enjoyed the absence of close scrutiny by neighbors and officials, and he took advantage of the fact that the area was a hunter's and trapper's paradise. He gained valuable experience in both hunting and trapping, as well as gained expertise in the geography of the northwest Montana frontier.[23]

Chance Beebe married Eva V. DeFord in Columbia Falls, Montana, on August 1, 1914. They lived for a few years on Chance's homestead, and in 1917, Chance was hired to begin working for Glacier National Park as a park ranger. Chance was a ranger from 1917 to 1920, and then began a long career as a government hunter, specializing in hunting mountain lions. During their time in Glacier Park, the young couple were stationed at the old Two Medicine, St. Mary, and Many Glacier ranger stations. The most detail about their lives comes from their time at St. Mary in 1918–1919.[24]

Life in the St. Mary ranger station included not only Chance and Eva, but two small children (Edward and Chauncey, Jr., born in 1915 and 1917, respectively). As was common up until the 1930s, Ranger Chance was "on call" twenty-four hours a day, seven days a week. Nonetheless, blurry photos of the family show they had time for recreation as well, including fishing, hiking, and ice skating on a frozen-over St. Mary Lake. Chance's patrol duties, in winter accomplished on snowshoes or a dog sled, kept him away from the ranger station for extended periods, with Eva left to fend for herself and her small children.[25]

Early Rangers of Glacier National Park

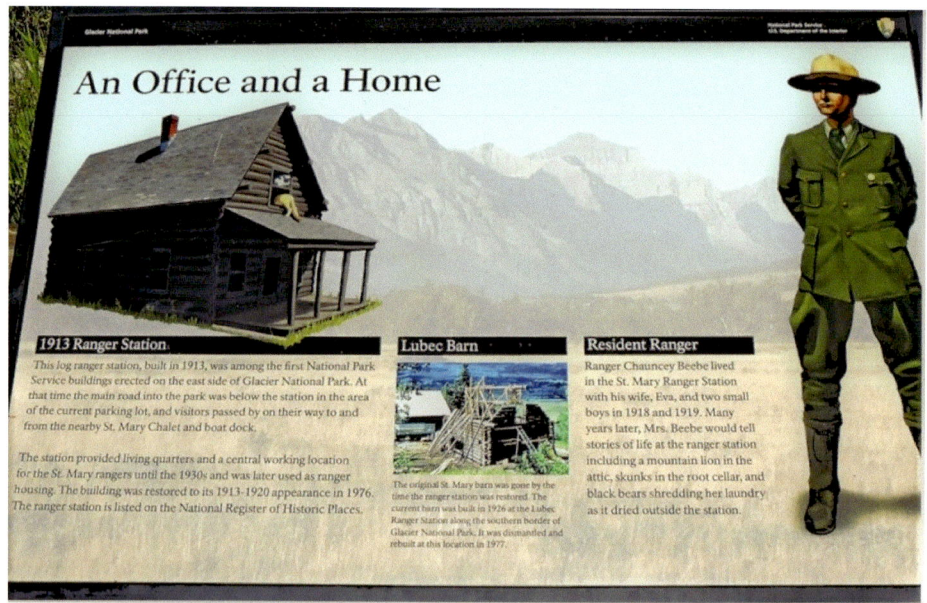

Chance Beebe and his wife and children were stationed at the St. Mary Ranger Station in 1918 and 1919. The building, constructed in 1913, was one of the first park structures on the east side of Glacier Park. (*NPS*)

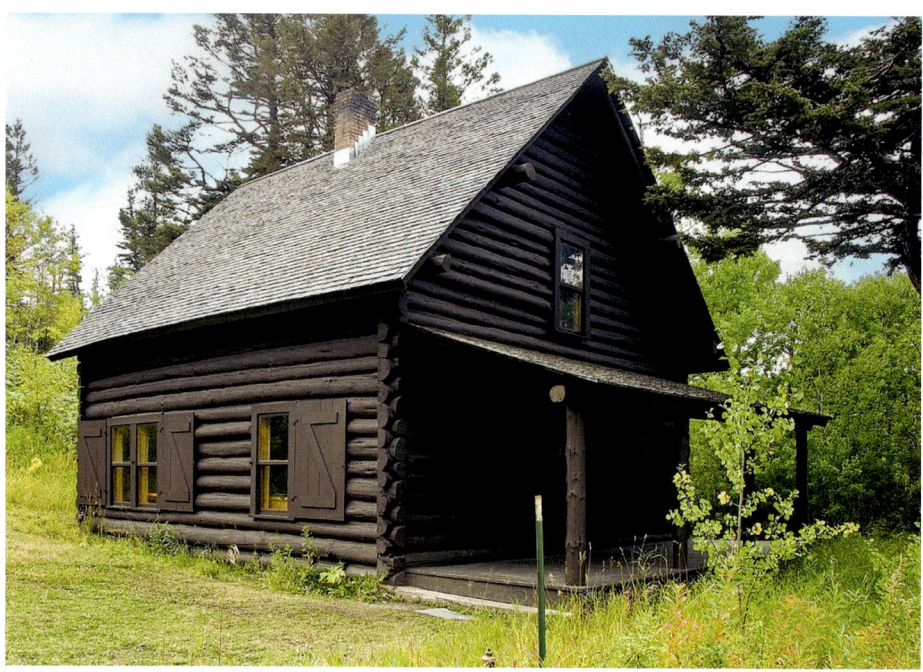

Photo of the St. Mary Ranger Station where Chance and Eva Beebe and their children lived for two years. (*Wikipedia, Creative Commons, photo by Acroterion, September 14, 2010*)

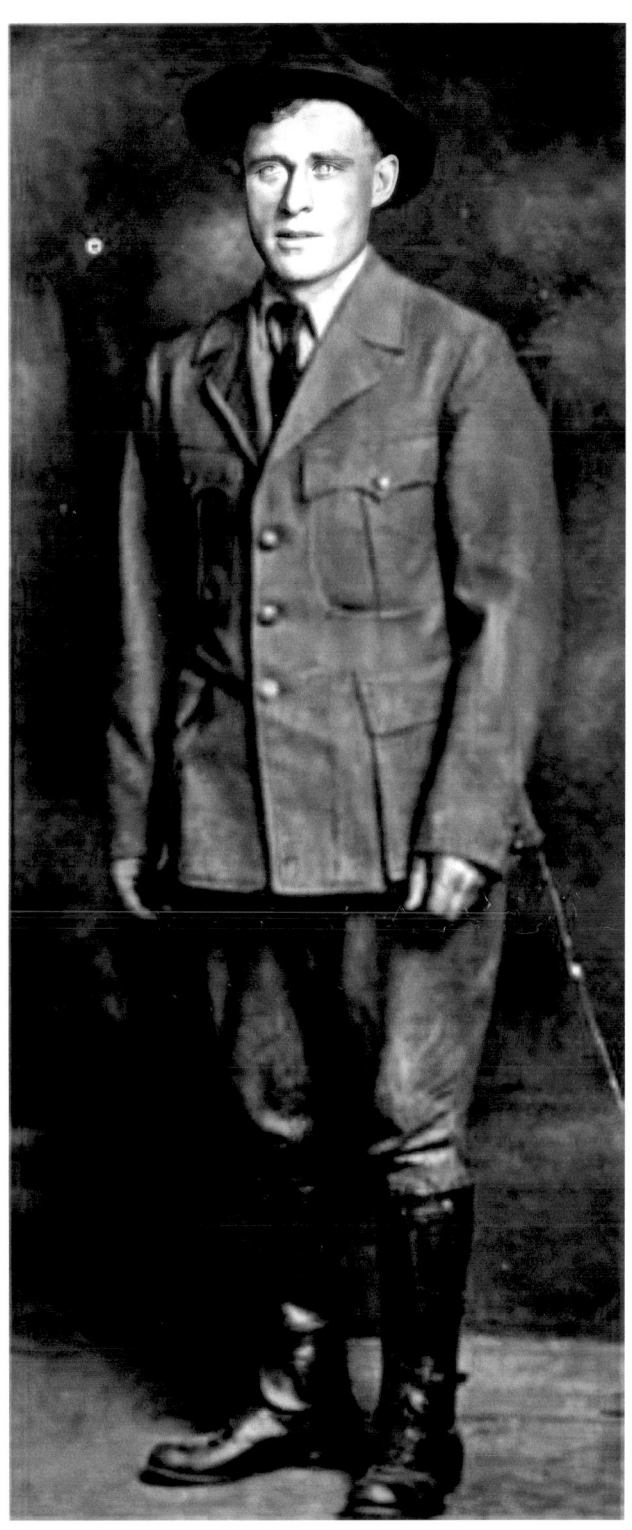

Chance Beebe models the new standardized 1920 park ranger uniform in Glacier National Park. (*GNP GLAC HPF 2681, photographer unknown*)

During the periods when Chance was away patrolling and carrying out his ranger duties, life was not always easy nor safe for Eva and the children. Encounters with skunks and black bears were not uncommon. Most significantly, a mountain lion entered the attic through an upper window (as illustrated on the park service ranger station sign) and threatened Chauncey, Jr., in his crib. Eva's entrance into the room, in response to the child's crying, scared the lion off. Eva took the children, locked the door to prevent the lion from coming downstairs, and made the short walk to the nearby (now razed) St. Mary Chalets, run by the Great Northern Railway, for safety. After Chance returned from patrol, he and Eva returned to the cabin station and found it surrounded by mountain lion tracks. The upper window through which the lion had entered was very quickly and permanently sealed.[26]

The St. Mary Chalets served as refuge for the Beebes during the winter, and Eva worked there as a caretaker in return for a small salary and food. During the summer season, Ranger Chance would meet the Glacier Park Transportation Company buses at the chalets and guide prominent visitors around the area. Well-known visitors for which he served as guide included the president of the Great Northern Railway James J. Hill, writer Mary Roberts Rinehart, conservationist George Byrd Grinnell and, especially noteworthy, Queen Mary and Prince Albert of Belgium. The royal couple ate lunch with the Beebes, and Queen Mary gave Eva $5 to purchase candy for the children.[27]

After 1920, Chance left the Park Service to work as a hunter of predatory animals ("varmints") that at the time were considered undesirable by the federal government. His hunting prowess was renowned and unparalleled, and he was particularly well known for his success in hunting mountain lions.

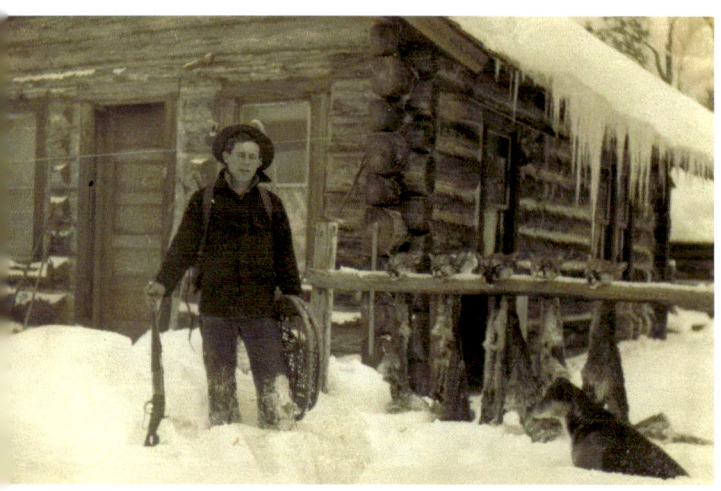 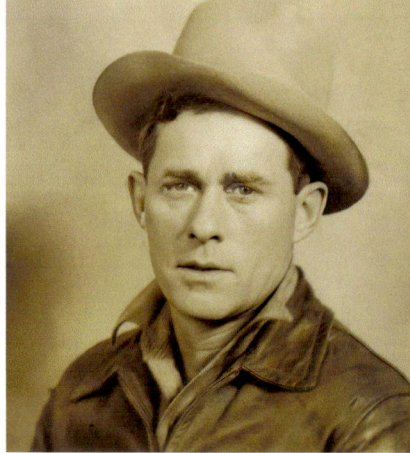

Above left: Chance Beebe, with snowshoes and a dog, at the Nyack Ranger Station, 1922. Note the five mountain lion carcasses/pelts aligned along the hitching rail. (*Early Columbia Falls History Facebook Page, July 9, 2019; photographer unknown*)

Above right: In the mid-1920s, Park Ranger Beebe left the National Park Service to work as a hunter/trapper for the U.S. Forest Service. (*Early Columbia Falls History Facebook Page, July 8, 2019; photographer unknown*)

4
Glacier Park Rangers of the 1920s and 1930s

The life of a ranger continued to be difficult in the 1920s and 1930s, although the isolation of the park's first decade began to relent a little. Roads slowly improved, although U.S. Highway 2 was not completed over Marias Pass on the southern end of Glacier Park until 1930. Going-to-the-Sun Road over Logan Pass, connecting St. Mary on the east to Apgar and Belton (West Glacier) on the west was not completed and dedicated until 1933. A telephone line connecting park headquarters in Belton to St. Mary over Hidden and Logan Pass was not completed until the summer of 1938. Rangers still patrolled year-round up until about 1940, so although technological improvements were slowly changing the nature of working in the park, rangers working in this period were still carrying out often-dangerous tasks in very isolated situations.[1]

Clyde Fauley

Clyde Fauley was known as among the very best of the early Glacier Park rangers, and his wife, Marie, was a ranger's wife for many years. They met in the summer of 1922, when Clyde was working as a temporary ranger at the Belton (West Glacier) entrance station and Marie Fratzke was working as a waitress at the nearby Belton Chalet. A Glacier Park summer romance led to their getting married in 1923.[2]

    Clyde was assigned in the fall of 1923 to the now-razed Paola Ranger Station along the Middle Fork of the Flathead River, about 20 miles southeast of Belton and 10 miles north-northwest of Essex and the present-day Walton Ranger Station. The only way to get to the station was via the Great Northern Railway, because in the early 1920s U.S. Highway 2 had not yet been extended into the Middle Fork valley east of Belton. From the railway line, a cable or trolley bucket was used to cross over the Middle Fork into Glacier Park on the east shore. Because of the inherent dangers in using a cable/trolley bucket, Fauley's wife, Marie, typically only crossed the river in the cable bucket to go to Kalispell to give birth and return to the ranger station (this occurred twice during their time at Paola). The couple left Paola in 1928, and later served at both the Two Medicine and Nyack Ranger Stations, the latter also along the Middle Fork and also reachable only by a cable bucket.

Early Rangers of Glacier National Park

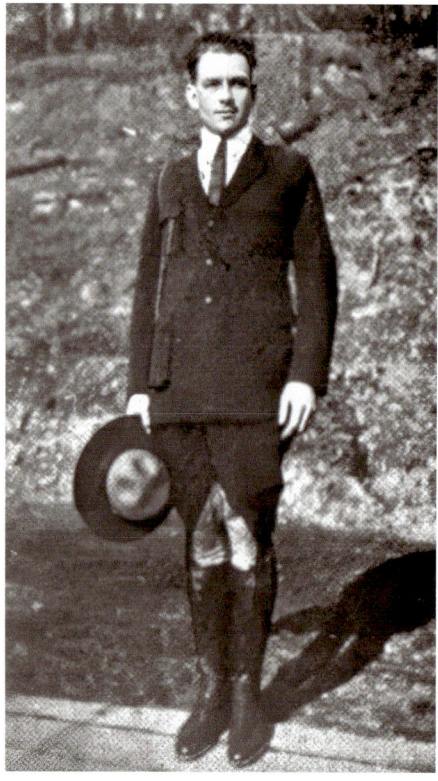

Ranger Clyde Fauley in uniform, from an article he wrote that was published in 1923 in the magazine *Hunter-Trader-Trapper*. (*Clyde Fauley-provided photo, circa 1920–1921*)

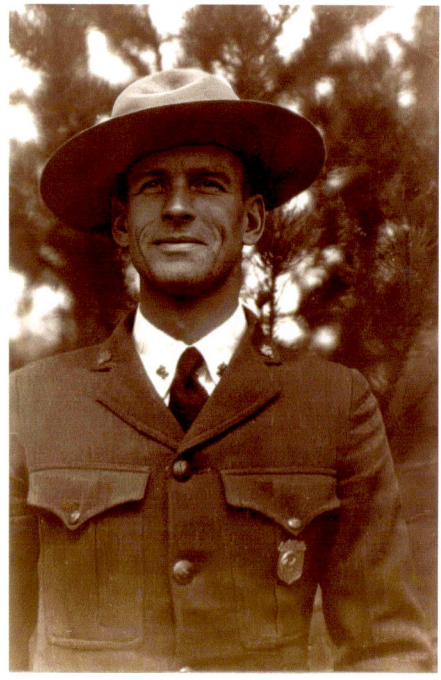

Clyde Fauley in his ranger uniform, *circa* mid-1930s. (*NPS, photographer unattributed*)

While at the Paola and Nyack Ranger Stations, Fauley had a couple of near-death experiences such as were alluded to in Chapter 1. While on patrol from the Paola Ranger Station sometime in the mid-1920s, Fauley barely escaped a massive snow avalanche near the junction of Muir Creek and the Middle Fork of the Flathead River; after just crossing a coulee on his snowshoes, hundreds of tons of snow swept past him and down into the Middle Fork below. In the winter of 1929, while on patrol working out of the Nyack Ranger Station, Fauley plunged through the ice of Harrison Lake while in his snowshoes. He was miraculously able to slowly and desperately pull himself to shore across the remaining thin ice while still in his snowshoes and make his way to the nearby Harrison Lake snowshoe cabin where he was able to build a fire and survive.[3, 4, 5]

Dan Huffine

Dan Huffine lived in and near Glacier National Park for decades, including living in East Glacier Park, running tourist camps first at Stanton Creek near the Nyack settlement and later at Essex near the Walton Ranger Station, and in later life in the Flathead valley. Huffine served as a ranger, but was not classified as a permanent park ranger, in Glacier National Park from September 1926 to May 1928. Stationed first at St. Mary and staying in the same ranger station cabin as the Beebes had done several years before, he was eventually assigned to the Cut Bank Ranger Station in 1927.

Dan met Doris Weaver, a young widow, in East Glacier in 1925, where he worked as a "gearjammer" (tourist bus driver), and she worked as a maid at Glacier Park Lodge. After initially disliking him, Dan won over the reluctant Doris such that they married on October 17, 1927. By the end of October, the newlyweds moved into the Cut Bank Ranger Station where they would spend the winter of 1927–28. From late October 1927 until May 31, 1928, the Huffines occupied the Cut Bank Station. Details of their life there, and some of Doris' adventures, are well described by John Fraley in his excellent book *A Woman's Way West*. After failing to achieve a coveted permanent ranger position in 1928, Dan Huffine left the employ of the Park Service, never to return.[6]

Francis X. "Frank" Guardipee

Francis X. Guardipee, known almost throughout his life as "Frank," was born on November 4, 1885, on the Blackfeet Indian Reservation at the Old Agency on Badger Creek, Montana. He attended the Carlisle Indian School in Pennsylvania, after which he attended the University of Washington and subsequently working at a variety of jobs in the eastern U.S. before finding employment on his native Blackfeet Indian Reservation in Browning as a forester in the 1920s. While working as a Blackfeet forester, Frank met Ethel Alma Kiernan, who went by Alma and who worked in the early to mid-1920s for several summers in Glacier Park at the now-razed Going-to-the-Sun Chalets. The couple married in 1929.[7, 8]

In 1930 (some sources state 1932, but they are outweighed by those stating 1930), Frank became the first Native American ranger in Glacier National Park. A 1970 federal government memorandum, released eight days after Frank's death, also stated that he was likely "the first full-blooded Indian appointed to a permanent ranger position in the National Park Service."[9]

Early Rangers of Glacier National Park

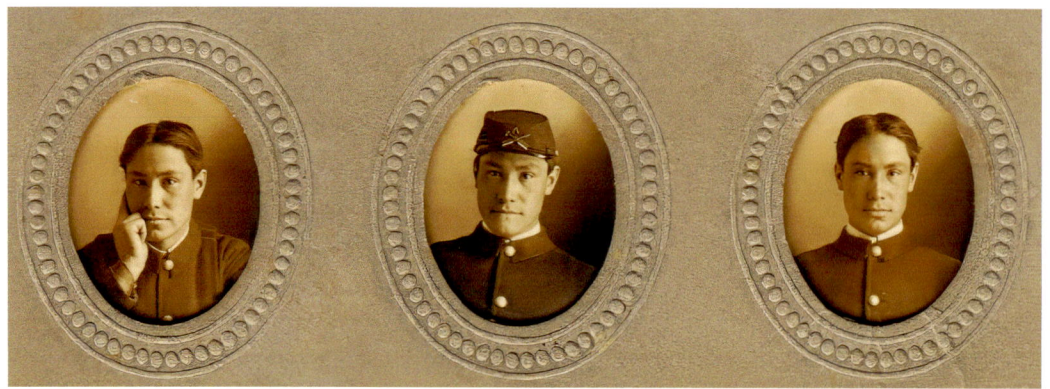

Photos of Francis X. "Frank" Guardipee, *circa* 1907, at the Carlisle Indian School of Pennsylvania, the same school where famous Olympic athlete Jim Thorpe was a student in the same period. (*National Archives RG 75, Series 1327, box 28, folder 1307, photographer unattributed*)

From 1930 until 1948, Alma and Frank lived in several Glacier Park ranger stations. Many summers were spent at the Two Medicine Ranger Station and winters at East Glacier. However, they were also stationed at Nyack, Lake McDonald, East Glacier, and for two years in the mid-1930s at the North Fork Ranger Station (now gone) near the junction of the Middle and North Forks of the Flathead River, where both Frank and Alma interacted with members of a nearby Civilian Conservation Corps camp. Frank apparently enjoyed the isolation of the Nyack camp the best, but Alma preferred having neighbors at East Glacier.[10]

During their years as a "ranger couple," Frank and Alma were typically on-call twenty-four hours a day. Because of the necessity of being able to see fires, calls to the ranger station informing Frank of a forest fire required him to rush out to try to put out the fires immediately. Alma noted that such calls almost inevitably came at night. In rushing out to fight fires, Frank would need to leave Alma alone at home for an unspecified period with their young son, Frank "Gunner" Jr. Frank also patrolled extensively, again leaving Alma to tend the homestead. In an oral history recorded in 1984, Alma noted that Frank would never go anywhere without his .38-caliber pistol at his side, because he had to be ready to pursue poachers at a moment's notice if he heard gunshots.[11]

Alma also described the difficulties associated with the Nyack Ranger Station cable bucket tram crossing of the Middle Fork of the Flathead River, similar to the one employed by the Fauleys at the Paola Ranger Station. She noted:

> … one had to climb a ladder roughly 12 feet high to a platform, and then enter the 3 × 4-foot bucket suspended by cable over the river. To move, a handle clawed at the wire cable and worked one's way across the often-raging Middle Fork. Alma described the river as "terrible." She also recalled that one of the first things Frank did upon moving to Nyack was to try and tighten the cable, which subsequently broke, hit him in the head, and knocked him off the platform. Alma had to arrange to get Frank to the hospital in Kalispell as a result of this mishap.[12]

Frank was a well-liked member of the Glacier Park ranger community, and served until his retirement in 1948, after which the couple moved to Browning where they lived

Glacier Park Rangers of the 1920s and 1930s

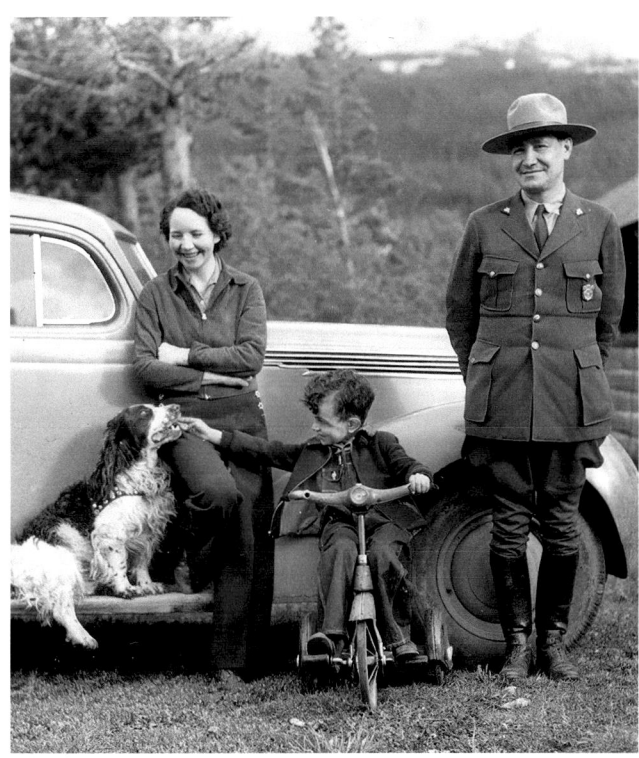

Right: Ranger Frank Guardipee with his wife, Alma Guardipee, and their son, Frank "Gunner" Jr., probably at the Lower Two Medicine Ranger Station on the east side of Glacier Park (that station no longer exists). (*Photo undated, courtesy of Ron Beard*)

Below: Frank Guardipee with puppies, at the Nyack Ranger Station on the west side of Glacier Park along the Middle Fork of the Flathead River. (*Photo undated, courtesy of Ron Beard*)

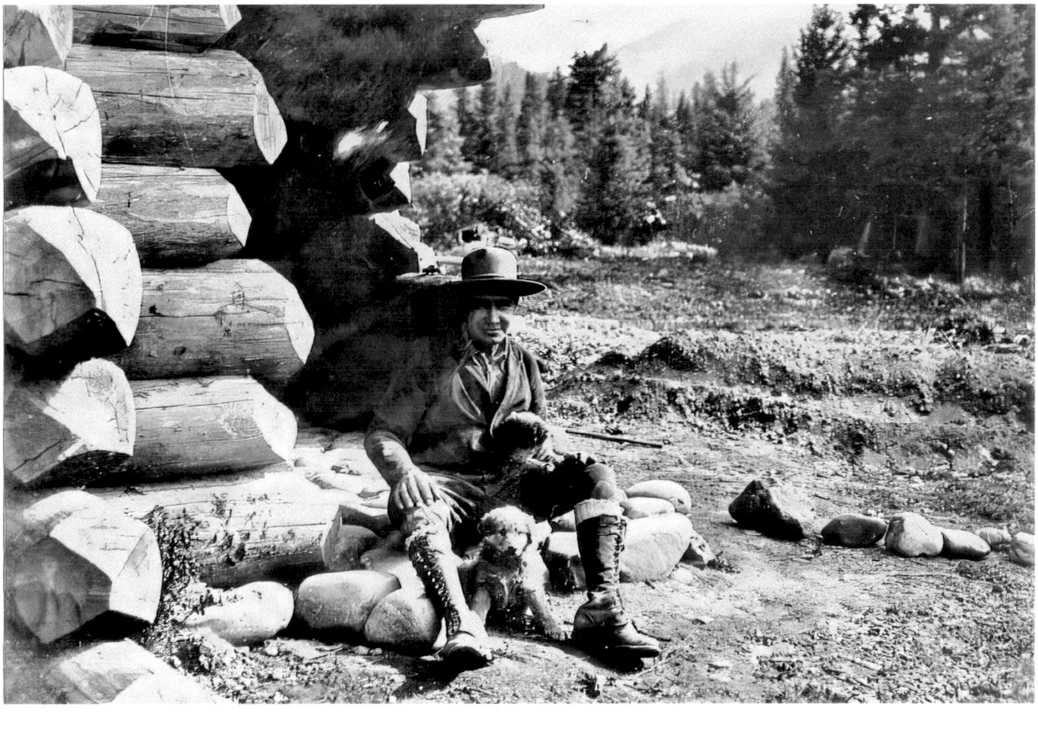

Early Rangers of Glacier National Park

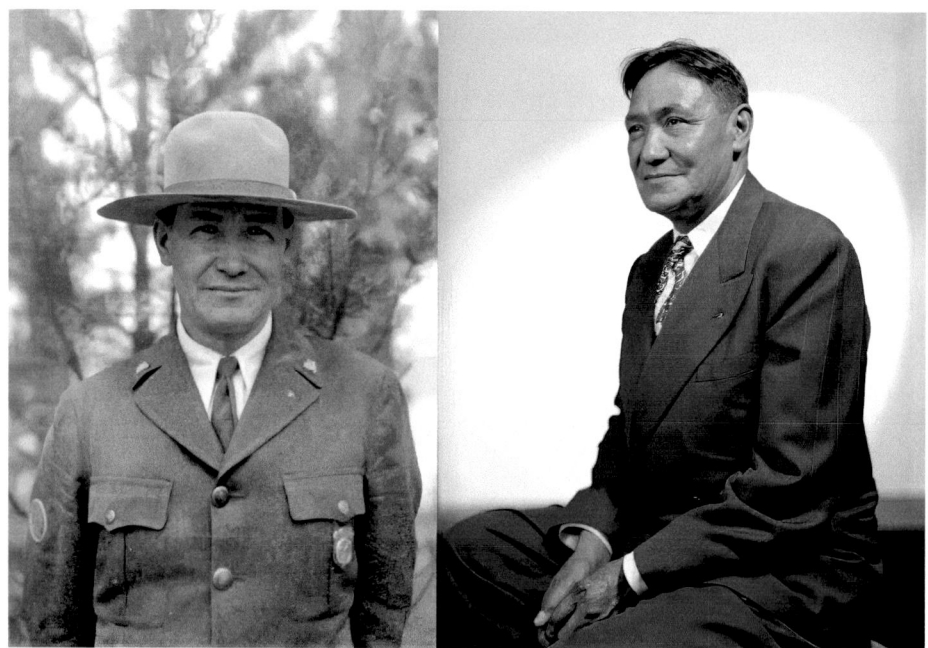

A comparison of photos of Ranger Frank Guardipee in 1935 and 1965. (*1935 photo, GNP; 1965 photo from Max Beard Family Collection, courtesy of Ron Beard. Photographers unattributed*)

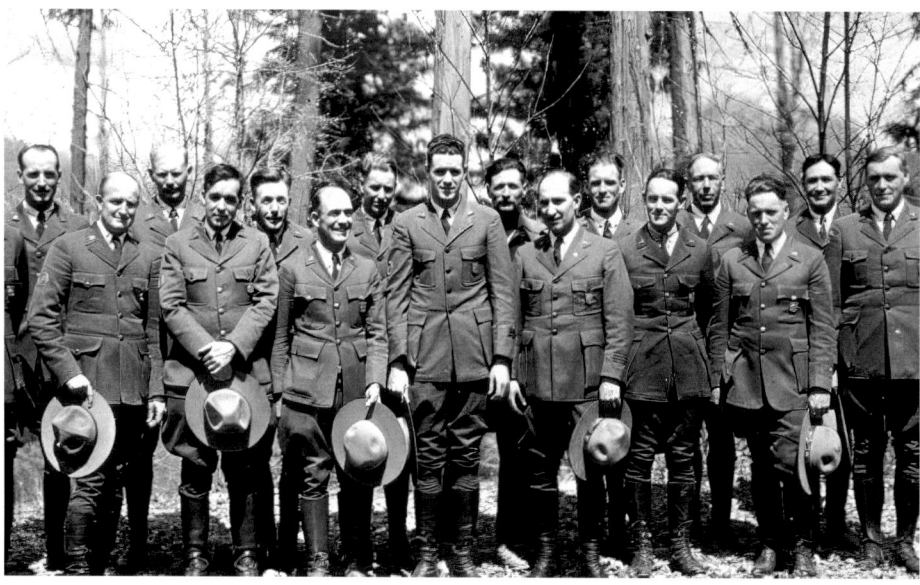

The Glacier National Park Ranger force for 1936. Frank Guardipee is in the rear, second from the right. Also shown are Elmer Ness, rear row third from left; Joe Heimes, front row far right; Ben Miller, front row second from left; and Clyde Fauley, back row and two over from Frank Guardipee. (*GNP Archives, photographer unattributed*)

Glacier Park Rangers of the 1920s and 1930s

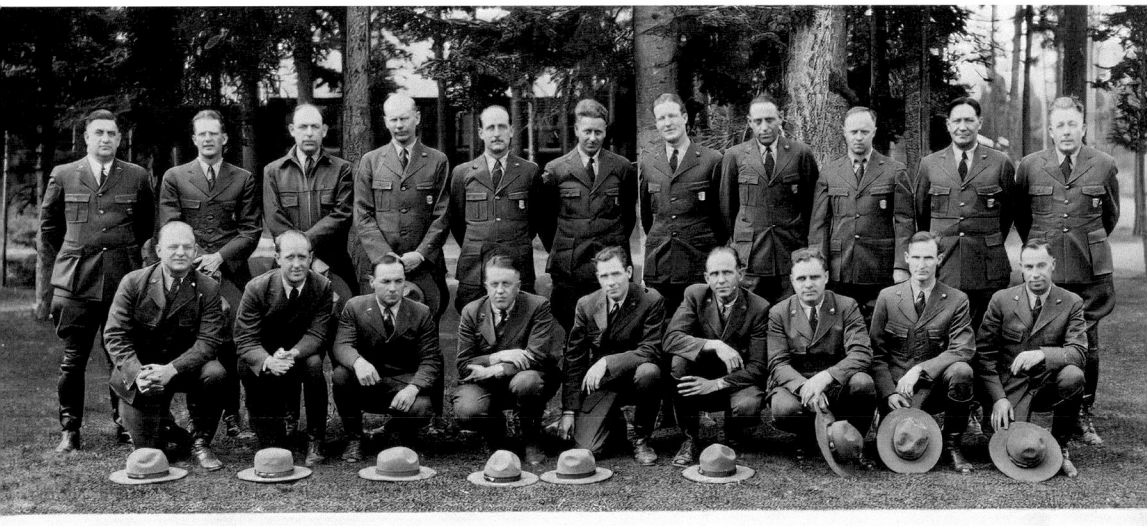

The Glacier National Park Ranger force, April 22, 1941. Frank Guardipee is standing, second from right. Frank Guardipee is flanked by Joe Heimes and Elmer Ness. (*GNP Archives, photographer unattributed*)

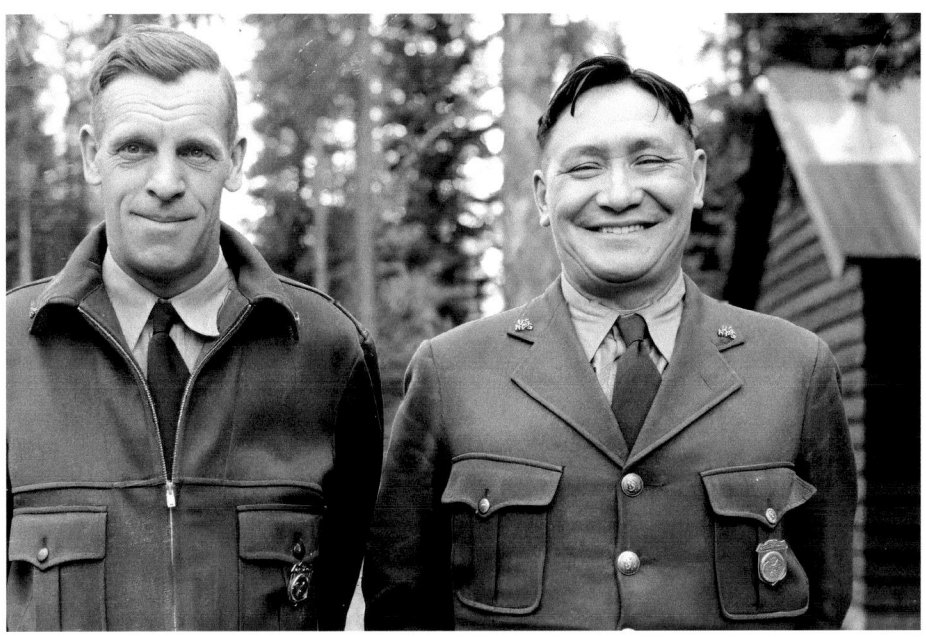

Ranger Frank Guardipee (right) with Ranger Ray Wedge, 1945. (*NPS, photographer unattributed*)

45

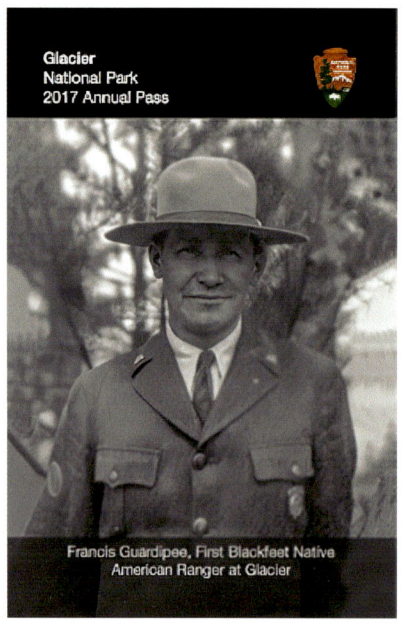

The annual entry pass for 2017 from Glacier National Park paid tribute to Frank Guardipee, the first Native American Ranger in the park. In fact, he was also the first Native American park ranger anywhere in the entire National Park Service. (*NPS, photographer unattributed*)

until Frank's death in 1970. On June 30, 2017, Glacier National Park honored Frank Guardipee's legacy as the first Native American ranger anywhere in the National Park Service by putting his photograph on the park's 2017 Annual Pass for visitors.

Joe Heimes and the Capture of Joe Cosley

Joe Heimes, along with Clyde Fauley and Hugh Buchanan, was one of the most highly regarded of all the Glacier Park rangers of the late 1920s and 1930s. His career as a Glacier Park ranger extended into the early 1960s. He was described in 1959 as "one of the few remaining old-time backcountry rangers," a "crusty fellow with a predictably dour attitude," and "a loner in the true sense of the word."[13]

In May 1929, however, Joe Heimes was a young man, a ranger stationed at Joe Cosley's old haunts, the Belly River Ranger Station just south of the Canadian border. Heimes had arrived in Montana in 1923 at age twenty-two, and he became a park ranger that year. His career lasted until his retirement in 1962, when he moved to a home on the west side of Flathead Lake near Somers, Montana.[14, 15]

Joe Cosley had returned to the area after World War One, where he continued to trap and poach on both sides of the border including in the Belly River and Mokowanis River valleys. Unfortunately for Cosley, on a spring day in May 1929, Joe Heimes found it necessary to break up a beaver dam that had flooded the wagon road (now a simple trail) leading along the Belly River from the Canadian border to the Belly River Ranger Station. In doing so, Heimes came across a camp and cache of furs not quite a mile south of the U.S.–Canadian border. He returned to the ranger station to report the find, and then returned to the camp to find Joe Cosley cooking his dinner. Heimes threatened to shoot Cosley if he moved, and after a sleepless night stand-off, forced Cosley to walk to Heimes' ranger station where he was met by another ranger and a Canadian park warden. Cosley was forced to snowshoe with Heimes and the other ranger over Gable Pass and down to Slide Lake and the Glacier Park boundary, where a waiting car took them southward to East Glacier and onto the Great Northern Railway to Belton for justice to be served (this so-called road no longer exists, except as the trail from the Chief Mountain Highway to the Glacier Park boundary and on to Slide Lake).[16]

In Belton, a quick trial found Cosley guilty of poaching, having been found with seven traps, three muskrat hides, and a beaver carcass in his possession. Cosley was fined $100 and given a suspended sentence of ninety days in jail. After the quick trial, Joe Heimes found out that a friend had paid Cosley's fine and Cosley was turned free, at which point he got a ride from Belton to the end of the road above Lake McDonald, and immediately started snowshoeing back to the Belly River on a route that would take him up McDonald Creek and over Ahern Pass into the headwaters of the Belly River. Heimes and another ranger boarded the eastbound Great Northern to Glacier Park Station (East Glacier) and drove at break-neck speeds to the Canadian border and around to the wagon road into the Belly River. Cosley was gone, having returned to another hidden cache which he cleared out, and from which he subsequently fled northward into Canada. Joe Heimes estimated that they must have missed Cosley by only a few hours, but Cosley was gone. Cosley moved northward and trapped in northern Alberta until his death in May 1944.[17, 18, 19]

Elmer Ness

We saw in Chapter 1 the dangers of backcountry patrolling by park rangers, and specifically the harrowing experience of Ranger Elmer Ness. That sparse report from Chapter 1 does not truly convey the life-threatening nature of Ranger Ness' experience. In an oral history interview given in 1975, Elmer's wife, Margaret, provided a much more thorough account:

> Elmer set out for the Kennedy Creek Ranger Station in November and planned to continue to the Lee Creek patrol cabin to take snow course readings and count wildlife. Because he expected to get to Kennedy Creek cabin for supper, he only took a candy bar with him in his trip over Gable Pass. Hard, icy snow had glazed over on the east face of the pass, however, and Elmer slipped and fell, hitting a boulder. The packboard he wore saved his life, Margarent said, by cushioning some of the force of his fall. With a smashed hip and two pelvic fractures, Elmer cut pine trees with a jackknife to fashion crutches. It took him three nights and four days to crawl back to the station, about four or five steep miles from the Belly River Ranger Station.[20]

Worried that he might draw criticism from Park Headquarters for the accident, Ness bravely spent two weeks with his wife's nursing at the Belly River Ranger Station before the pain became intolerable. They finally radioed for help, and the assistant chief ranger made it to the station to evacuate the Nesses. Elmer subsequently spent nearly four months in the hospital recovering. The Nesses were transferred to the St. Mary Ranger Station in 1934, and Elmer became district ranger there in 1938 until 1940. He was

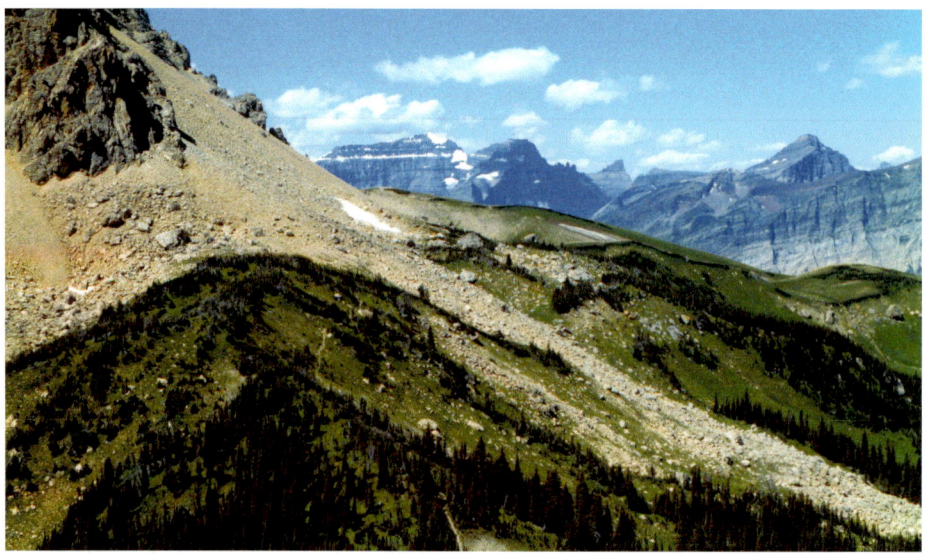

Ranger Elmer Ness suffered a life-threatening accident at Gable Pass on November 13, 1933, described in the text. This photo looks down upon Gable Pass from above. The pass is visible at bottom center, and a trail leading up toward Gable Mountain at upper left is visible. (*Photo by author, photo taken July 19, 1998*)

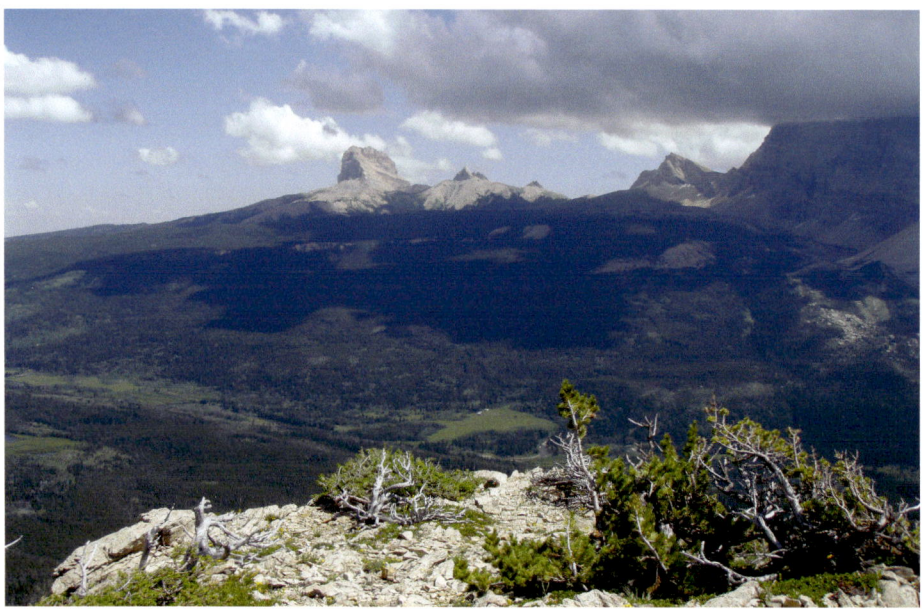

The Belly River Ranger Station, where Elmer Ness was stationed in 1933, is visible at lower center, on the light-green fan-shaped landform to the left of the protruding foreground twig. Gable Pass is the low point on the ridge at upper right-center. Ranger Ness had to make it from the pass back to the ranger station to survive after his accident. (*Photo by Jon J. Kedrowski, photo taken July 25, 2009*)

Glacier Park Rangers of the 1920s and 1930s

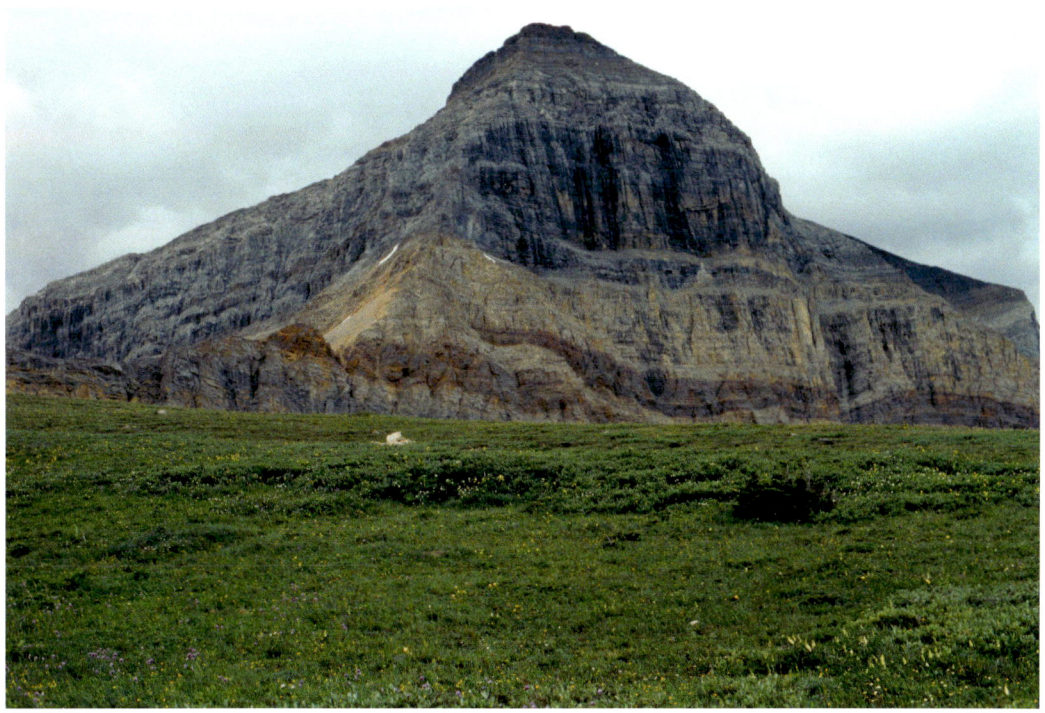

The trail from Gable Pass to the Belly River Ranger Station goes along the base of Gable Mountain seen here, where a hiker in mid-November, i.e. Ranger Elmer Ness, would be exposed to blowing snow, strong winds, and rockfalls. (*Photo by author, photo taken July 30, 2002*)

subsequently transferred to park headquarters and became assistant chief ranger for the park until his retirement in 1956.[21, 22]

Hugh Buchanan

Hugh Buchanan was another highly regarded ranger with a long career in Glacier Park. He put in thirty years with the National Park Service and served in several locations in the park, including the Nyack Ranger Station in 1928–1929, at Lake McDonald in the early 1930s, at Polebridge in the early to mid-1930s, and at Walton as District Ranger in 1935 and 1938–1940. Buchanan was highly respected by the locals in the Middle Fork of the Flathead River valley. Buchanan allowed the local residents to shoot and take an occasional deer to feed their families, but he drew the line at those residents inviting friends of theirs from outside the valley to do so. He also became friends with Dan Doody's widow at Nyack, Josephine Doody, and respecting her status as a ranger widow, he looked the other way and tolerated her occasional poaching and of course her on-going moonshining.[23]

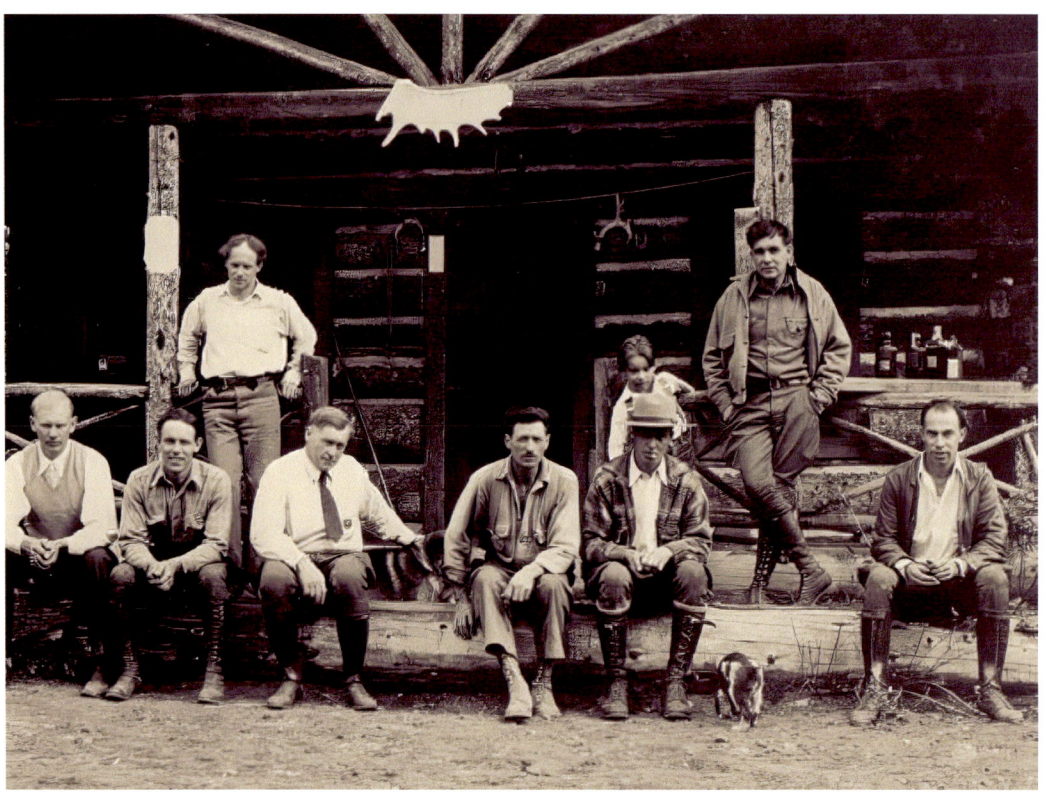

Park west-side rangers get together for Thanksgiving at the Kishenehn Ranger Station in 1933. From left to right, Elmer Fladmark, Park headquarters (Belton); Channing Howell, Fish Creek; Joe Heimes (location unspecified in 1933, but not at his usual Belly River station); Ray Newbury, Lake McDonald; Andy Fleutsch, Kishenehn; Hugh Buchanan, Polebridge; Ben Miller, Walton; Hugh Peyton, Logging Creek. The boy is not identified. (*Photographer unidentified; GNP Archives 42736*)

5

Glacier Park Ranger Stations Past and Present

Early rangers were expected to patrol, on average, 10 miles a day every day of every month regardless of the weather—an average of roughly 300 miles per month over territories of roughly 100 square miles to each ranger. To do so in spring through autumn on foot or horseback would have been challenging enough. To do so in the dead of a Glacier Park winter is mind-boggling. Snowshoes were required for several months of the year, and the snowshoes of this era were not the lightweight, easily portable items of today. Rather, they were massive wooden monsters with webbing. The first two photos in this chapter give you a feeling for how incredibly heavy these snowshoes must have been, making the wintertime 10 miles plus per day on patrol that much more remarkable.[1]

In order to support park rangers in their patrols, ranger stations were positioned within the circumference of the park boundaries. Rangers lived year-round in these log stations, and the stations were heavily stocked with provisions to support the rangers in their duties around the station and to allow them to embark on their 300-miles-per-month patrols. Distances between ranger stations were typically well in excess of 10 miles, and the patrols of rangers did not typically take them from their own station to another station, but rather around the territory surrounding their own station. A supporting network of backcountry snowshoe cabins was, therefore, necessary to support the patrolling missions of each ranger. The ranger stations were primarily built in the park's first decade, and some like the Lake McDonald Ranger Station predated the establishment of Glacier Park in 1910. By the early 1920s, it became apparent that the supporting snowshoe cabin network was vitally necessary, and nearly all the park snowshoe cabins were built in a flurry between about 1925 and 1931. This chapter examines the network of park ranger stations, beginning in the southeast corner of Glacier Park in Glacier Park Station (today's East Glacier Park) and travelling counterclockwise around the perimeter of the park until returning to East Glacier. This same pattern will be used in the following chapter in examining the distribution and role of the park snowshoe cabins.

Early Rangers of Glacier National Park

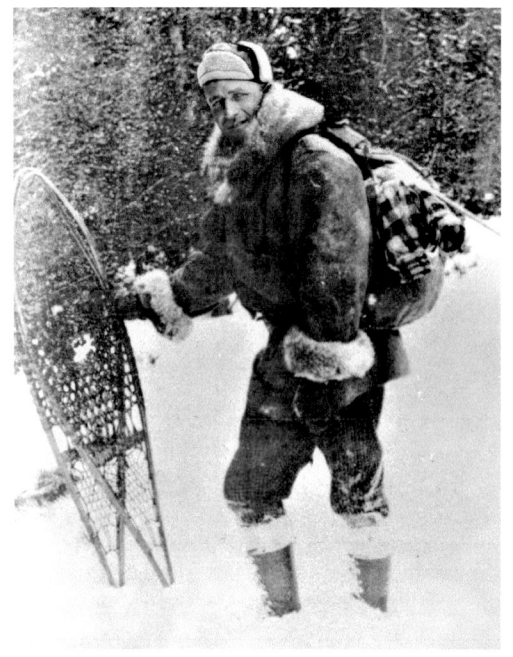

Unidentified park ranger, from the cover of *Glacial Drift—Notes from Glacier National Park*, January 1934. The oversized snowshoes were the standard in the 1930s. (*Photographer unidentified, GNP Archives*)

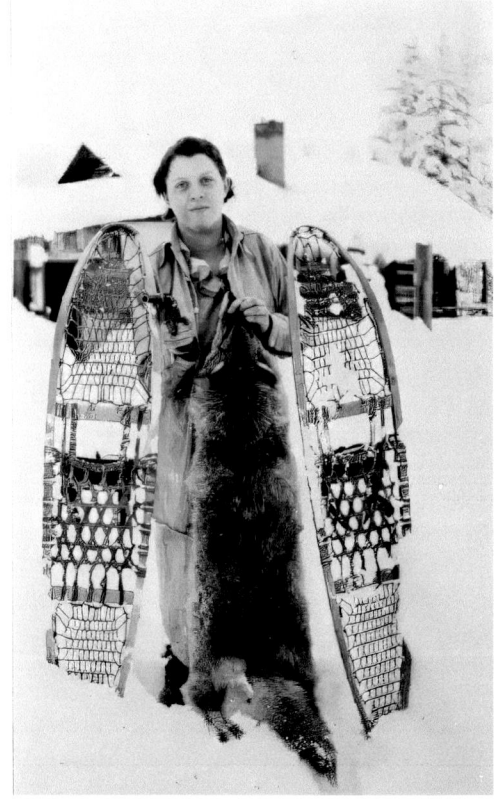

Mary Ellen Miller, wife of Park Ranger Glenn Miller, shows off a coyote pelt shot by her husband while the couple was stationed at the Kishenehn Ranger Station in the winter of 1935–1936. Note that Mrs. Miller also had the standard oversized snowshoes of the 1930s. (*GNP Archives*)

Glacier Park Ranger Stations Past and Present

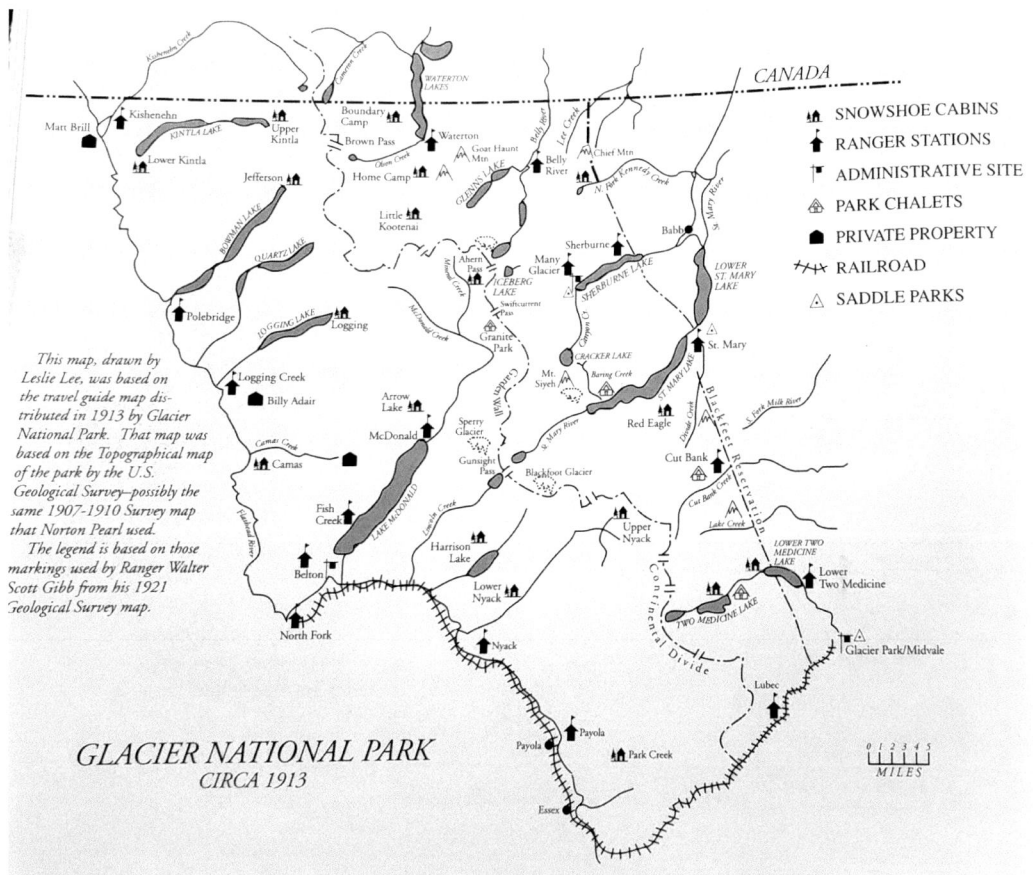

Map showing the location of ranger stations *circa* 1913 and snowshoe cabins *circa* early 1930s (nearly all the park snowshoe cabins were built in the period of the mid-1920s to about 1931). Nearly all the snowshoe cabins shown still exist, and the map does not show the Fielding cabin just north of the railroad on the southern end of the park. With respect to the ranger stations, several of those shown no longer exist, including the North Fork, Nyack (outbuildings still survive), Paola (shown as Payola on the map), Lubec, and Lower Two Medicine Ranger Stations. The Waterton station was destroyed in the Great Flood of 1964 and was replaced by the current Goat Haunt Ranger Station at the same location on the southern end of Upper Waterton Lake. (*Map drawn by, and courtesy of, Leslie Lee*)

East Glacier Ranger Station

East Glacier/Glacier Park Station was, until the completion of Going-to-the-Sun Road in 1933, the beating heart of the eastern half of Glacier Park. It served as the district headquarters for the rangers' contingent on the eastern side of the mountains until that distinction was moved to St. Mary in 1933 upon completion of Sun Road.

The East Glacier Ranger Station is located north of Glacier Park Lodge along Montana Highway 49. It comprises, with several surrounding buildings, the East Glacier Ranger Station Historic District. The ranger station served as the district headquarters office as well as the home for the ranger stationed there. Not constructed until 1921, the building continues to serve as the ranger station there at the present time. The fire cache in the historic district was constructed by Civilian Conservation Corps workers in 1935, but for the Two Medicine area. The building was moved from there to East Glacier in 1948.[2]

North-northwest of the East Glacier Ranger Station once stood the Lower Two Medicine Ranger Station, on the shore of Lower Two Medicine Lake (on the Blackfeet Reservation, not within the park boundary). The photo of Park Ranger Frank Guardipee and his family, in the previous chapter, is the only known photo of the Lower Two Medicine Ranger Station.

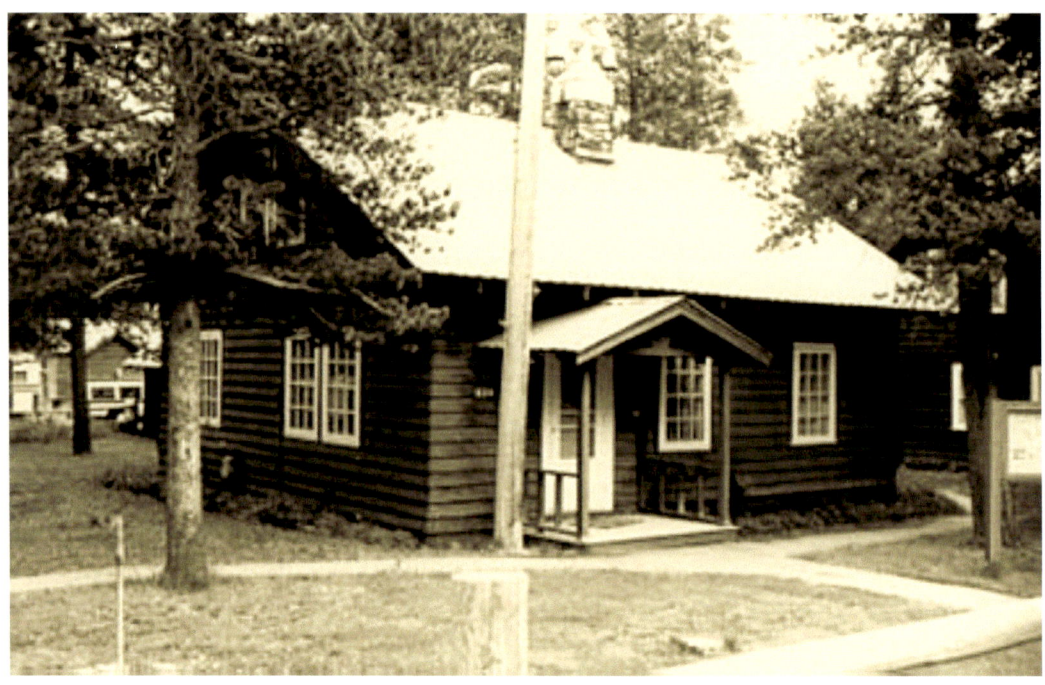

A view of the combined Ranger Office and residence of the East Glacier Ranger Station Historic District. (*Undated public domain photo, photographer unattributed*)

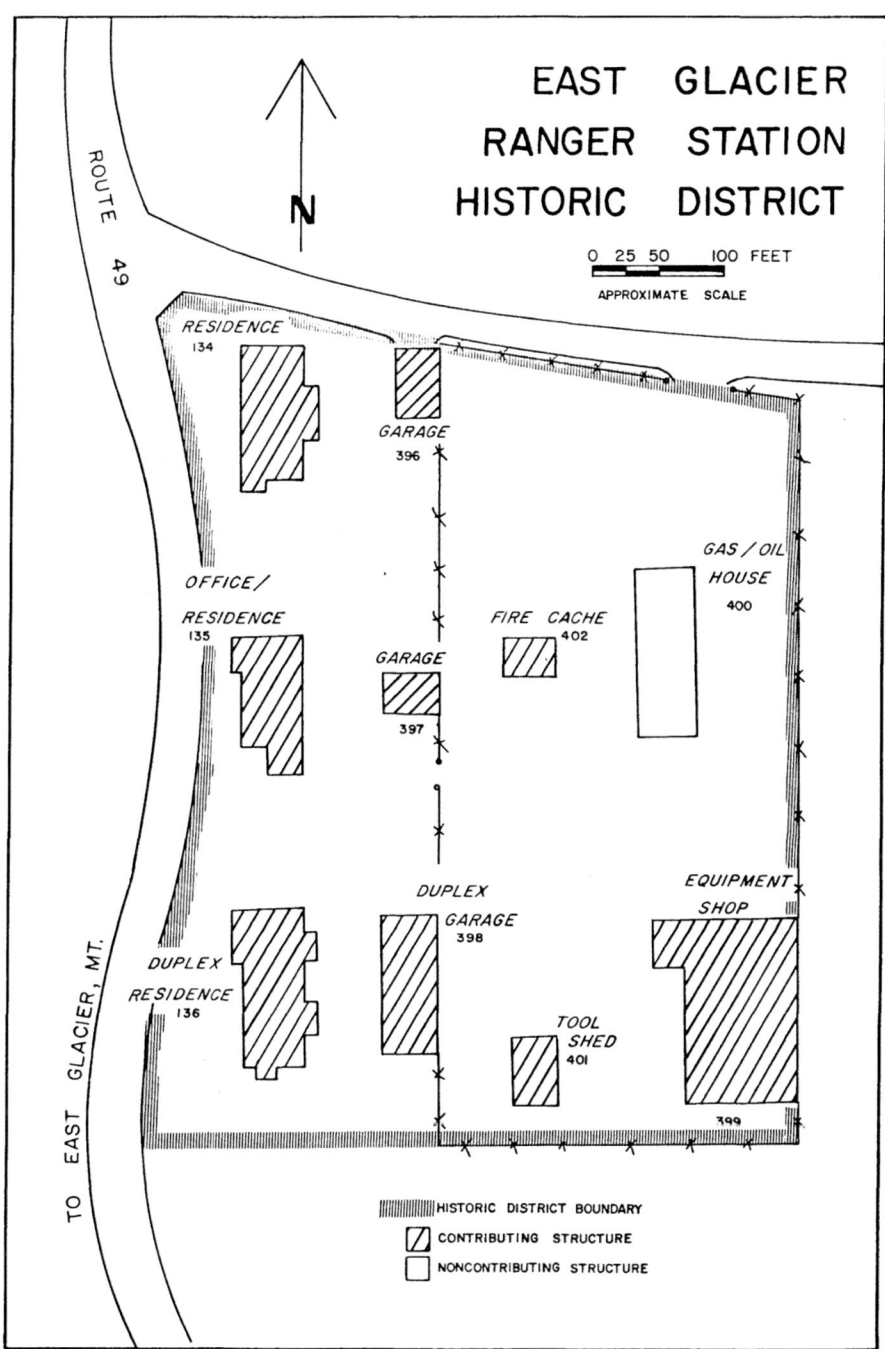

Map of the East Glacier Ranger Station Historic District. The size of the district is attributable to the fact that it served as the Park's east-side district headquarters until replaced by St. Mary upon the completion of Going-to-the-Sun Road in 1933. The ranger office is the building at left center. (*NPS, 1984*)

Cut Bank Ranger Station

The Cut Bank Ranger Station was built in 1917; it was one of the first structures funded and completed under the authority of the new National Park Service (founded in 1916). The ranger stationed there was to patrol the Cut Bank valley and surrounding areas and interact with park visitors at the nearby Cut Bank Chalets operated by the Great Northern Railway. A barn and woodshed were added to the ranger station district in 1935, both built by the Civilian Conservation Corps.[3]

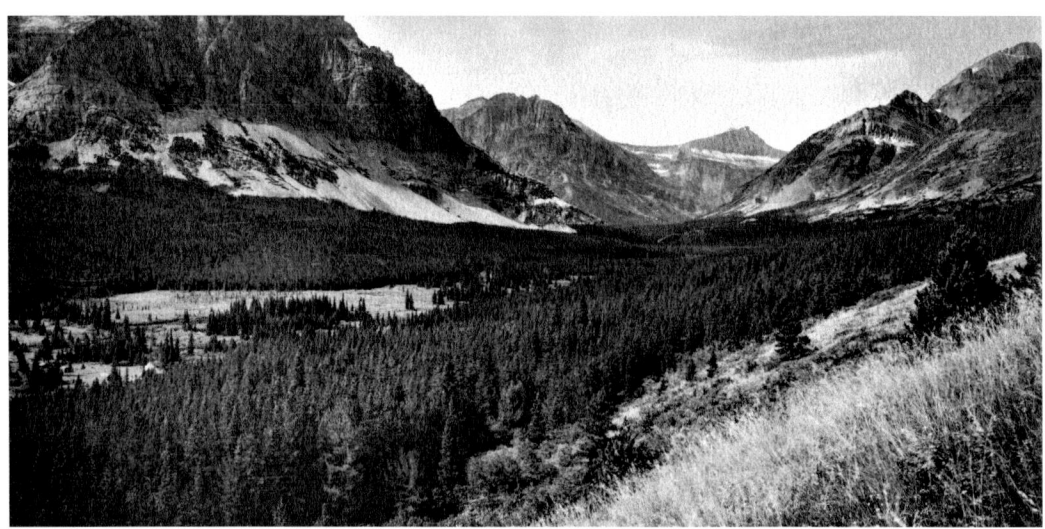

The Cut Bank valley, location of the Cut Bank Ranger Station, where Doris Huffine and her ranger husband were stationed during the winter of 1927–28. The station is located to the right (north) of Cut Bank Creek. (*Fred H. Kiser, OHSL ba020876*)

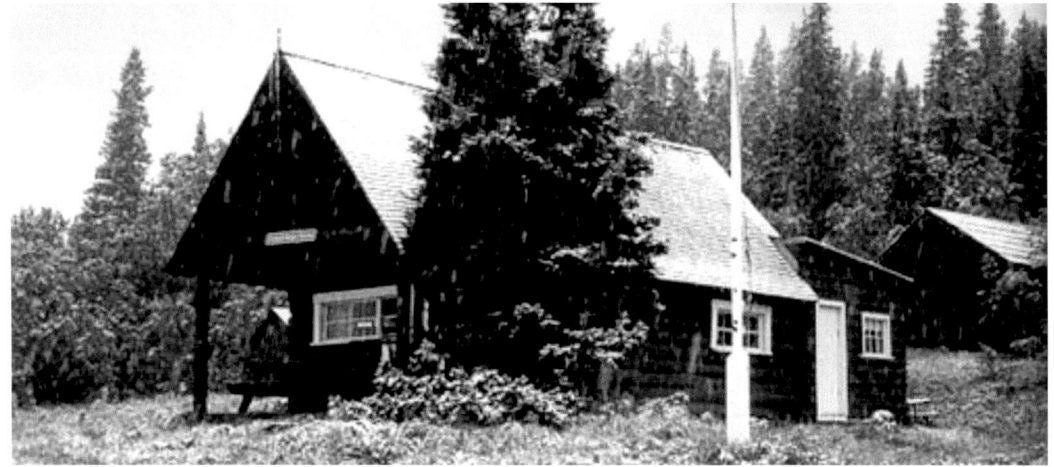

Cut Bank Ranger Station, immediately north of Cut Bank Creek, during a light snowstorm. (*NPS photo, undated*)

Glacier Park Ranger Stations Past and Present

Right: The Cut Bank Ranger Station, with barn/woodshed in the rear. The barn and woodshed were built in the 1930s by the Civilian Conservation Corps and were designed to match the architecture of the pre-CCC ranger station. (*Photo undated, NPS*)

Below: Side view of the Cut Bank Ranger Station, looking toward the southwest. (*GNP photo, undated*)

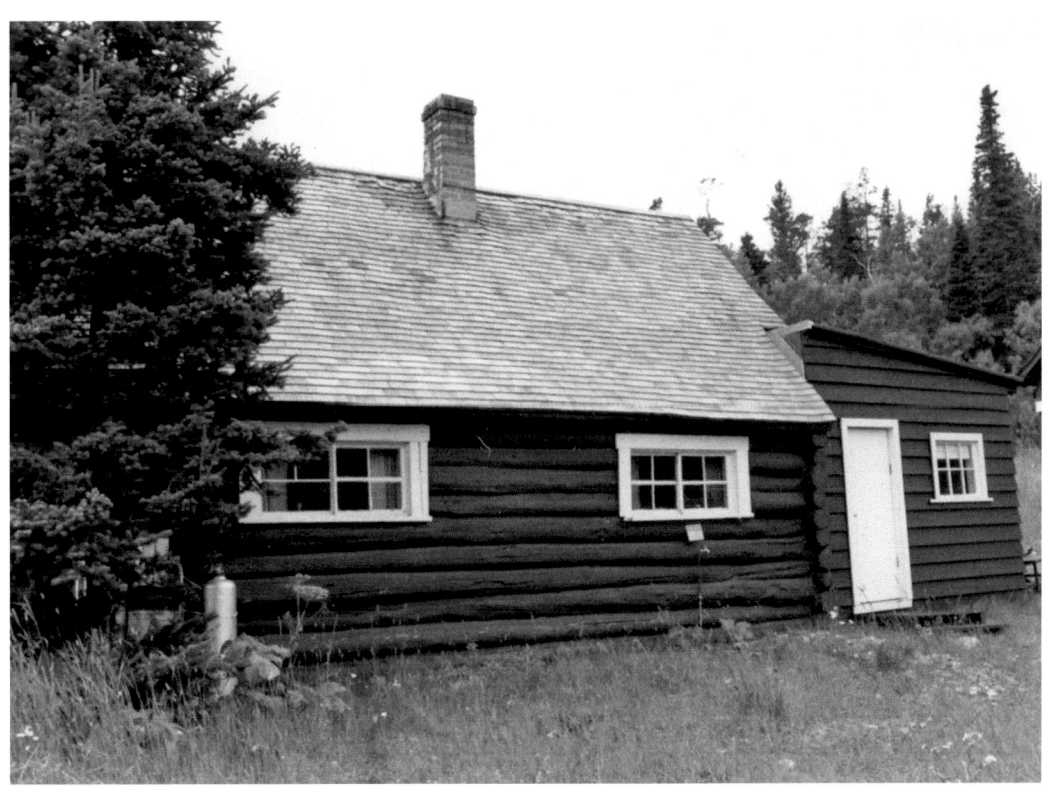

St. Mary Ranger Station

Roughly 17 miles north of the Cut Bank Ranger Station is the St. Mary Ranger Station. In this instance, I am referring to the original Ranger Station established in 1913 rather than the present-day district headquarters office and ranger station a half mile or so away. Also referred to as the "Old St. Mary Ranger Station," this original station replaced a pre-park cabin used by the first St. Mary Park Ranger, William Burns, who worked there from 1910–1913. It was one of the first buildings built in the new national park on the eastside of Glacier and was built by the first district ranger assigned there.[4, 5]

Built prior to the creation of the National Park Service in 1916 and its eventual imposition of standardized designs, the Old St. Mary Ranger Station's two-story design is unique for Glacier Park. Recall that it was upstairs on the second floor where Eva Beebe encountered a mountain lion that had come in through the upper window and was threatening her young child. Refurbished somewhat in 1954, the station was fully restored in 1975–1976. A dedication ceremony, attended by Eva Beebe, was held on July 11, 1976.

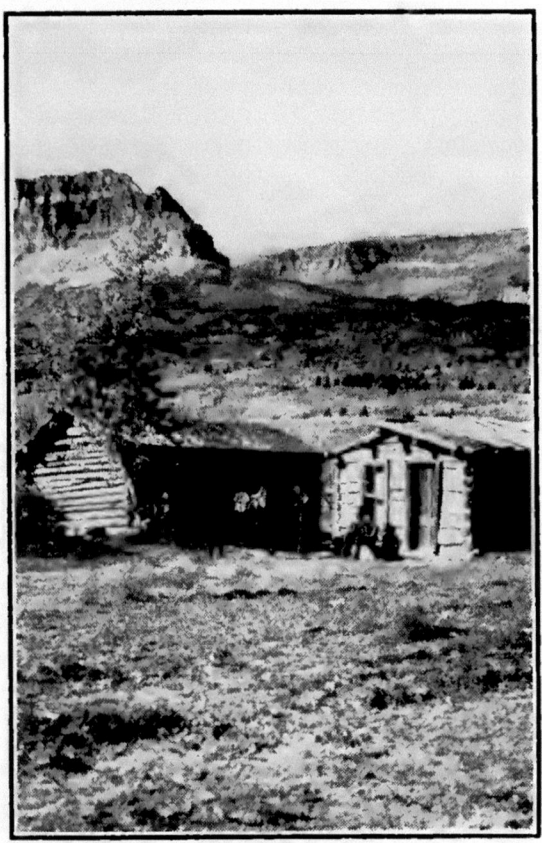

"Down the grass-grown street was the cabin that Ranger Burns called his home."

Pre-park-establishment ranger station at St. Mary, home of Ranger William Burns who served as a guide to early tourist parties. View is northward to Singleshot Mountain (left) and East Flattop Mountain (right). (*Photo by Tom Dillon, circa 1910, from his "Over the Trails of Glacier National Park" published in 1911*)

Glacier Park Ranger Stations Past and Present

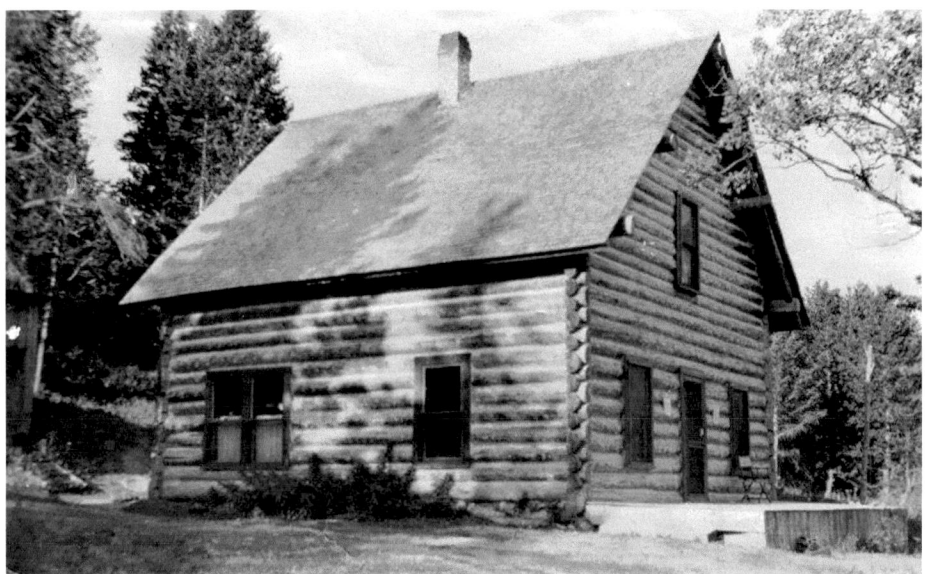

Early photo of the park service St. Mary Ranger Station. Photo is undated here, but it is dated as 1918 in the 1976 restoration dedication pamphlet (shown below). (*Photo unattributed, from the "Early Columbia Falls History" Facebook page, August 17, 2019*)

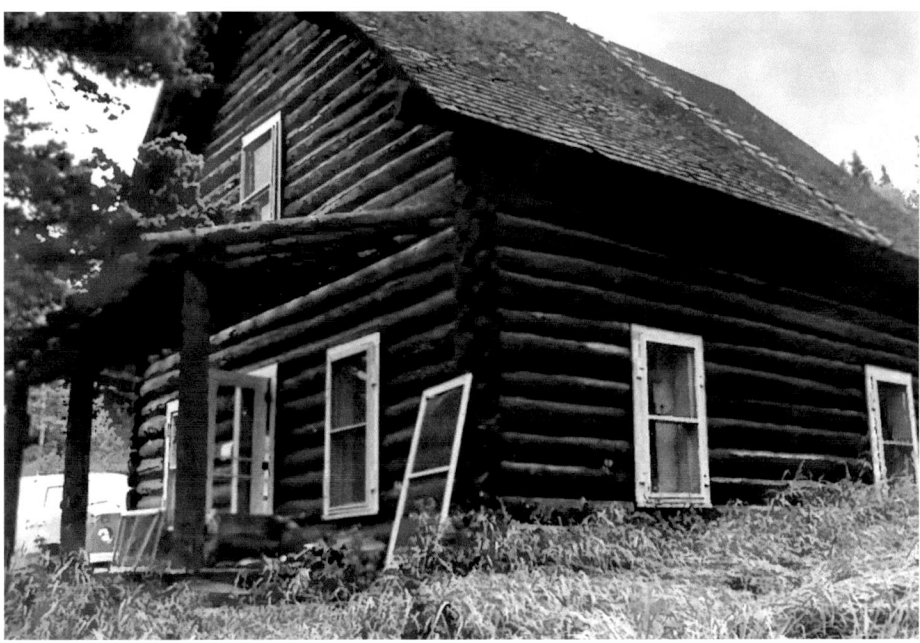

St. Mary Ranger Station undergoing restoration in 1975. View is the front of the station, from a different angle than shown in the previous photo. Note that a porch overhang roof had been added between the time of the two photos. (*Photo by Lance Williams for GNP, August 1975*)

Early Rangers of Glacier National Park

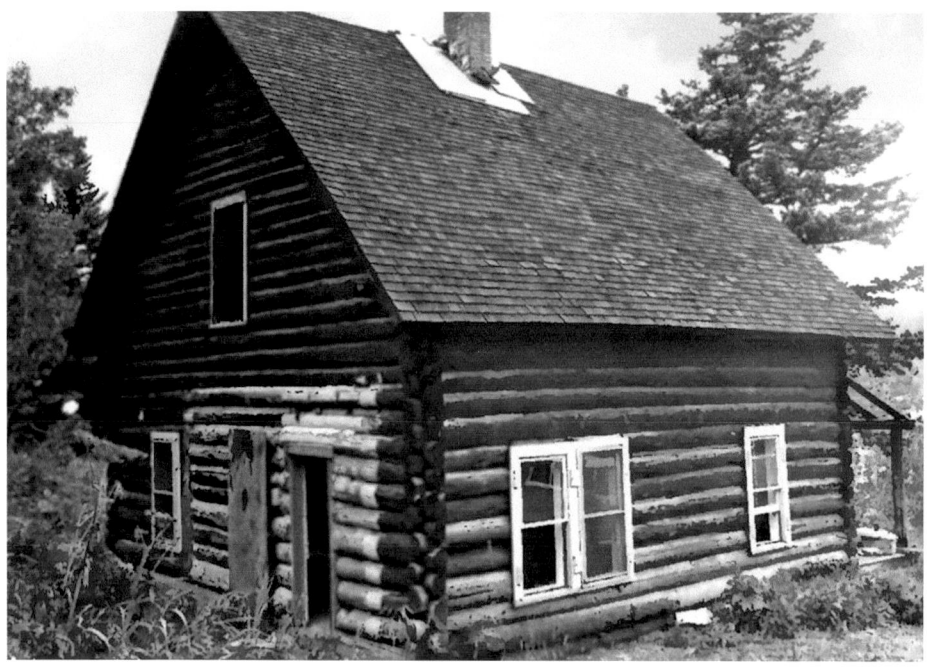

View of the side and rear of the St. Mary Ranger Station, looking toward St. Mary Lake (unseen in distance). (*Photo by Lance Williams for GNP, August 1975*)

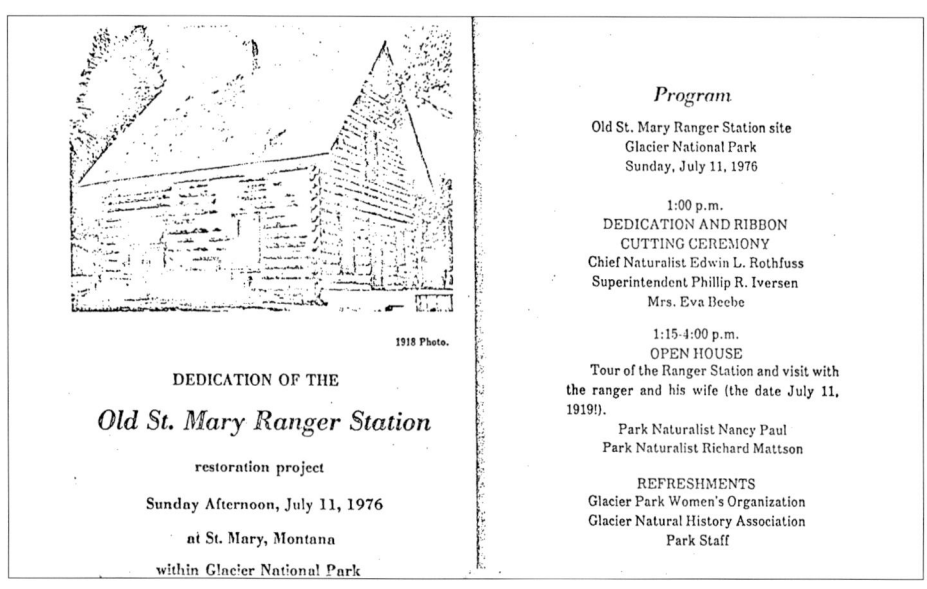

The 1976 station restoration dedication program for the St. Mary Ranger Station. A stylized drawing-like image of the station from the 1918 photo shown previously is on the cover page. Mrs. Eva Beebe, one of the first ranger wives to live in the station in the years 1918–1919, was part of the dedication ceremony. (*GNP/NPS, program designer unattributed*)

Lake Sherburne Ranger Station

The Lake Sherburne Ranger Station is adjacent to the entrance/checking station along the road entering the Swiftcurrent valley leading up-valley to the Many Glacier Hotel and, further on, the Swiftcurrent camp store, campground, and ranger station. The Sherburne station anchors the Sherburne Ranger Station Historic District. The station is very similar to those at Belly River and Lake McDonald. It was built in 1925. The entrance station was constructed in 1928, and buildings surrounding the ranger station date to the 1930s.[6]

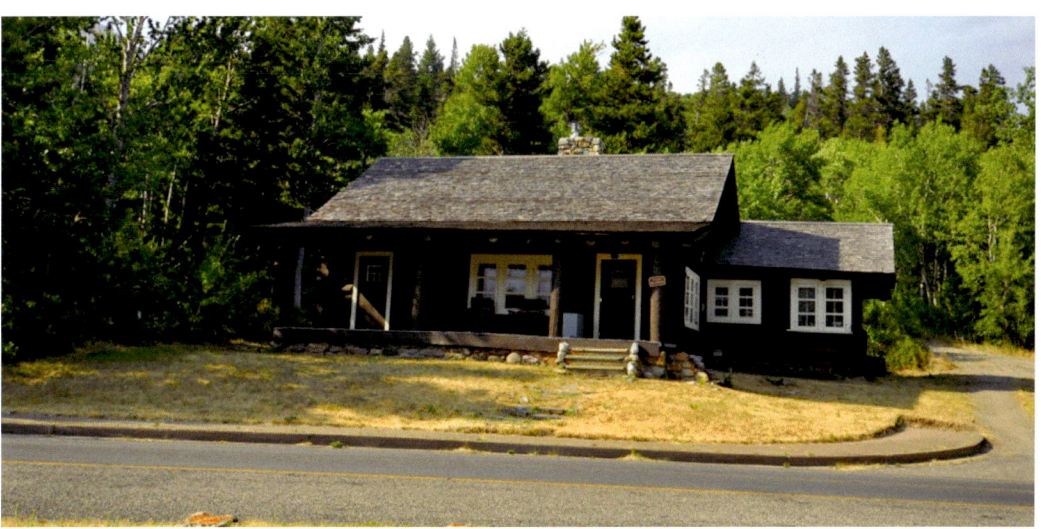

Above: Lake Sherburne Ranger Station, adjacent to the entrance station to the Many Glacier/Swiftcurrent valley (next photo). (*Photo from Creative Commons, by Magicpiano, photo taken August 2, 2017*)

Below: Many Glacier entrance station, adjacent to the Lake Sherburne Ranger Station (in trees on left). (*Lance Olivieri photo for NPS, photo taken 1975*)

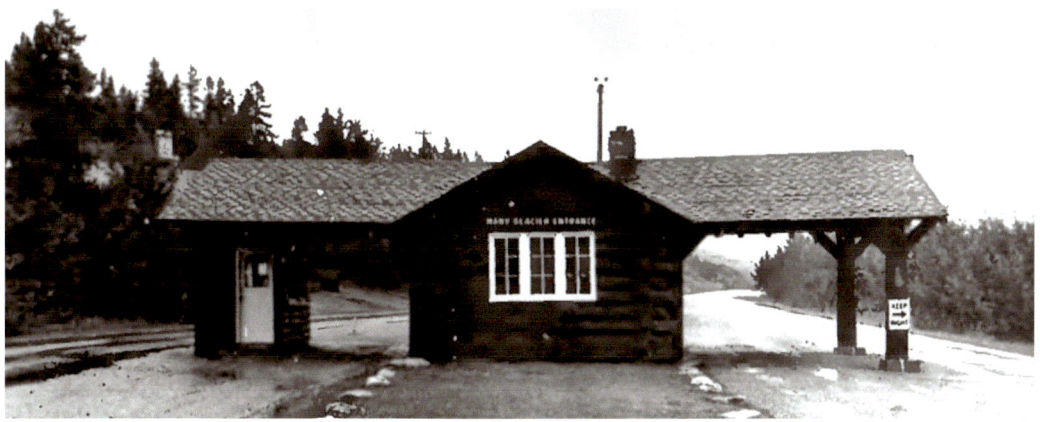

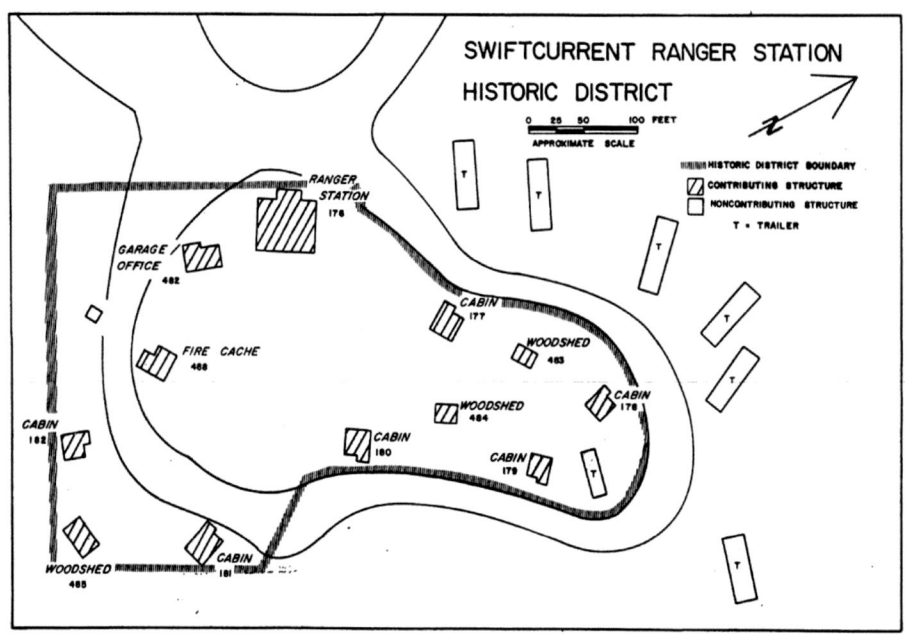

Map of the Swiftcurrent Ranger Station Historic District, in the Many Glacier valley about a mile up-valley beyond the turn-off to the Many Glacier Hotel. (*GNP, undated*)

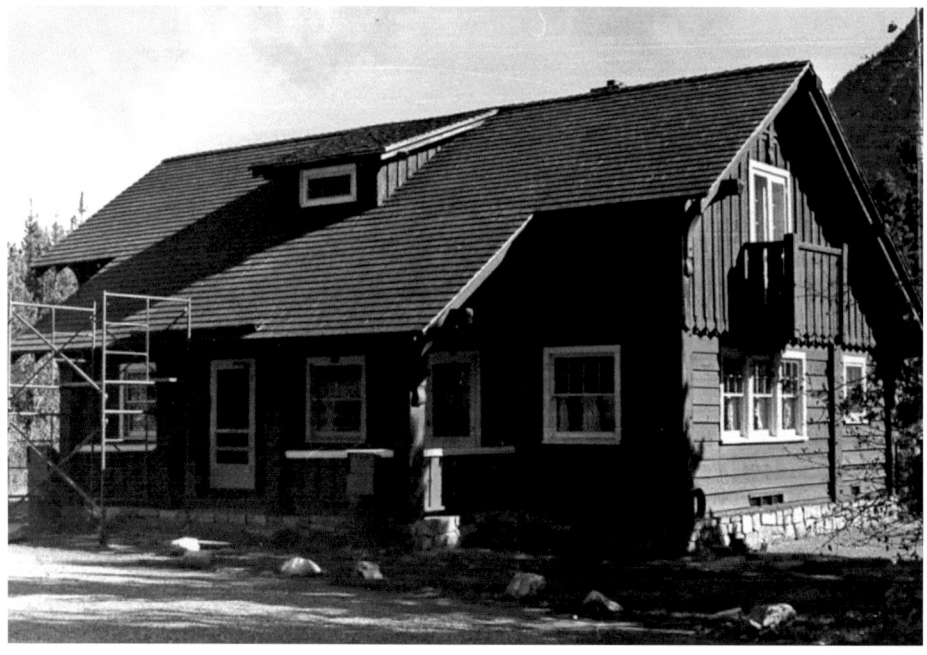

Swiftcurrent Ranger Station, undergoing renovations in 1975. (*Photo by Lance Williams for GNP*)

Swiftcurrent Ranger Station

The Swiftcurrent Ranger Station Historic District, directly east of the Swiftcurrent/Many Glacier Campground, is comprised of the ranger station there and numerous surrounding structures and outbuildings. The district is unique in Glacier Park because it all dates to one year, completed in 1938. This unusual tightly clustered dating of the structures is because the entire ranger station and associated buildings were destroyed by the Heaven's Peak fire that swept into and through most of the Swiftcurrent valley in August 1936. The station and surrounding structures are basic, Park Service-style structures of no striking appearance.[7]

Belly River Ranger Station

The Belly River Ranger Station, home to ranger icons such as Joe Cosley, Joe Heimes, and Elmer Ness, is located in one of the most beautiful valleys in Glacier Park. However, Joe Cosley never lived in the current station, which was built in 1925. The still-existing barn, however, was built in 1912 and may have been the actual "station" that Joe Cosley lived in during his days there. Views from the station include a sweeping view of multi-crested Gable Mountain, and a view across the Belly River and up the Mokowanis valley to Glacier Park's highest peak, Mt. Cleveland.[8]

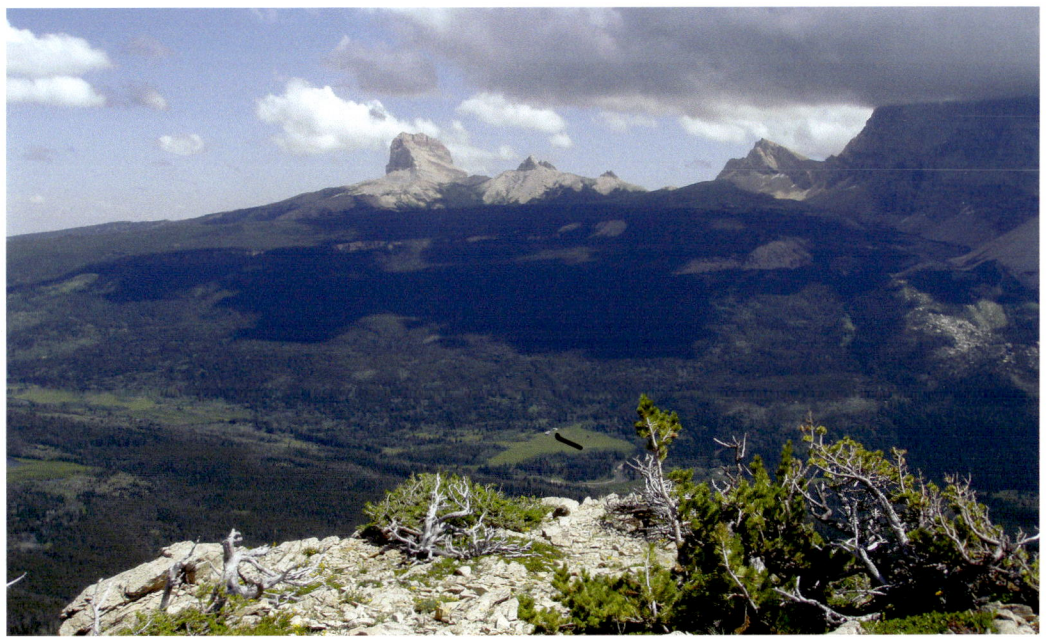

The black line points to the Belly River Ranger Station complex, with the Belly River located just below the station. Chief Mountain is the mountain on the left. Gable Pass, site of Ranger Elmer Ness's infamous injury, is the low point at upper right-center. (*Photo courtesy of Jon J. Kedrowski, photo taken July 25, 2009*)

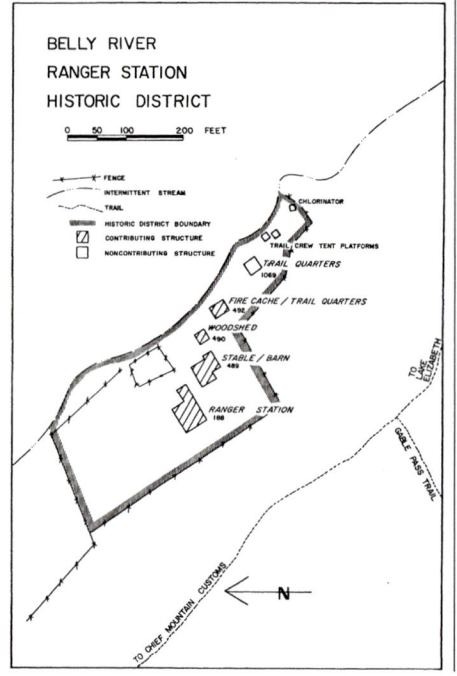

Left: Map of the Belly River Ranger Station Historic District. The ranger station and barn are the two structures visible on the previous photo. (*GNP, undated*)

Below: The Belly River Ranger Station office building. Gable Mountain is the multi-crested peak in the background. (*Photo courtesy of Jon J. Kedrowski, photo taken July 24, 2009*)

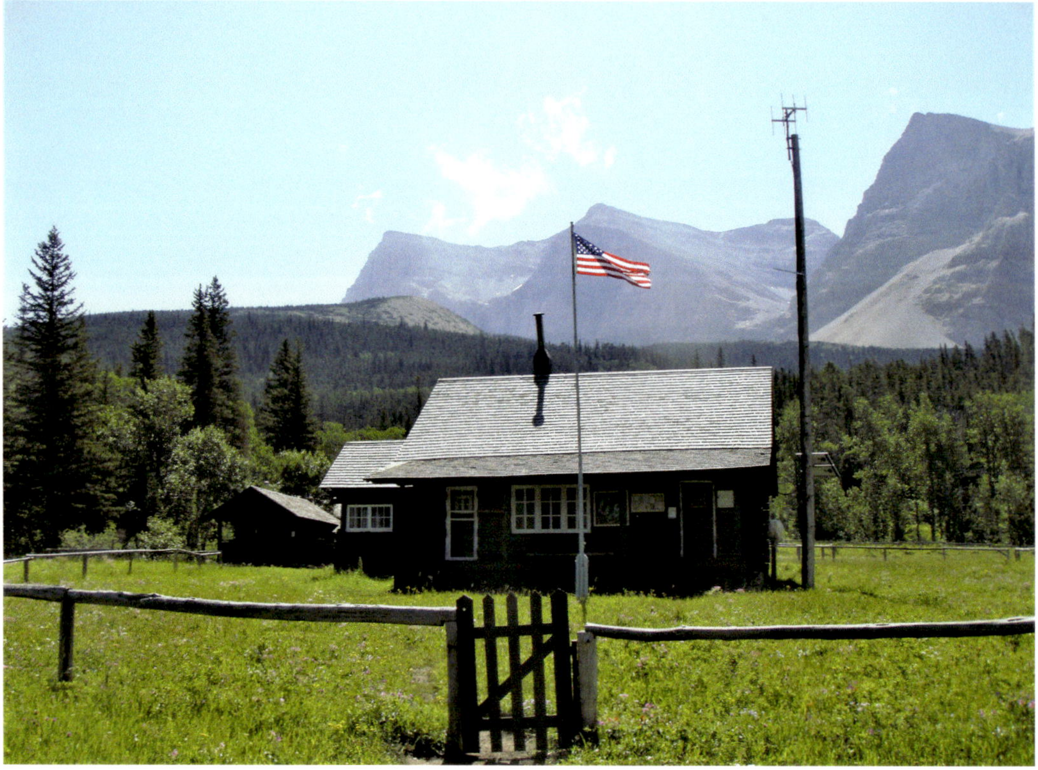

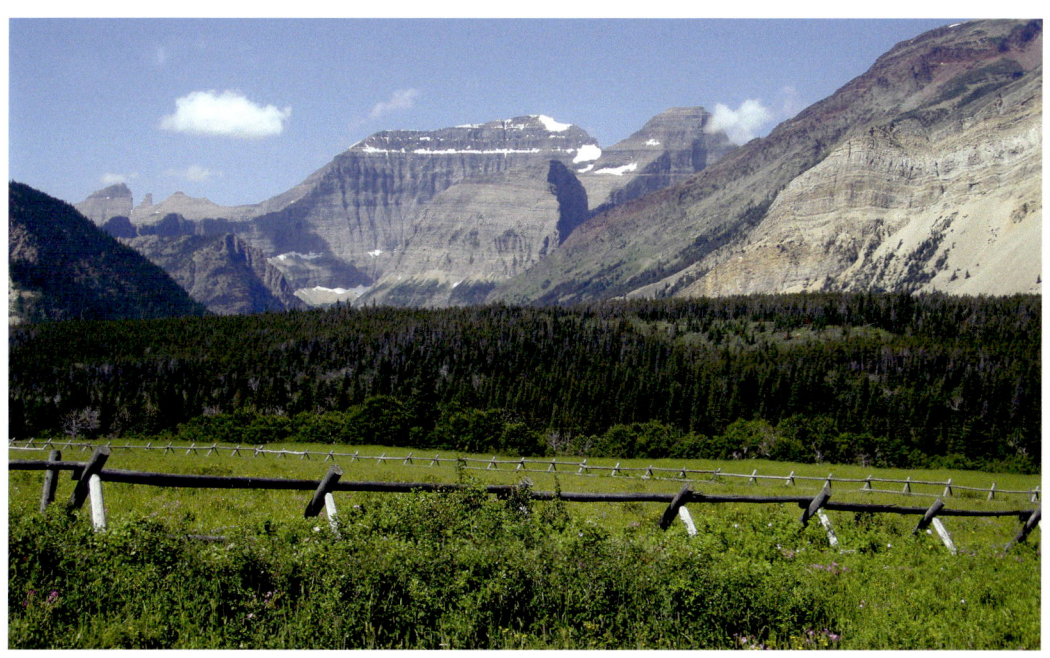

View from the Belly River Ranger Station up the Mokowanis River valley. Mt. Cleveland, the highest peak in Glacier National Park, is at center rear with a horizontal snow patch running across its face. (*Photo courtesy of Jon J. Kedrowski, photo taken July 24, 2009*)

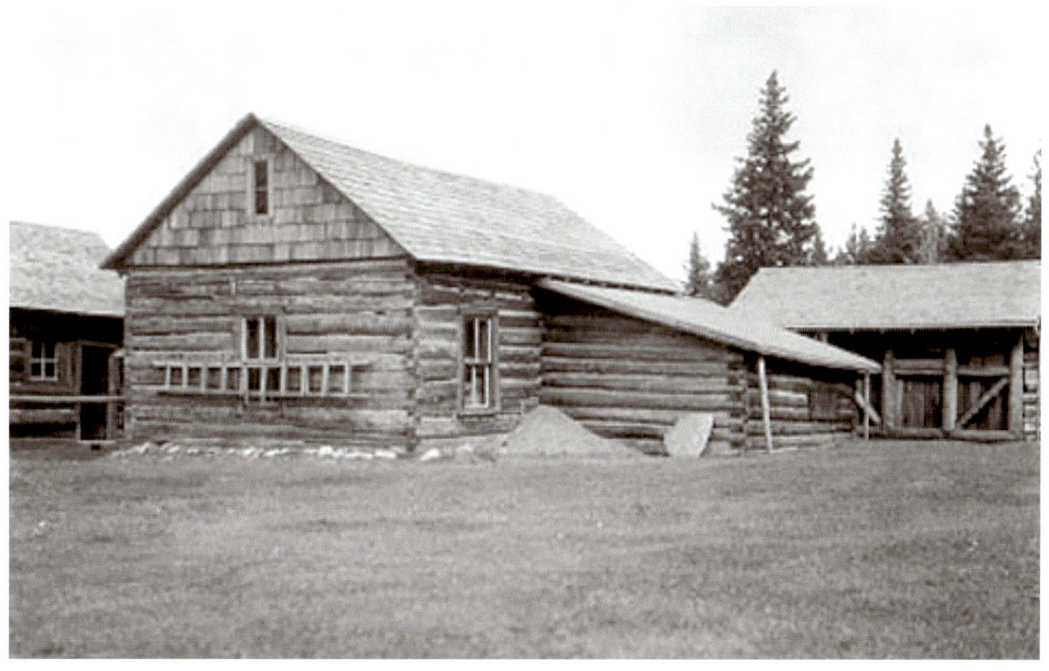

The barn at the Belly River Ranger Station. (*Undated public domain photo, photographer unknown*)

Waterton/Goat Haunt Ranger Station

The original Waterton Ranger Station was built before 1914, when it appears in a photograph taken by early park photographer R. E. Marble. It appears to have been a solitary, one-story log cabin. The station was destroyed in the Great Flood of June 1964, when the raging Waterton River removed the station. Because of the importance of its position monitoring comings and goings across the nearby Canadian border, it was quickly replaced by the current Goat Haunt Ranger Station built approximately on the same location. The station handles immigration needs for visitors arriving and departing there from and to Waterton Lakes National Park in Alberta, Canada.

Ranger Stations along the North Fork of the Flathead River

The ranger stations within Glacier Park and east of the North Fork of the Flathead River range from the extremely isolated Kishenehn Ranger Station near the Canadian border to the busy Polebridge Ranger Station that acts as the entry point for visitors to the popular campgrounds and hiking trails at Kintla, Bowman, Logging, and the Quartz Lakes. The ranger stations in the North Fork area include Kishenehn, Kintla Lake, Bowman Lake, Polebridge, and Logging Creek. Note that neither the Kintla Lake nor Bowman Lake stations appear on Leslie Lee's map shown near the beginning of this chapter. Reasons for these omissions are discussed below.

The Kishenehn Ranger Station is the closest Glacier Park station to Canada, being only 3 miles south of the border, and rangers stationed there were supremely isolated from the rest of the park but expected to monitor poaching and border excursions from the north. Winter isolation there was, as seen in Chapter 1, potentially deadly. After Ranger McAfee's suicide in the winter of 1926, the Park Service tried to post married couples to the station to alleviate the desperate isolation one individual could feel there.

The Kishenehn historic district is among the smallest in Glacier Park, being comprised simply of the station, constructed in 1921 (replacing the original station built in 1913 but destroyed by fire in 1919); a barn, woodshed, and fire cache built in 1934–35; and a pit toilet possibly built in 1922. However, numerous digging scars around the station suggest the toilet has been moved numerous times in the station's history. By about 1940, the station was no longer staffed, but it is still available for backcountry patrol use by rangers. It is no longer accessible by road from the Inside North Fork Road (the road was extended to the station on a branch road off the road to Kintla Lake in 1931) but requires hiking in today because that 1931 road extension has been abandoned.[9]

Moving south to the Kintla Lake Ranger Station, we encounter a station with a unique, pre-Park history. The current ranger station occupies a building built in approximately 1900 by the Butte Oil Company, which was involved in exploration for oil along the shore of Kintla Lake. This same company was responsible for construction of the Inside North Fork Road that still exists today, built by the company to bring oil-exploration equipment into the area.[10]

It is not clear what year Glacier National Park took over the Butte Oil Company building and established the ranger station, but it is noteworthy that it does not appear on Leslie Lee's *circa* 1913 map of ranger stations and snowshoe cabins. Nor is there

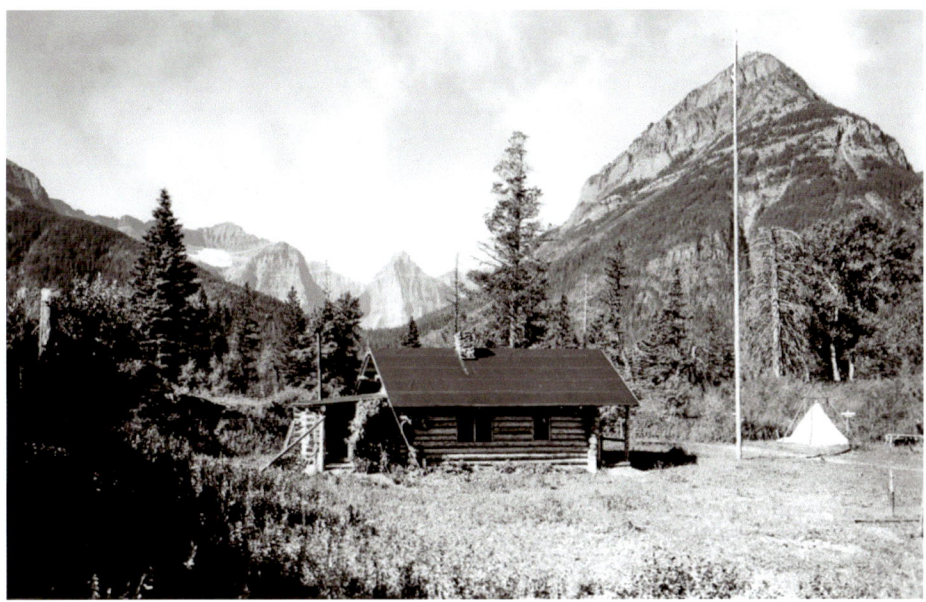

Waterton Ranger Station, 1914, at the southern end of Waterton Lake in the United States (the northern half of the lake extends northward into Waterton Lakes National Park, Alberta). *(Photo by R.E. Marble, GNP Archives GLAC 5979)*

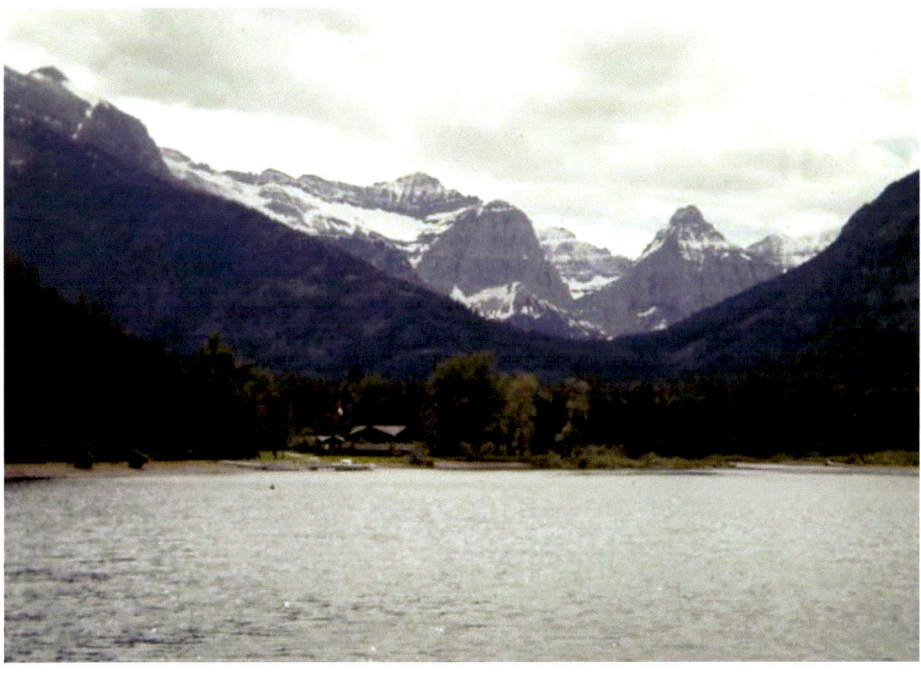

Approaching the Goat Haunt Ranger Station by boat, located where the former Waterton Ranger Station stood prior to the Great Flood of 1964. *(Photo by author, taken in June 1973)*

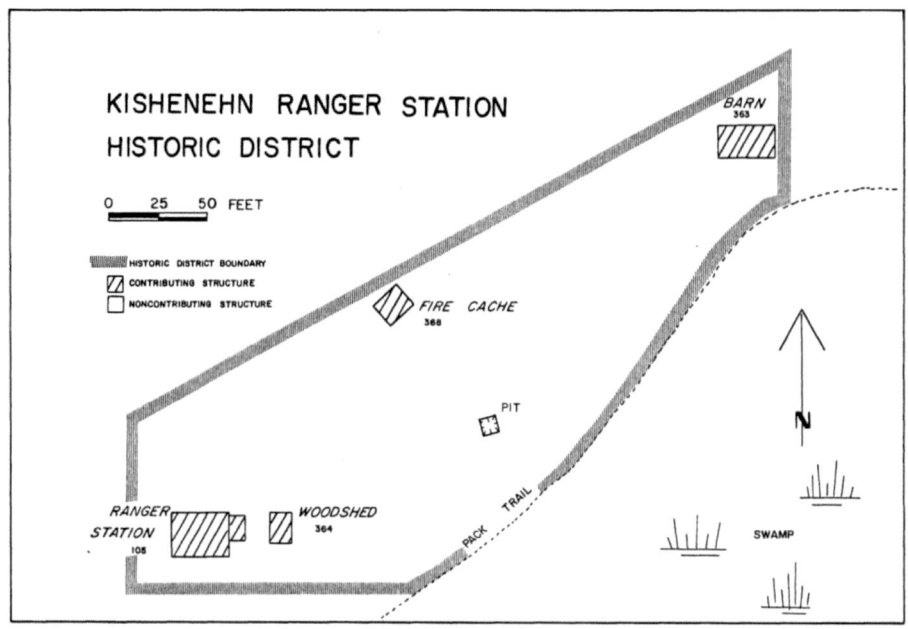

Map of the Kishenehn Ranger Station Historic District. (*GNP, undated*)

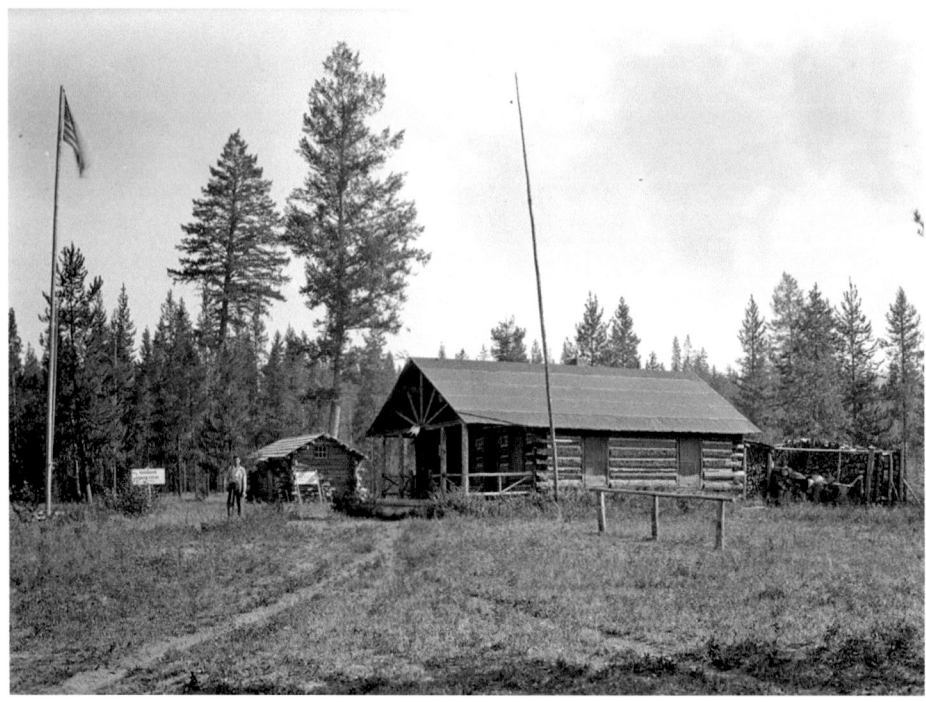

Ranger Andy Fleutsch stands in front and to the left of the Kishenehn Ranger Station, August 7, 1932. (*Photo by George Grant, GNP GLAC Grant 185*)

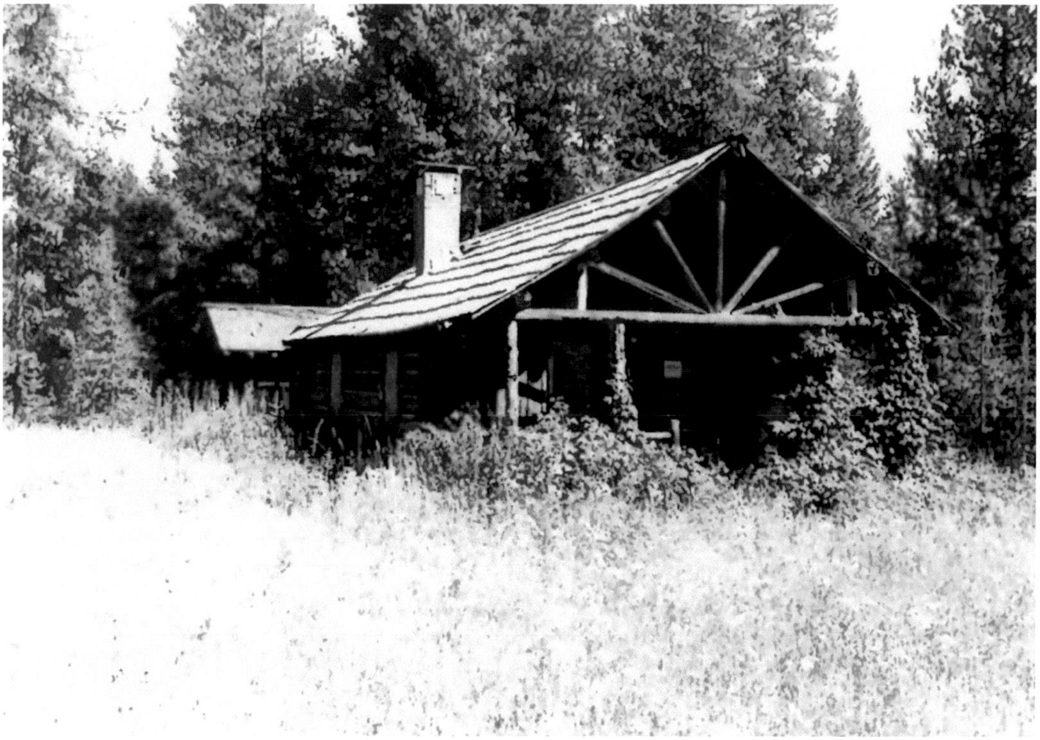

Above: Kishenehn Ranger Station, August 1975. (*Photo by Lance Williams for NPS*)

Right: The rustic interior of the Kishenehn Ranger Station. (*Photographer unattributed and undated, GNP*)

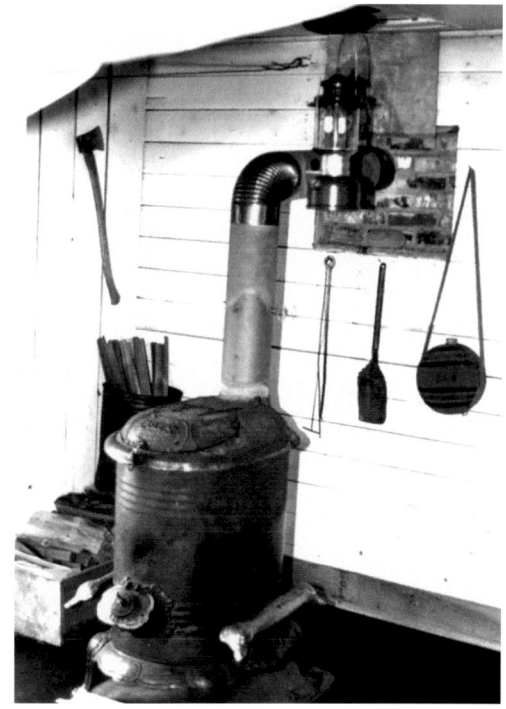

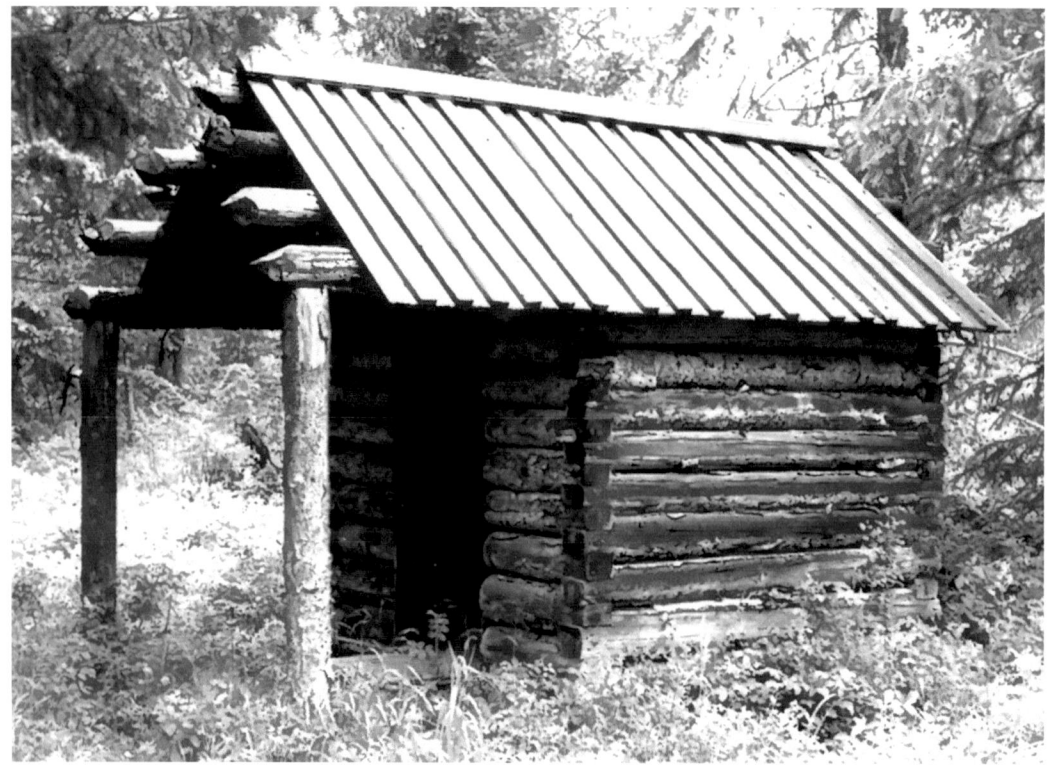

The Kishenehn Ranger Station pit toilet, a typical facility for backcountry ranger stations in Glacier National Park. (*GNP photo, undated*)

a ranger from Kintla Lake at the 1933 Thanksgiving gathering at nearby Kishenehn Ranger Station (shown in the photo at the end of the previous chapter of this book). Given that the Kintla Lake Ranger Station boathouse and fire cache were both constructed in 1935, it seems likely that it was sometime in the mid- to late 1930s when Kintla Lake Ranger Station began to operate under the auspices of Glacier Park.[11]

The Bowman Lake Ranger Station also has a unique history, not pre-dating Glacier National Park or the National Park Service but having been built not by either governmental entity. Instead, the building that now serves as the Bowman Lake Ranger Station was built by the Culver Military Academy of Culver, Indiana, as part of an outdoor camp known as Skyland Camp, with cabins and other buildings operated as a concession through a contract with the National Park Service. The building that would become the ranger station, known as the Rainbow Lodge, served as the mess hall and gathering lodge for the boys. Although a popular tourist camp for a few years, mismanagement doomed the endeavor such that by 1940 the concession contract was cancelled by the Park Service, and all the buildings of Skyland Camp except for the Rainbow Lodge were removed. The building became a ranger station in 1940, at the end of the time period covered in this book, and it has a much more substantial look to it than most of the Park Service-designed ranger stations.[12]

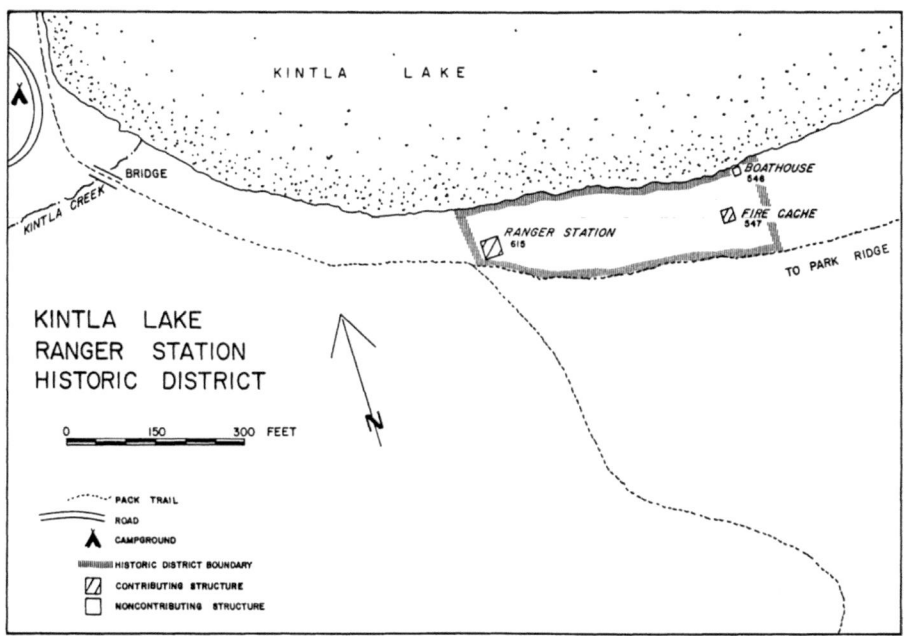

Map of the Kintla Lake Ranger Station Historic District, on the southern edge of Kintla Lake in northwestern Glacier National Park. The boathouse is on the shore of the lake, east of the ranger station. (*GNP, undated*)

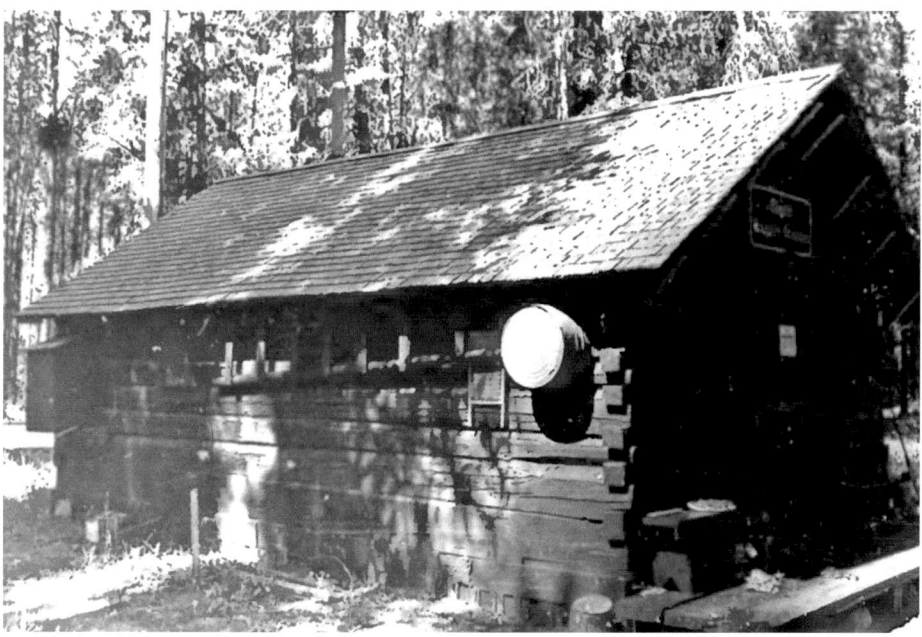

The Kintla Lake Ranger Station in 1975. The rustic look remains today. (*Photo by Lance Olivieri, for NPS Regional Office, Denver*)

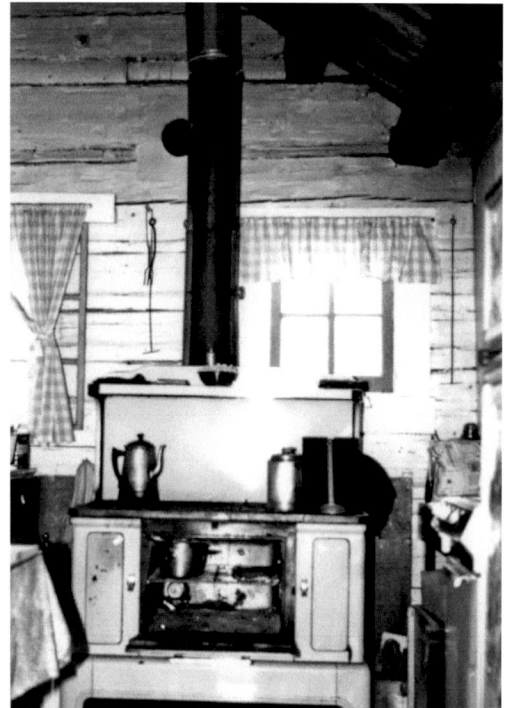

The rustic interior of the Kintla Lake Ranger Station, focused on the kitchen stove. (*GNP photo, no photographer attributed, undated*)

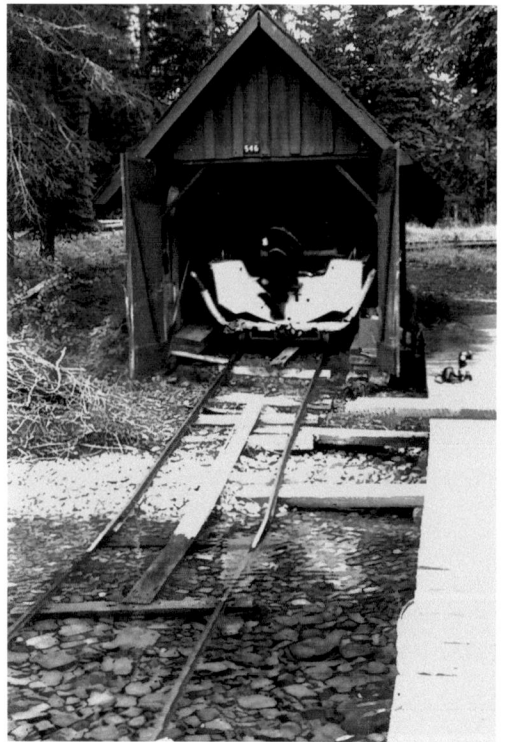

Boathouse at the Kintla Lake Ranger Station. The boat is wheeled out to the lakeshore on the tracks in the foreground. (*Unattributed GNP photo, undated*)

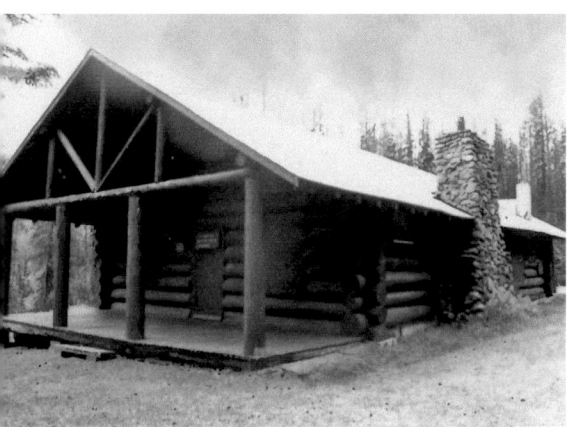 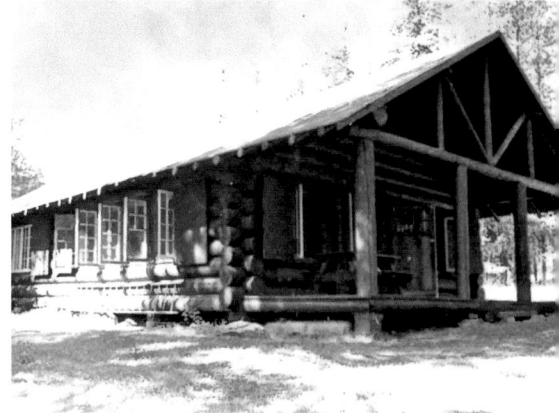

Above left: View of the Bowman Lake Ranger Station. Its much more substantial appearance attests to its original function as the Culver Boys' Military Academy Messhall prior to being taken over by the National Park Service. (*Photo unattributed, taken September 25, 1983, GNP*)

Above right: Photo of the opposite side of the Bowman Lake Ranger Station than shown in the previous photo. Again, the more substantial nature of the non-Park Service origin of the structure can be noted, with the many windows atypical for a Glacier Park ranger station. (*Photo by Lance Olivieri for GNP, photo taken in July 1975*)

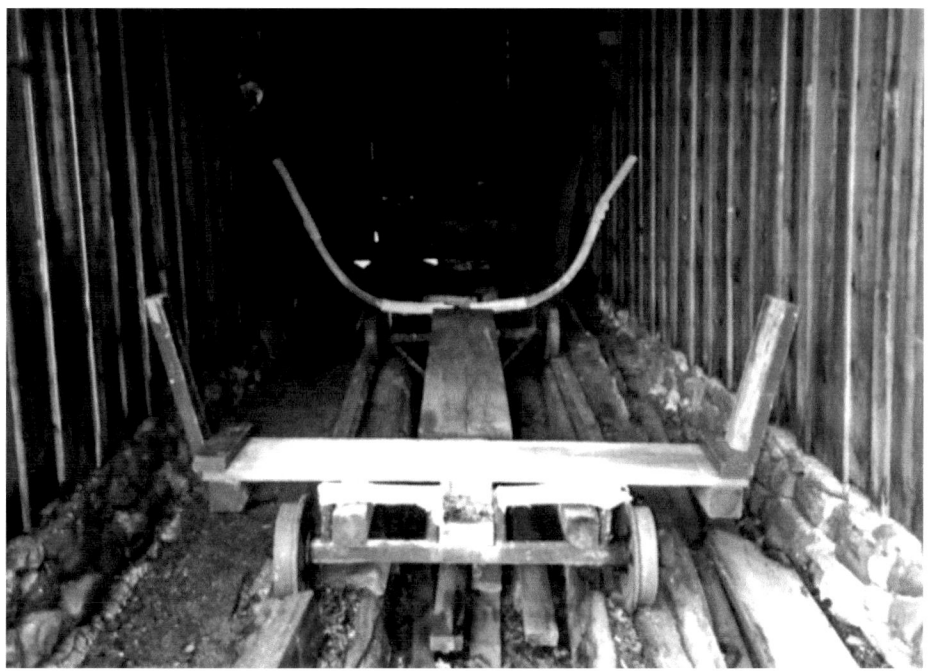

The boat-conveyance device at the Bowman Lake Ranger Station, similar to the tracked system at the Kintla Lake Ranger Station boathouse. (*Undated and unattributed photo, GNP*)

The Polebridge Ranger Station, along with the Polebridge Mercantile across the North Fork of the Flathead River, serves as the hub of the North Fork valley and the small community of Polebridge. The Polebridge historic district is among the largest in the entire park. It includes the ranger station and residence, built in 1922, a barn and oil house built in 1926, the Polebridge entrance/checking station built in 1935, and a number of additional buildings of unspecified dates of construction. The station and district are located at the confluence of Bowman Creek and the North Fork of the Flathead River. The district was substantially altered in its nature and completeness by the Red Bench Fire of 1988. Four contributing buildings in the district—the barn, the oil house, the fire cache, and the garage—were destroyed by the fire.[13, 14]

Minor controversy exists as to whether the first female ranger in the National Park Service served at the Polebridge Ranger Station. Mary Sullivan, wife of Park Ranger Thomas J. Sullivan, was hired in 1924 as the registration checking agent in the entrance/checking station at Polebridge. She carried out these duties in summers from 1924 until 1930, only in the summer visitation season. She was hired as a park ranger, although the paperwork of her hire clearly stated that her duties were simply those of a registration clerk during the tourist season. Readers can draw their own conclusions as to whether this situation fit the bill of a park ranger, in that she was indeed hired as a park ranger, but did not carry out typical park ranger duties and only worked in tourist seasons.[15]

The Logging Creek Ranger Station is the final ranger station positioned along the Inside North Fork Road (the Fish Creek Ranger Station shown on Leslie Lee's map no longer exists, but it was located somewhere in the general confines of today's Fish Creek campground located on a spur road just off of the Inside North Fork Road). Currently,

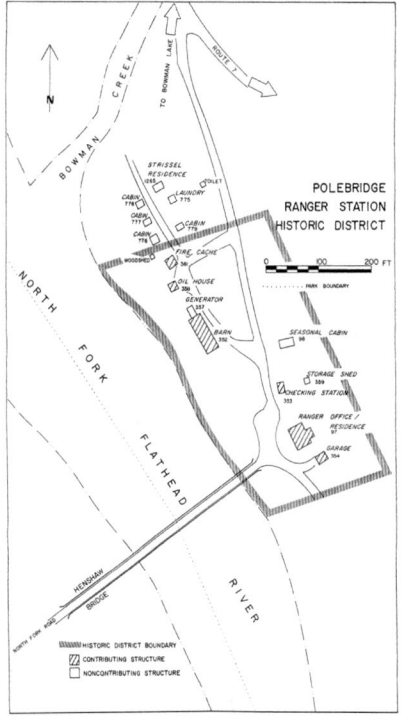

Map of the Polebridge Ranger Station Historic District, just south of the point where Bowman Creek flows into the North Fork of the Flathead River. Route 7, shown partially with an arrow pointing east-southeast, leads to the Logging Creek Ranger Station and points beyond, although as of this writing it is closed between Logging Creek and Camas Creek because of road damage from flooding. (*GNP, undated*)

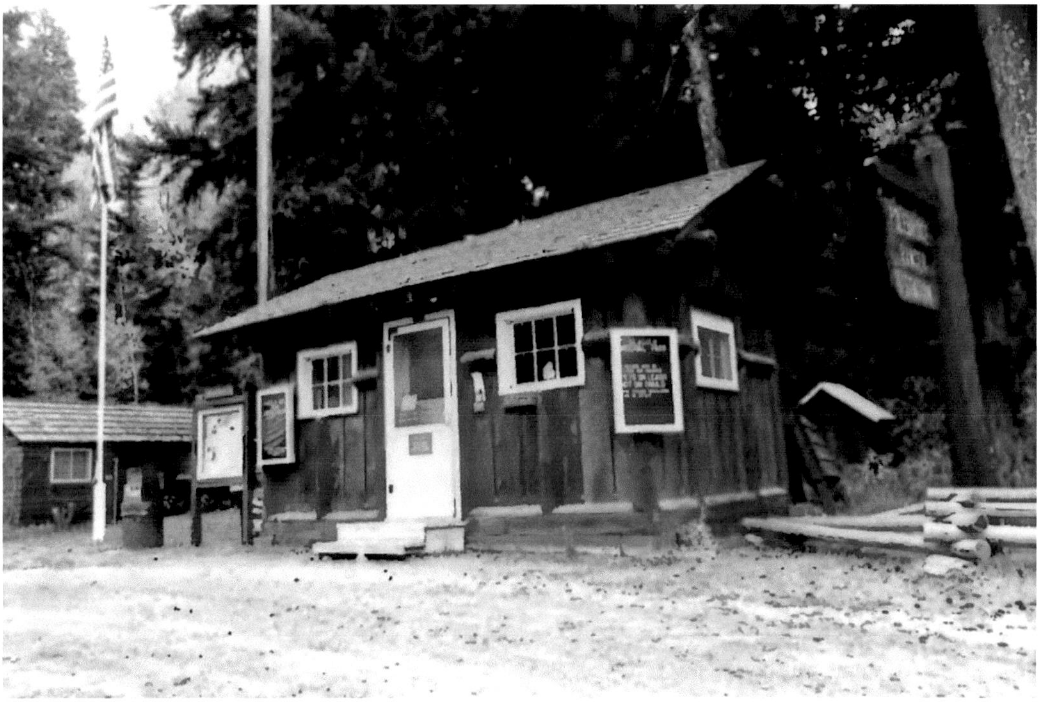

Polebridge Entrance/Checking Station in the Ranger Station Historic District. (*GNP, photo taken September 25, 1983*)

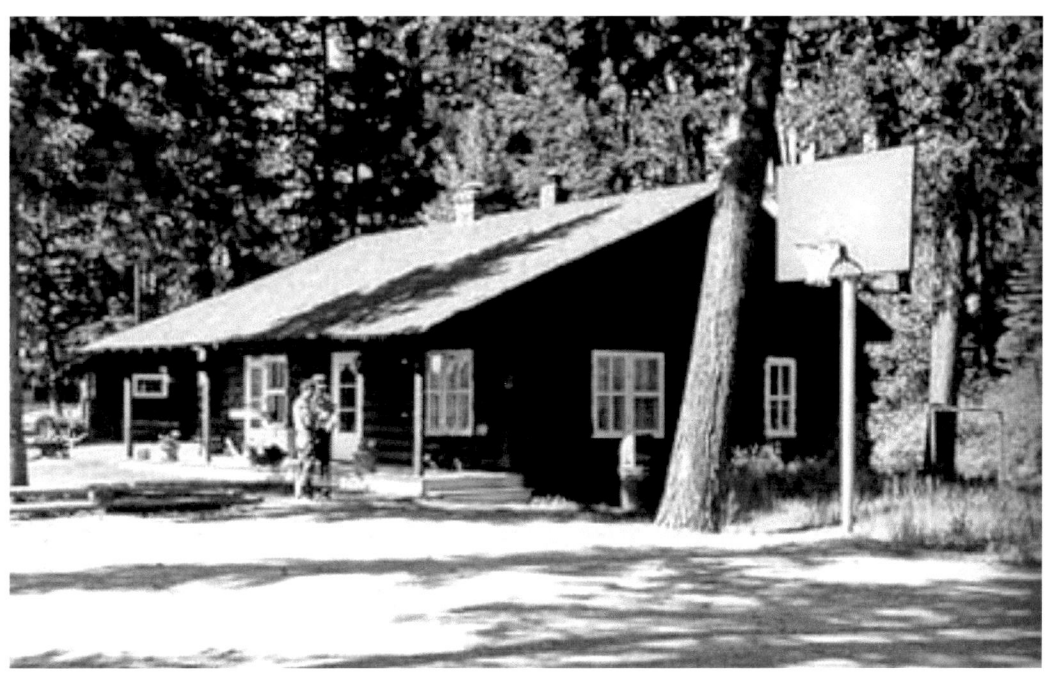

Polebridge Ranger Station and residence. (*Public domain photo, undated and unattributed*)

the Logging Creek station can only be accessed from the north, from Polebridge, because of the closure of a stretch of the Inside Road south of Logging Creek. The ranger station and historic district are about 3 miles southwest of the mouth of Logging Lake.

The Logging Creek Ranger Station was constructed in 1907, serving as an administrative location for the Forest Service in the pre-Glacier Park days prior to 1910. Its placement was very close to Adair's Mercantile, the precursor to the modern Polebridge Mercantile across the river. It is the oldest continuously operating administrative site in the park and was remodeled in the 1930s. All the surrounding buildings in the historic district date to the 1930s.[16]

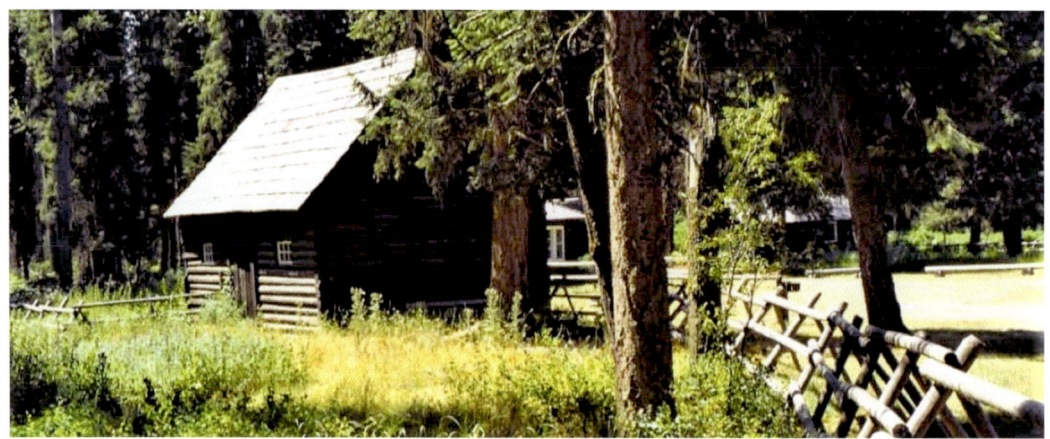

Above: View looking past the Logging Creek Log Barn (left center) toward the Logging Creek Ranger Station/residence. (*Photo by author, photo taken July 26, 1994*)

Below: The Logging Creek Ranger Station and residence. (*Public domain photo, undated and unattributed*)

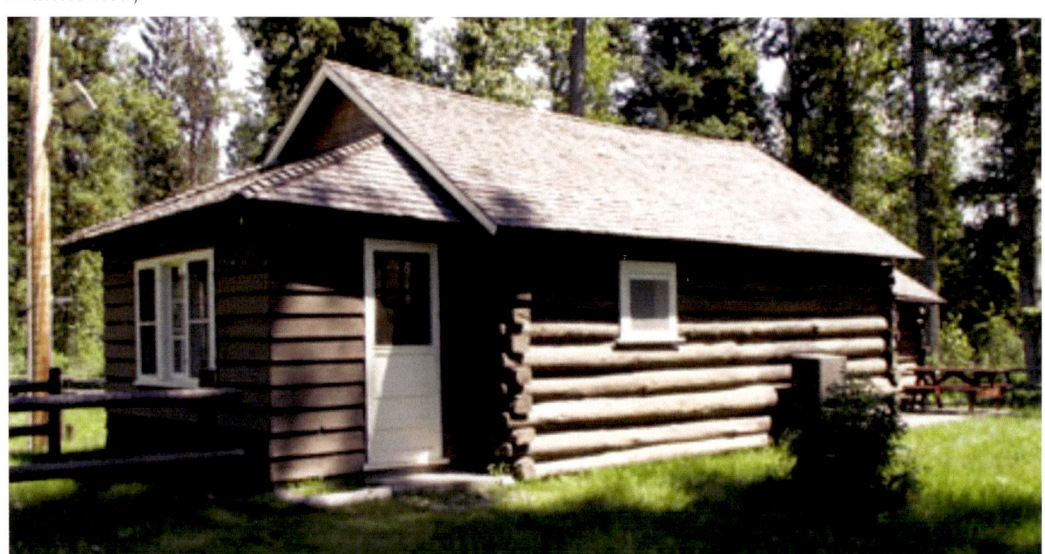

Glacier Park Ranger Stations Past and Present

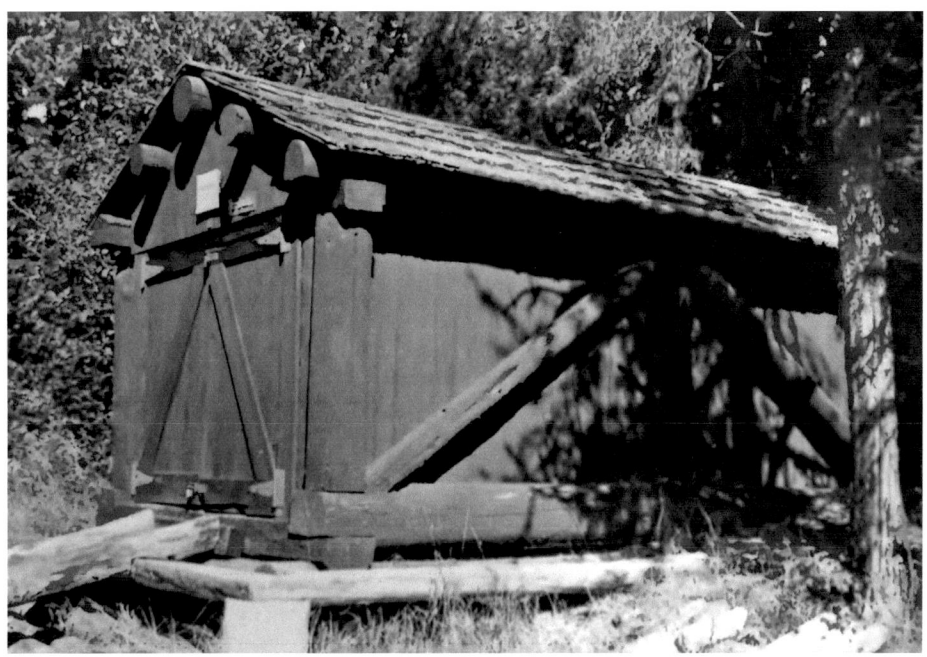

Above: The boathouse on the lower end of Logging Lake, reached only by trail from the Logging Creek Ranger Station Historic District. The hike from the district to the lakeshore and boathouse is roughly a 3-mile trek along the north side of Logging Creek. (*GNP photo, photographer unattributed, 1981*)

Right: Map of the Logging Creek Ranger Station Historic District, southeast of Polebridge along the Inside North Fork Road (Glacier Route 7). (*GNP, undated*)

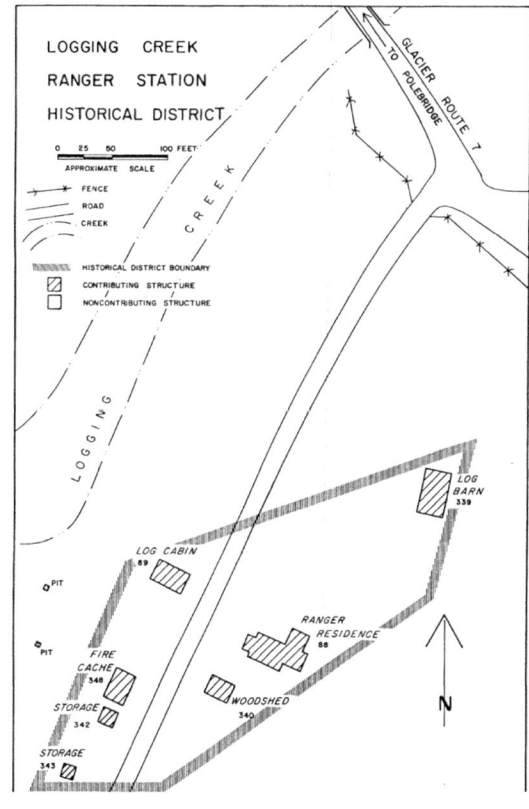

At the head of Lake McDonald sits the Upper Lake McDonald Ranger Station and Historic District. It is located west of McDonald Creek, about a half mile west of Going-to-the-Sun Road on a small spur road. The station building was constructed in 1924 as both an office and residence and is very similar in style to the Sherburne and Belly River Ranger Stations, following the same general Park Service plans of the period. The other buildings in the historic district were built during the 1930s. The boathouse was burned and lost in the Howe Ridge fire of August 2018. A fire also broke out on the roof of the ranger station, but it was extinguished quickly; the ranger station was saved.[17, 18]

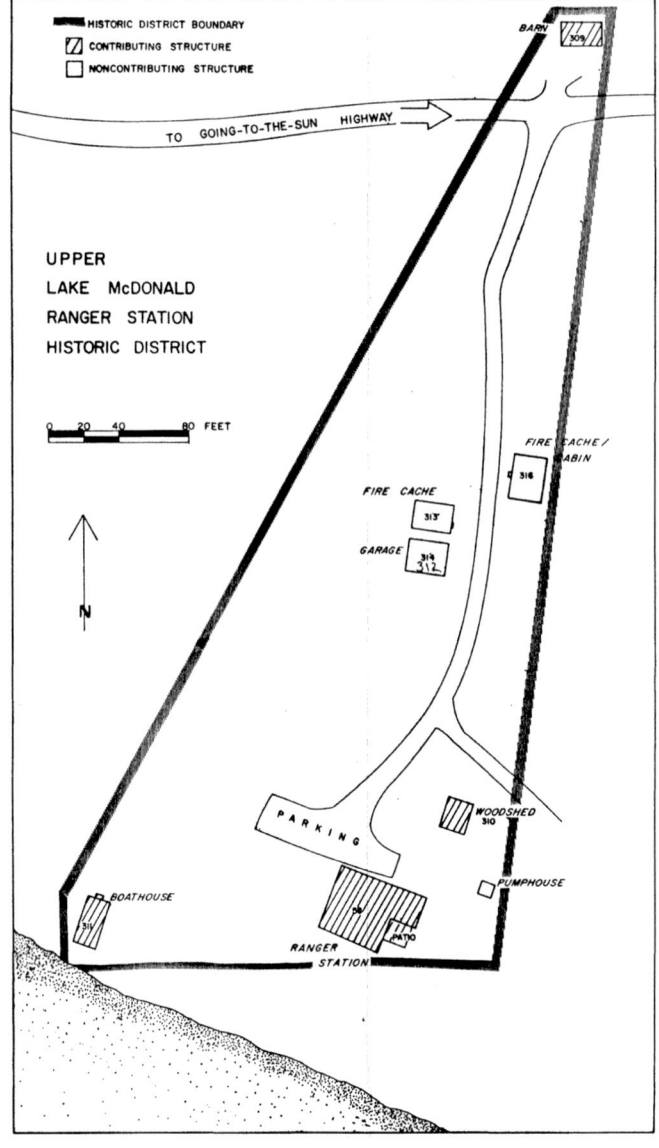

Map of the Upper Lake McDonald Ranger Station Historic District, located at the head of Lake McDonald northwest of the inlet where McDonald Creek enters the lake. (*GNP, undated*)

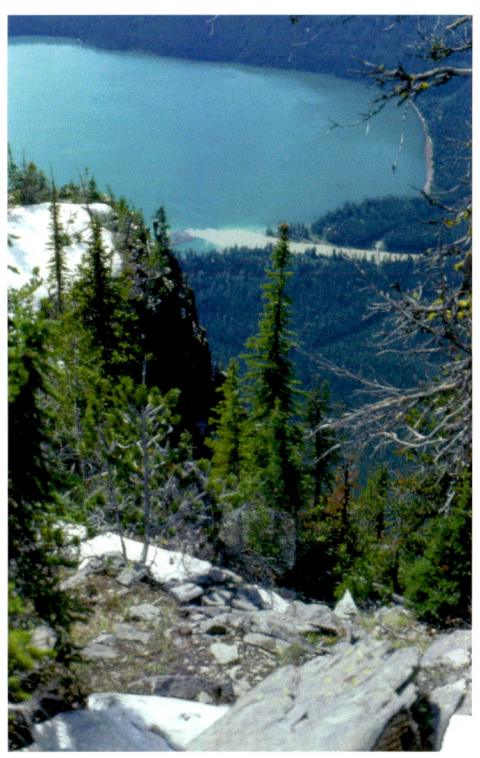

Right: View from the Mt. Brown Lookout down to the Upper Lake McDonald Ranger Station Historic District, to the right of the small branch hanging down almost vertically across the lake near the lakeshore. The district is reached via a small road that crosses McDonald Creek from Going-to-the-Sun Road at the head of Lake McDonald. McDonald Creek, seen here charged with sediments because of the June 1975 flood, is seen flowing right to left into the lake. (*Photo by William Marienau, photo taken in late June 1975*)

Below: The Upper Lake McDonald Ranger Station. The sign hanging from the building, near center of photo, simply reads "Lake McDonald Ranger Station." (*Creative Commons photo by Magicpiano, photo taken August 2, 2017*)

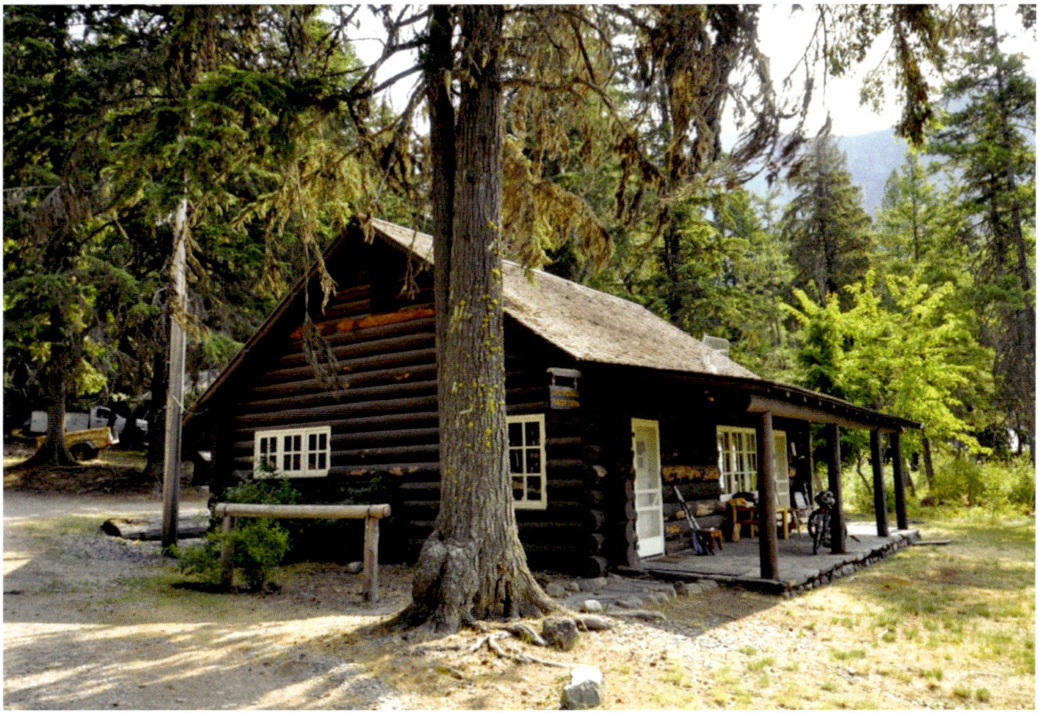

From the Middle Fork to Lubec

From Belton (West Glacier) back to East Glacier Park, only one ranger station currently exists. Other stations, shown on Leslie Lee's map, had brief histories alluded to in the discussions in Chapter 4 of individual rangers including Clyde Fauley at the Paola and Nyack Ranger Stations, Frank Guardipee at the Nyack and North Fork Ranger Stations, and Hugh Buchanan at Nyack.

Little is known about the North Fork Ranger Station, located at the confluence of the Middle Fork and the North Fork of the Flathead River, beyond the fact that Frank Guardipee had been stationed there. No information could be located as to when it was razed by the Park Service, nor could I locate any photos of the North Fork Ranger Station.

The Nyack Ranger Station was built sometime after Nyack Ranger Dan Doody was fired by Glacier National Park for poaching in 1916. Doody operated during his time as ranger out of his homestead rather than a ranger station. The Nyack Ranger Station was located "a stone's throw" upstream from the Doody homestead. Today, the station has been removed, likely in the 1960s during a widespread purge in the park of abandoned buildings (the last ranger served there in 1951). Remaining are the station's fire cache (constructed in 1928) and the station barn (constructed in 1935).[19, 20]

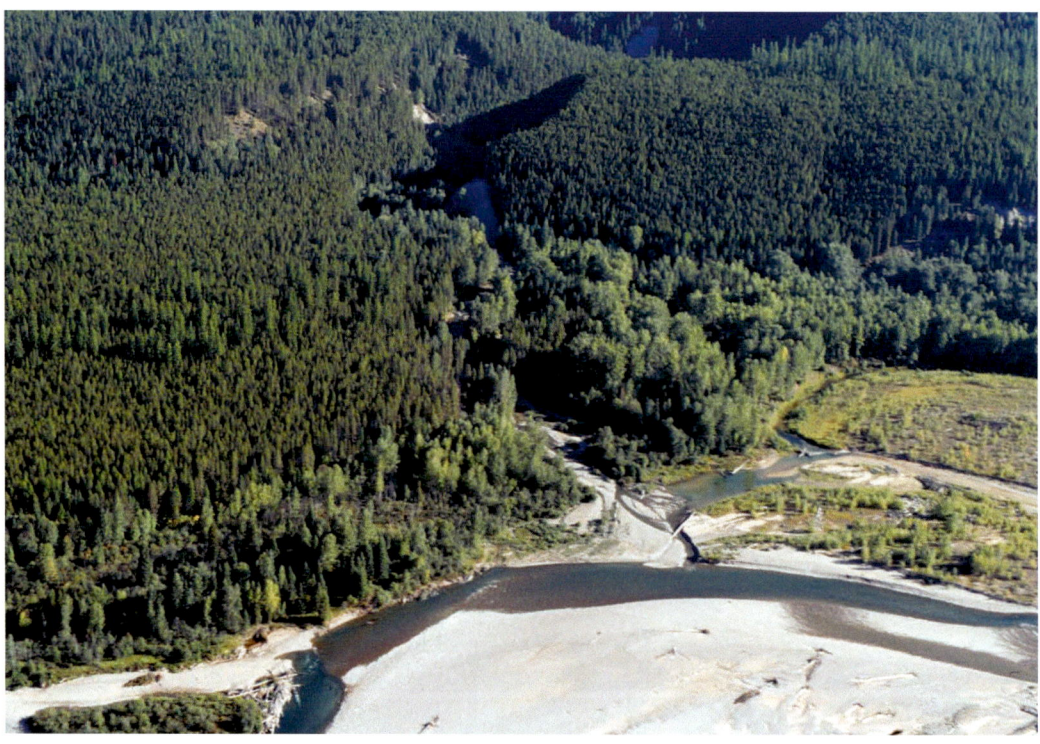

Aerial view of Nyack Creek (in canyon at upper center and center) where it flows into the Middle Fork of the Flathead River. The Nyack Ranger Station was located just off the right edge of the photograph. (*Photo by author, photo taken September 19, 2002*)

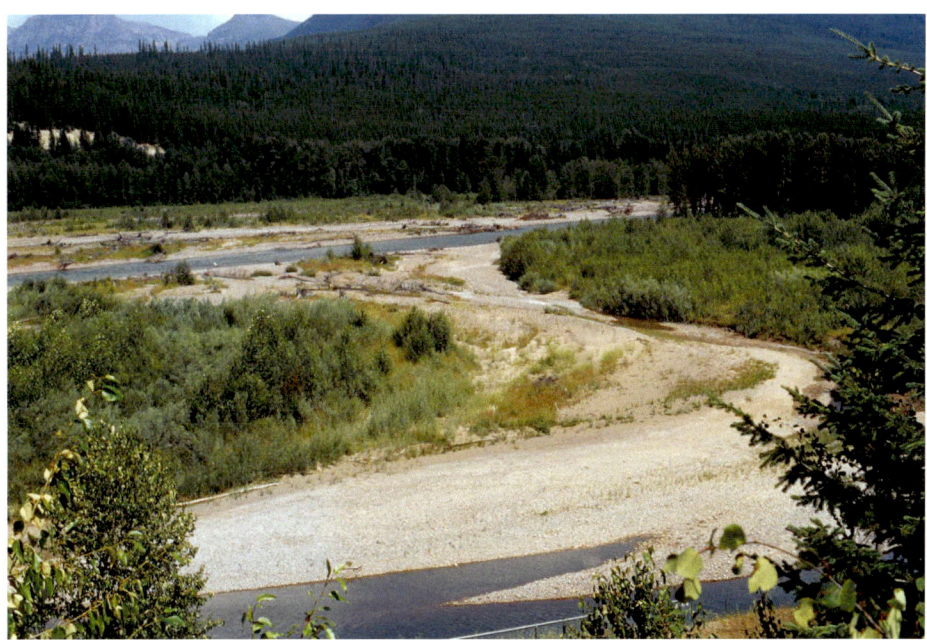

Ground view looking across the Middle Fork of the Flathead River to the approximate location of the Nyack Ranger Station behind the trees at center right. (*Photo by author, photo taken July 24, 1994*)

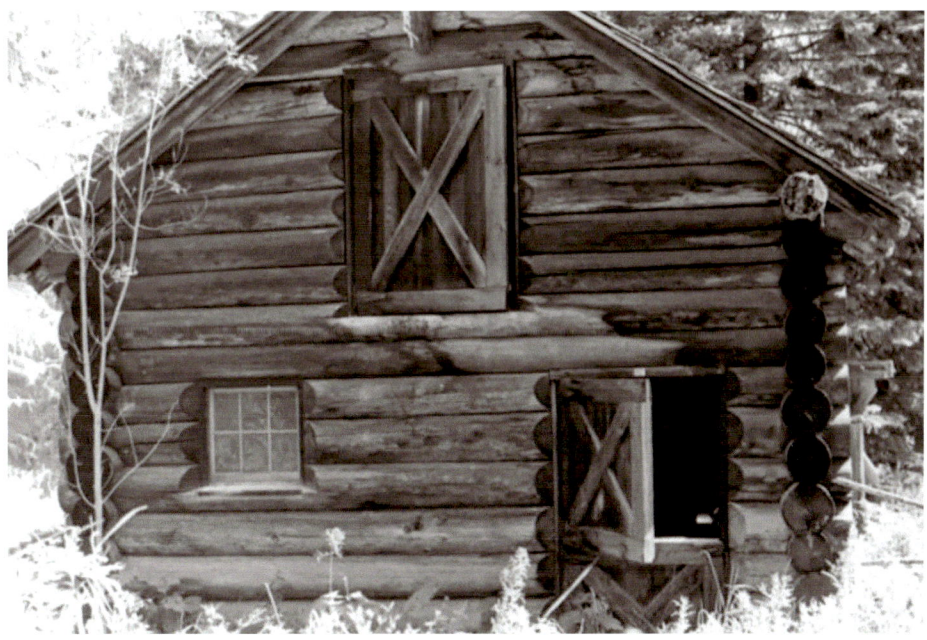

The Nyack Ranger Station barn, one of two remaining structures from the former ranger station. (*GNP, photographer unattributed, photo taken in 1982*)

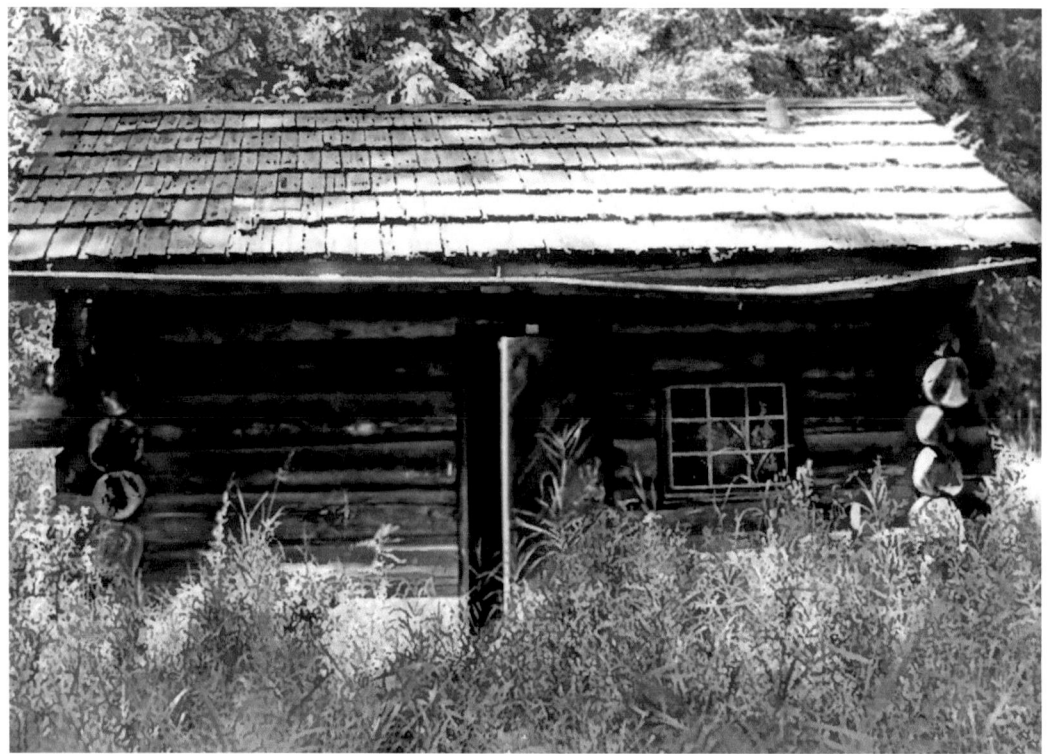

The Nyack Ranger Station fire cache, mis-identified in some online descriptions as a cabin. (*GNP, photographer unattributed, photo taken in 1982*)

The Paola Ranger Station, now gone, was active from 1913 to 1932. Bruce Miller was the last ranger assigned there, and he closed the station for good on August 15, 1932. The station had fallen out of favor with the Park Service because of its isolation and difficult access via the cable bucket system across the Middle Fork. During most of its existence, the station bucket crossing could only be reached via the Great Northern Railway until U.S. Highway 2 reached the area around 1930. After its closure in 1932, the Walton Ranger Station, 6 miles upriver, was built to cover the southern reaches of the park. Walton had the advantage that it could be reached by the new Highway 2 and did not require a river crossing except by bridge. The Paola Ranger Station and woodshed were burned by the park administration in January 1966.[21]

The Walton Ranger Station, constructed in 1932, was designed to be larger and more impressive looking to viewers passing by the station on the recently opened U.S. Highway 2. The station is unique in Glacier Park, although a similar structure built along the same design exists in Yellowstone National Park. It still serves its purpose today, although vegetation has grown up and partially obscures the view of the station from the highway. Outbuildings around the ranger station were constructed in the 1930s and 1940s.[22]

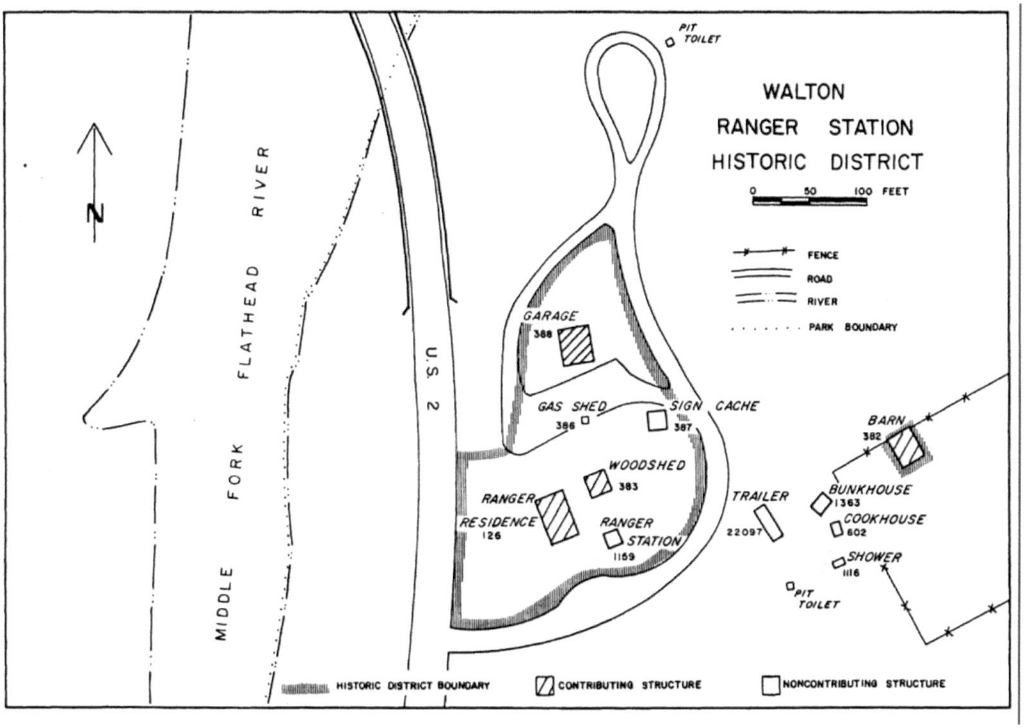

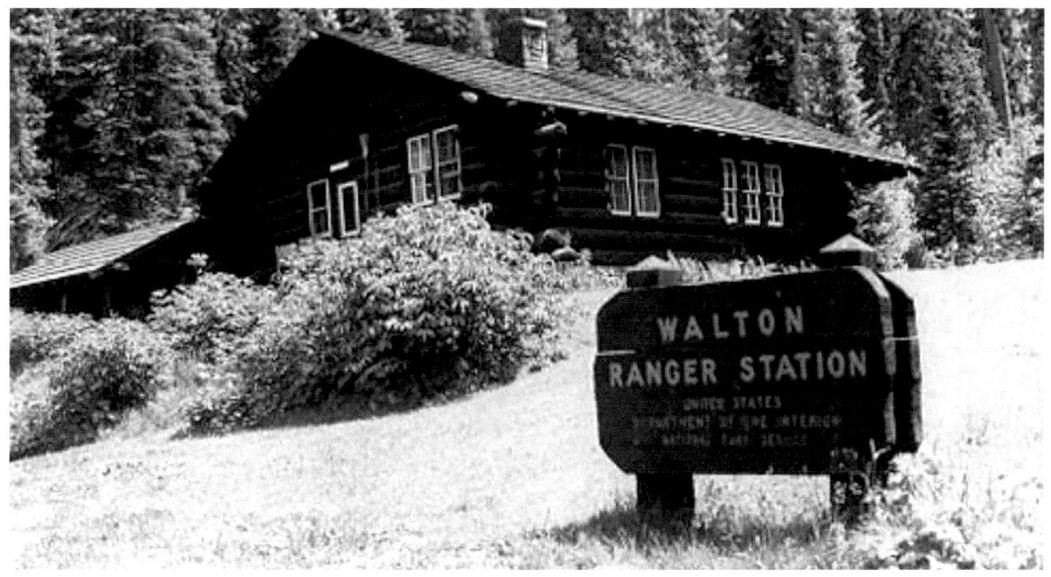

Map of the Walton Ranger Station Historic District, located just inside Glacier Park adjacent to the Middle Fork of the Flathead River near the park's southernmost point. (*GNP, undated*)

The classic log-cabin style of the Walton Ranger Station. (*Public domain photo, undated and unattributed*)

The final stop in this tour of ranger stations around Glacier National Park is the Lubec Ranger Station, located east of the Continental Divide about 10 miles southwest of Glacier Park/East Glacier. The U.S. Forest Service built a storage shed at this site, and that shed served as a (small!) ranger station until the National Park Service built a new, full-sized station in 1929, converting the original station into a tool shed. A barn was constructed at the site in 1931. The station served until 1971, when it was abandoned. In 1977, the station and the tool shed/original station building were burned by the National Park Service. The barn was rescued, and moved to the Old St. Mary Ranger Station site, because of its similarity to the former barn that existed in St. Mary. The barn continues to reside today adjacent to the Old St. Mary Ranger Station.[23]

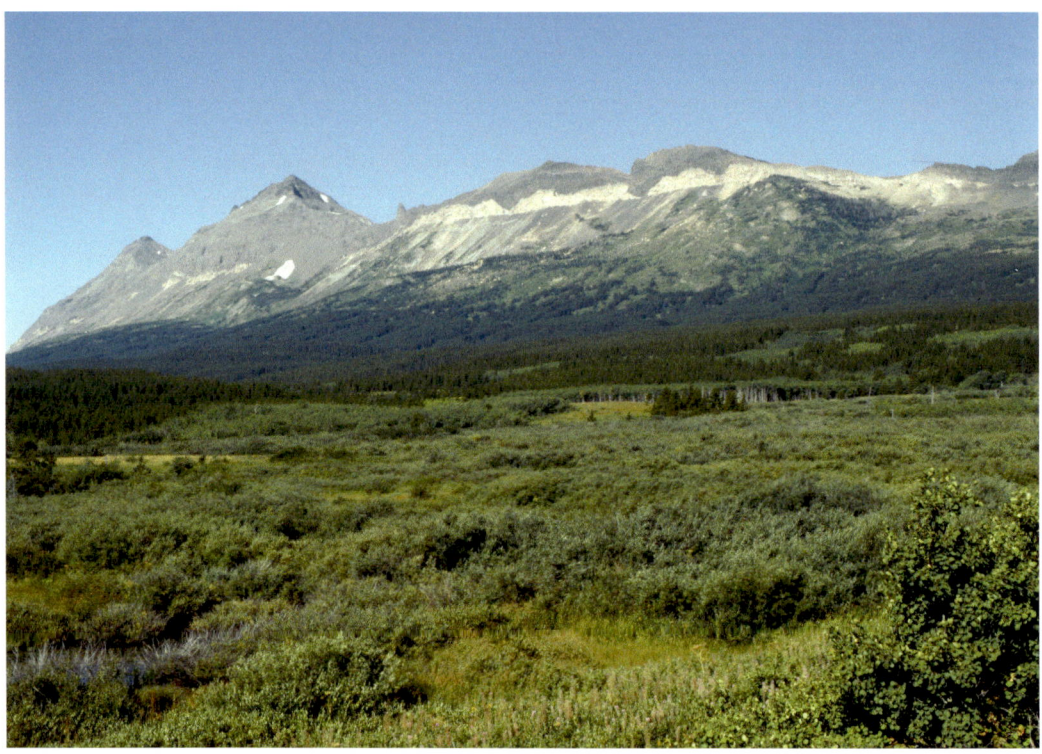

General scenery along the start of the Firebrand Pass trail, in the vicinity of the location of the former Lubec Ranger Station. View is to the southwest. (*Photo by author, photo taken August 21, 1991*)

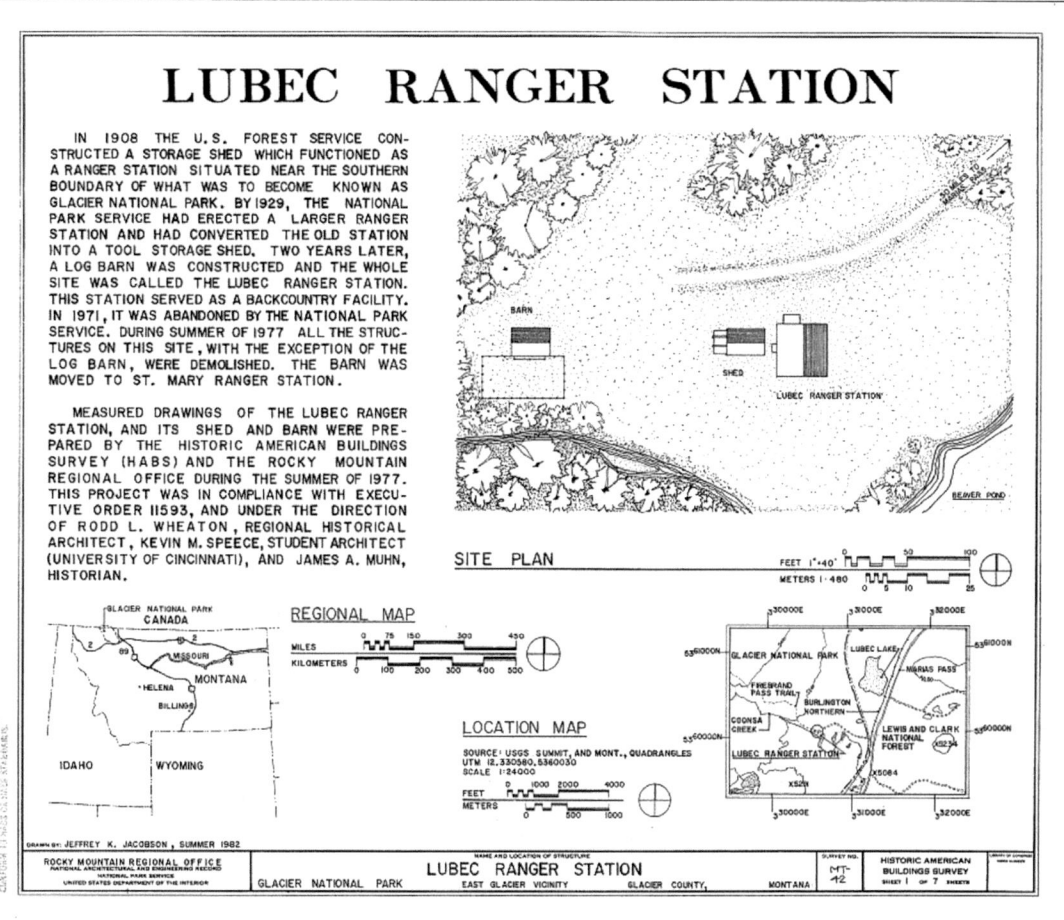

Map of the former Lubec Ranger Station, southwest of East Glacier and west of the tracks of the (then) Great Northern Railway, along the trail to Firebrand Pass in Glacier Park. (*Library of Congress, HABS MONT,18-GLACE.V,1-*)

6
Glacier's Backcountry Patrol/ Snowshoe Cabins

In this final chapter, I will again take the reader on a counterclockwise tour from Glacier Park/East Glacier, visiting the backcountry patrol cabins. Also frequently called snowshoe cabins (a moniker especially relevant on the snowier west side of the park), many of these small structures were constructed by the National Park Service in the late 1920s and on up to about 1935. Those cabins are not, therefore, shown on Leslie Lee's map in Chapter 5 of this book, but are described in this chapter. Some of the cabins shown on Leslie Lee's map are virtually unknown and unphotographed, such as those shown on the map in the Two Medicine valley. Because of the presence of roads penetrating eastside valleys, and the somewhat reasonable distances separating eastside ranger stations, fewer patrol cabins were built east of the Continental Divide. The isolated nature and greater length of many of the western park valleys dictated the building of many more snowshoe cabins west of the divide. The patrol/snowshoe cabins were built to support year-round ranger patrols originating from the network of ranger stations described in the previous chapter, with each patrol cabin being placed roughly one day's hiking or (especially) snowshoe travel from the originating ranger station and from each other. The cabins are still used for occasional backcountry patrols today; also, they are occasionally used by trail crew members who are working on fixing a trail a long way up one of the west side's glacial valleys.

Patrol Cabins East of the Continental Divide

The Baring Creek Patrol Cabin, also frequently known as the Sun Camp Fireguard Cabin, was located just east of Sunrift Gorge along Going-to-the-Sun Road. It was used primarily by rangers based out of the no-longer existing Sun Camp Ranger Station complex built in 1928 that was designed to provide support to and protection for the nearby Going-to-the-Sun Chalets, built and operated by the Great Northern Railway, at Sun Point. The cabin was built in 1935, and when the ranger station was abandoned after World War Two, the patrol cabin became important for rangers patrolling the St. Mary valley. The cabin was unfortunately destroyed in the Reynolds Creek fire of 2015.[1]

Glacier's Backcountry Patrol/Snowshoe Cabins

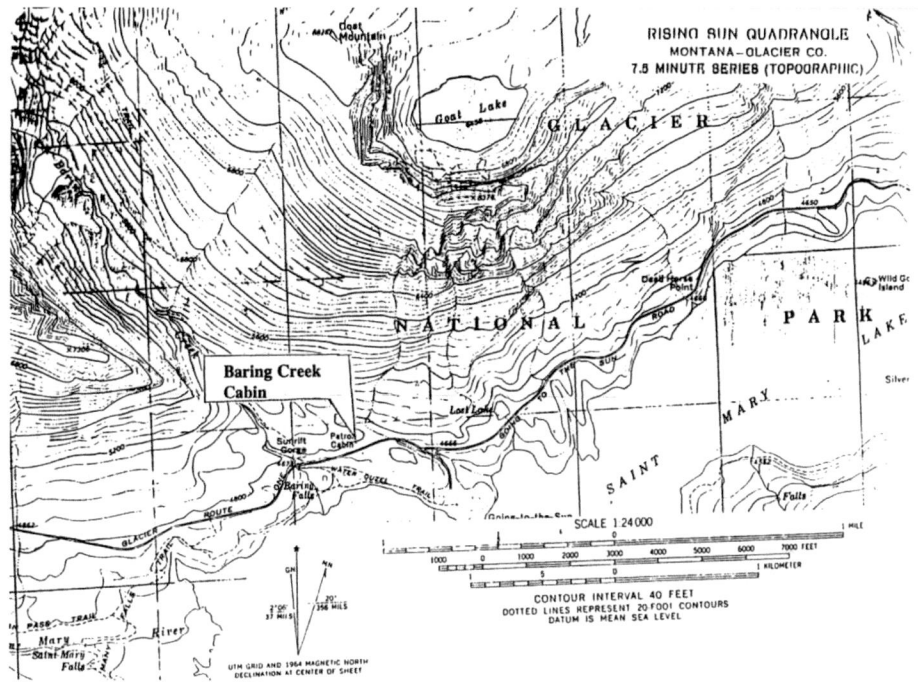

Location map for the Baring Creek Patrol Cabin, also known as the Sun Camp Fireguard Cabin. The cabin was destroyed in the Reynolds Creek fire of 2015. (*USGS base map, modified by NPS to indicate cabin location*)

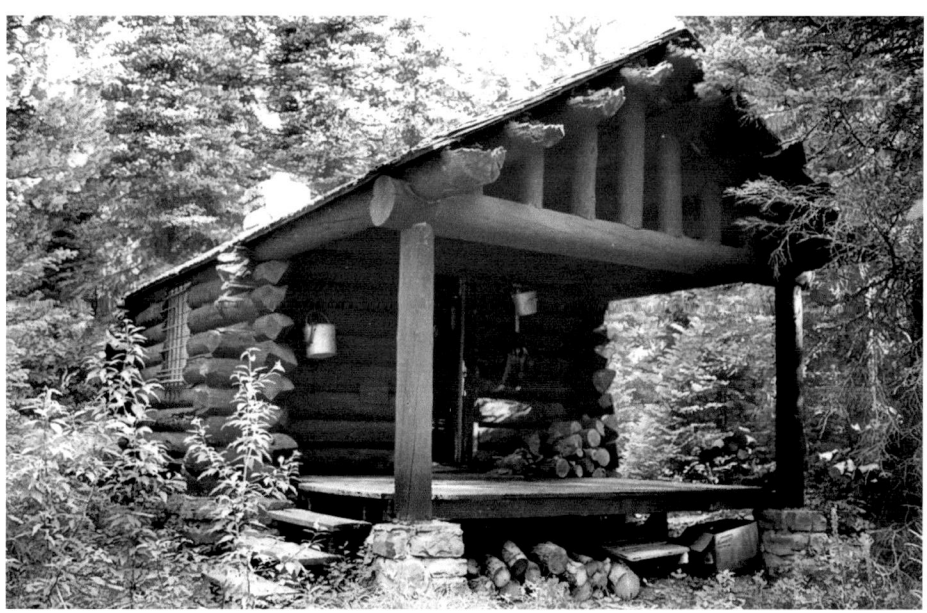

Front view of the charming and rustic Baring Creek/Sun Camp cabin. (*Leroy Dudley, photographer for GNP, photo taken in July 1988*)

Early Rangers of Glacier National Park

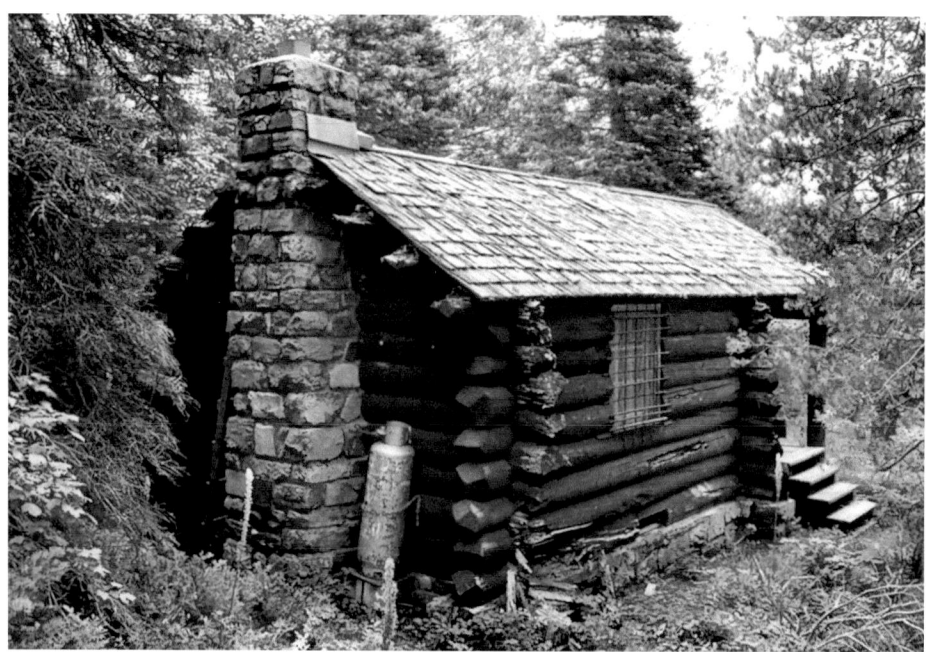

Rear view of the Baring Creek/Sun Camp cabin, also photographed in July 1988. (*Leroy Dudley, photographer for GNP*)

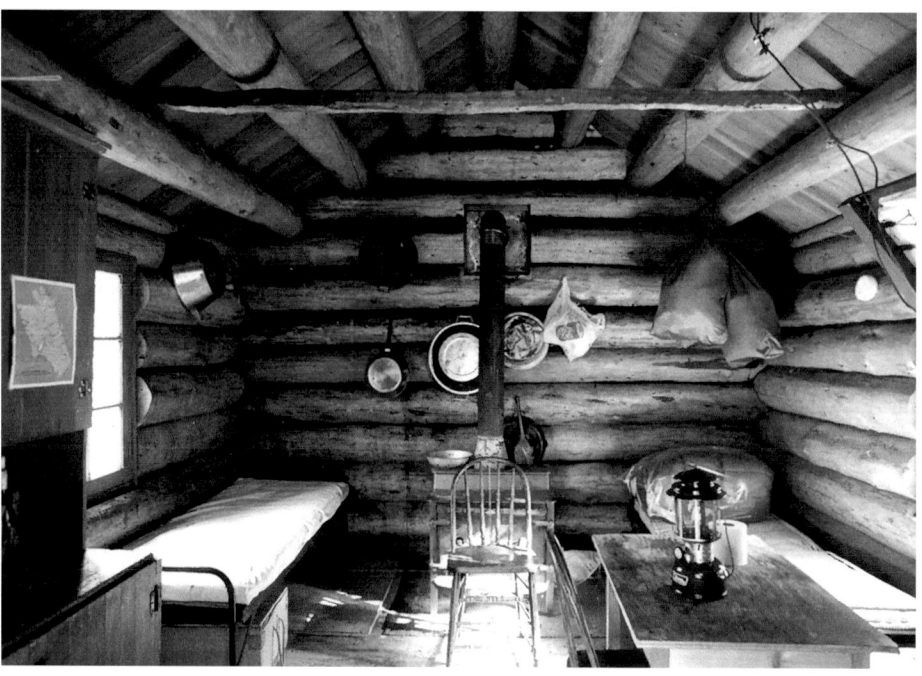

The tidy, rustic interior of the Baring Creek/Sun Camp cabin. (*Leroy Dudley, photographer for GNP, photo taken in July 1988*)

Glacier's Backcountry Patrol/Snowshoe Cabins

The Slide Lake patrol cabin, also known as the Otatso Creek cabin, is located in northeastern Glacier Park adjacent to Otatso Creek, along the hiking trail to Slide Lake, about a mile inside the park border with the Blackfeet Indian Reservation. At the time of Leslie Lee's map, the creek was known as the North Fork of Kennedy Creek. The Slide Lake cabin, along with the Fielding cabin on the southern end of the park, are the only two patrol cabins in the park with a frame construction rather than made of logs.[2]

About 8 miles north of the Slide Lake patrol cabin, the Lee Creek patrol cabin is just south of the U.S./Canadian border along Lee Creek. It is closely adjacent (about six-tenths of a mile northward) to the present-day Chief Mountain International Highway, but it is rarely seen by visitors as they hurry along to or from Waterton Lakes National Park across the border in Alberta. Built in 1925–1927, it is still used occasionally by rangers on backcountry patrol.[3]

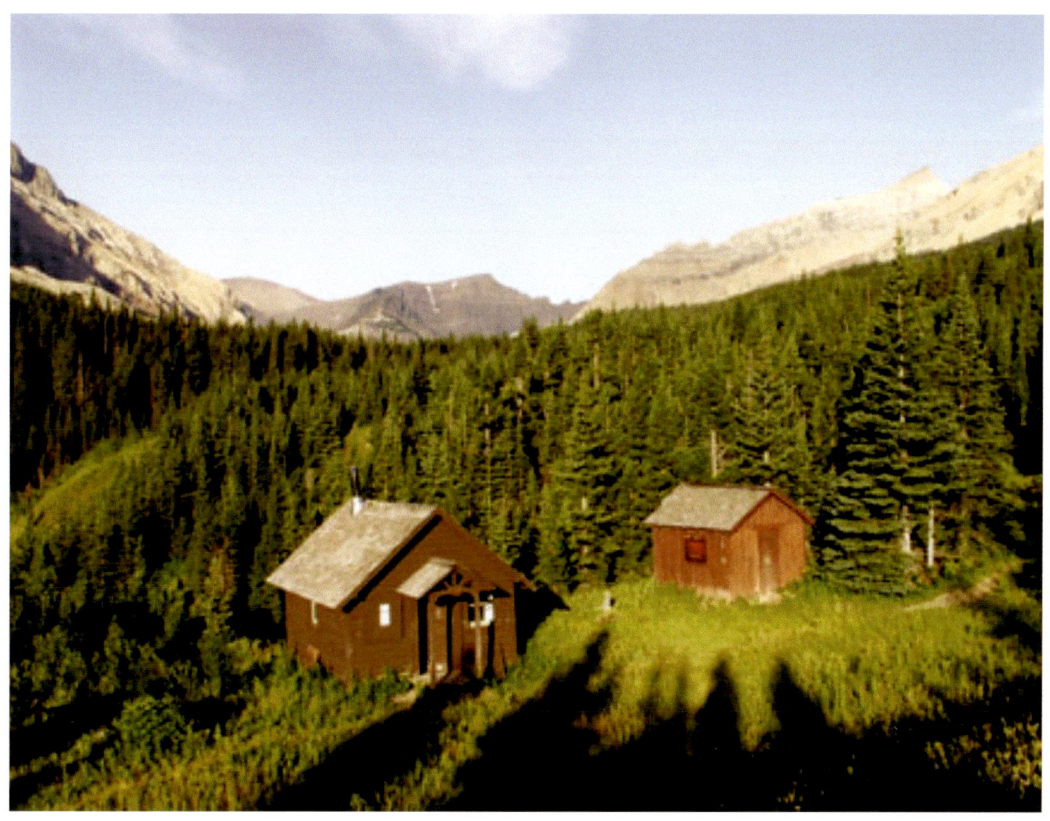

The Slide Lake/Otatso Creek backcountry patrol cabin (left) and fireguard cabin/woodshed in far northeast Glacier National Park. (*Public domain photo, undated and unattributed*)

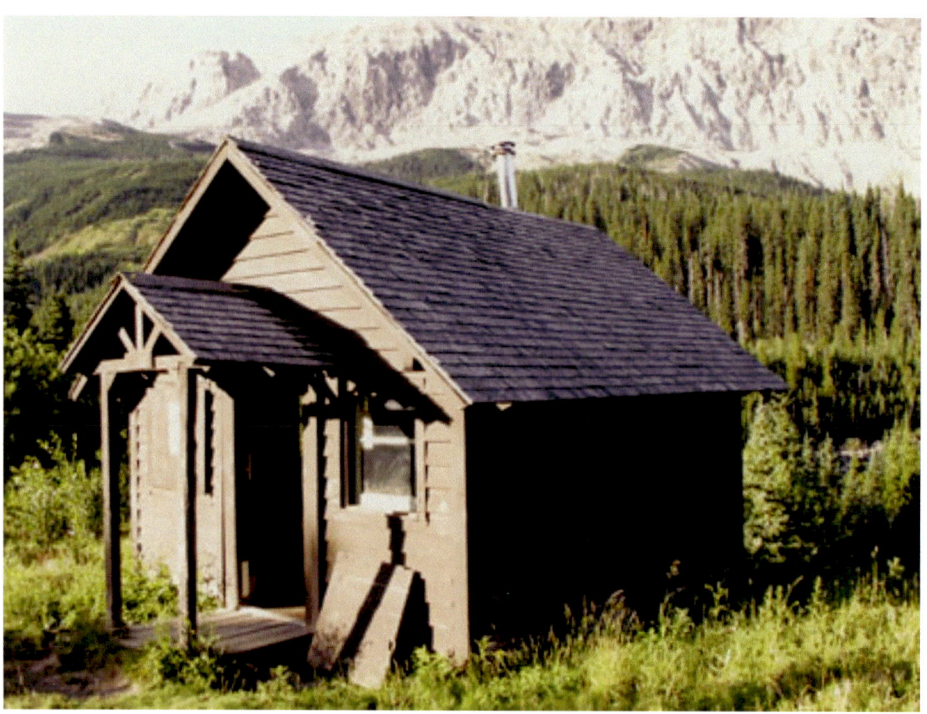

Another view of the main Slide Lake/Otatso Creek backcountry patrol cabin, with Yellow Mountain in the background. (*Public domain photo, undated and unattributed*)

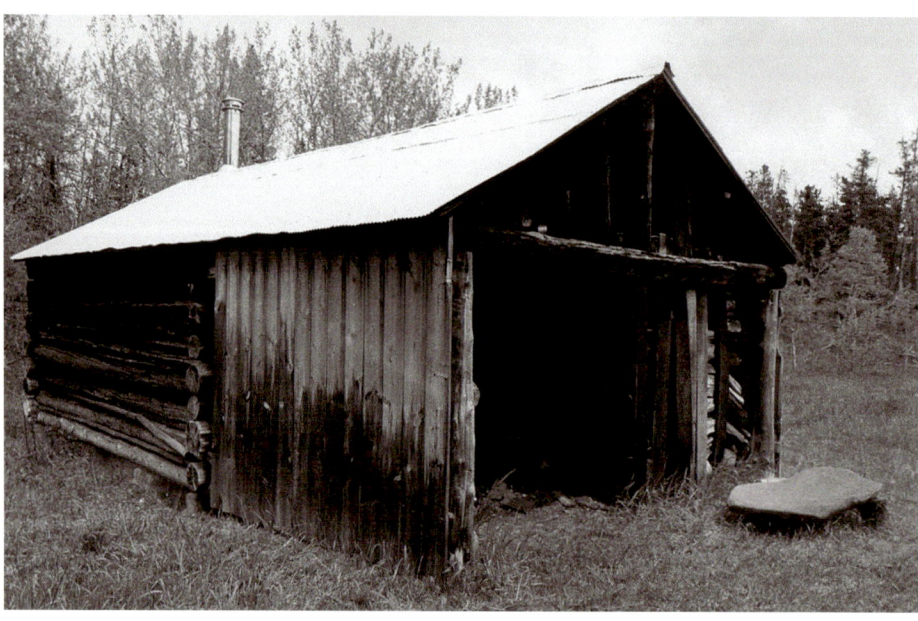

The front of the Lee Creek patrol cabin, almost directly north of the Slide Lake cabin and located adjacent to Lee Creek near the Canadian border north of Chief Mountain. (*Photo by Somer Hileman for GNP, photo taken June 5, 2000*)

Glacier's Backcountry Patrol/Snowshoe Cabins

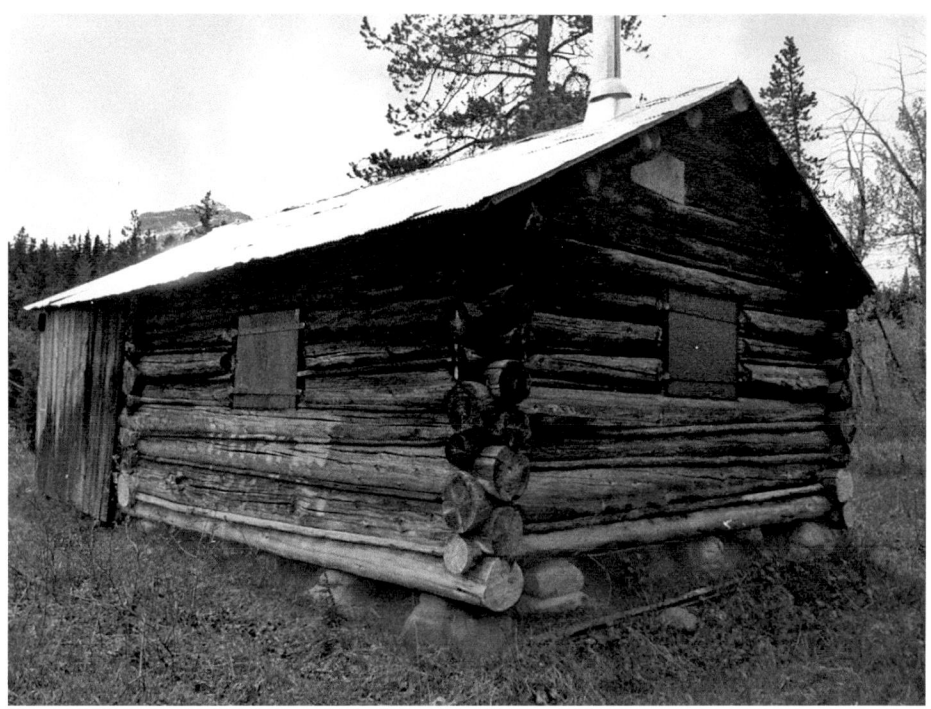

A rear view of the Lee Creek patrol cabin. Note the complex, interlocking/overlapping log work. (*Photo by Somer Hileman for GNP, photo taken June 5, 2000*)

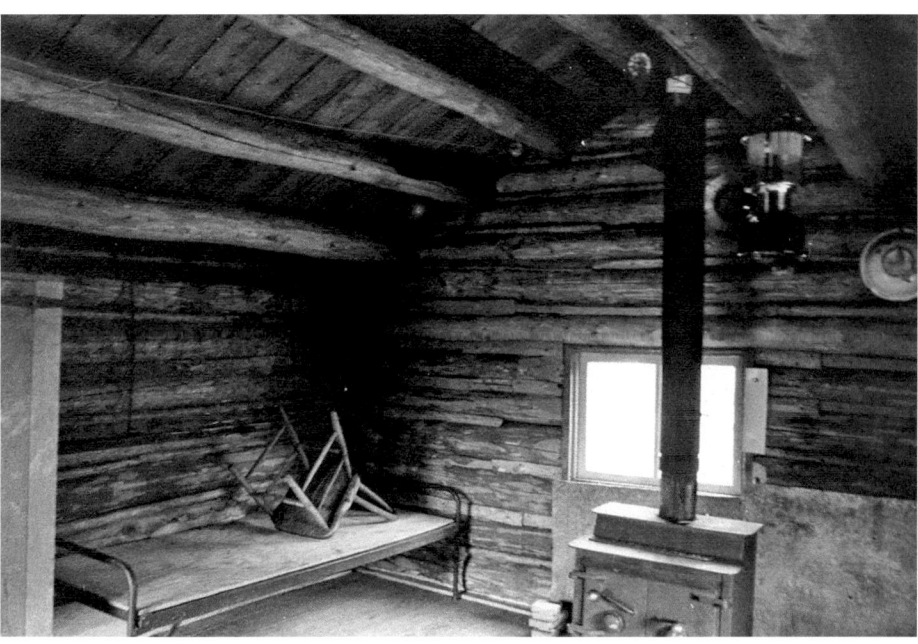

The spartan interior of the Lee Creek patrol cabin. (*Photo by Somer Hileman for GNP, photo taken June 5, 2000*)

For a ranger on patrol from Waterton Lake to Granite Park, or vice versa, three snowshoe/patrol cabins are encountered along the general journey. Two are located in the Waterton River valley, Pass Creek and Kootenai Creek (see image captions for their alternate names on Leslie Lee's map), and Cattle Queen (labeled Ahern Pass on Lee's map) in the headwaters of the McDonald Creek valley across the Continental Divide and discussed in the next section.

The Pass Creek cabin is listed as having been constructed in 1938, and the Kootenai Creek cabin in 1926, but their presence of Leslie Lee's map suggests they were pre-dated by earlier rough cabins used in the first two decades of the park. They are of similar design and appearance. The Pass Creek cabin serves the lower Waterton valley and Little Kootenai allowed access to nearby Stoney Indian Pass and the Fifty Mountain region of the Northern Highline Trail.[4, 5]

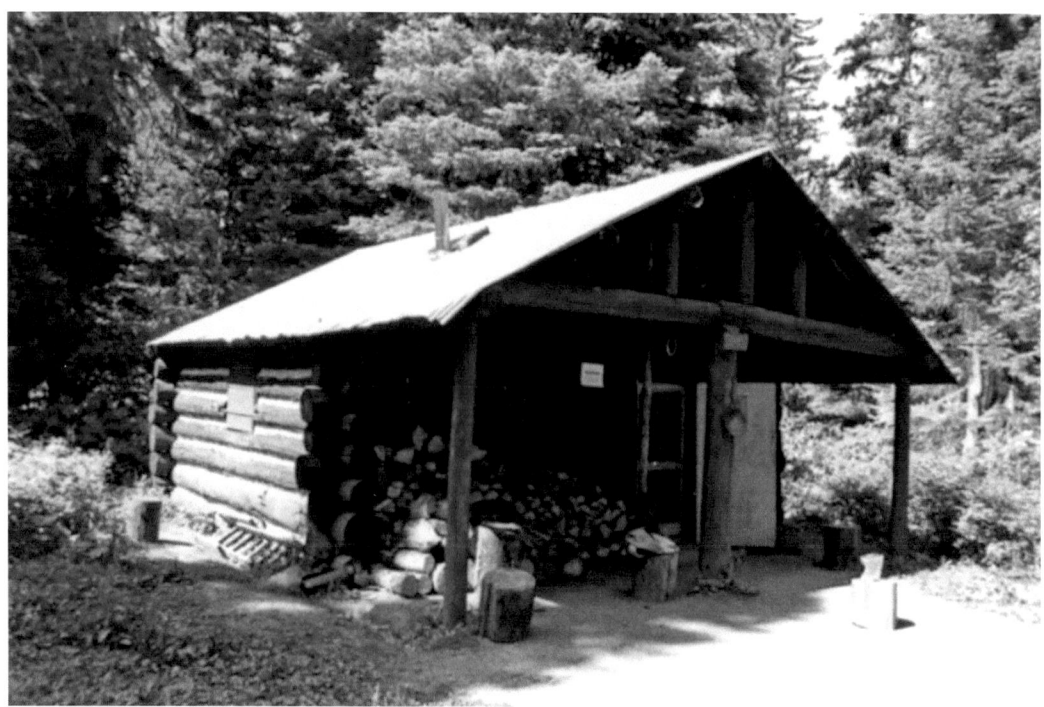

Exterior of the Pass Creek patrol cabin, located at the junction of the Waterton River and Pass Creek in northern Glacier Park south of the Goat Haunt Ranger Station. This location is labeled as "Home Camp" on Leslie Lee's map of ranger facilities in existence in 1913. (*Photo by Historical Research Associates for GNP, photo taken in August 1982*)

Glacier's Backcountry Patrol/Snowshoe Cabins

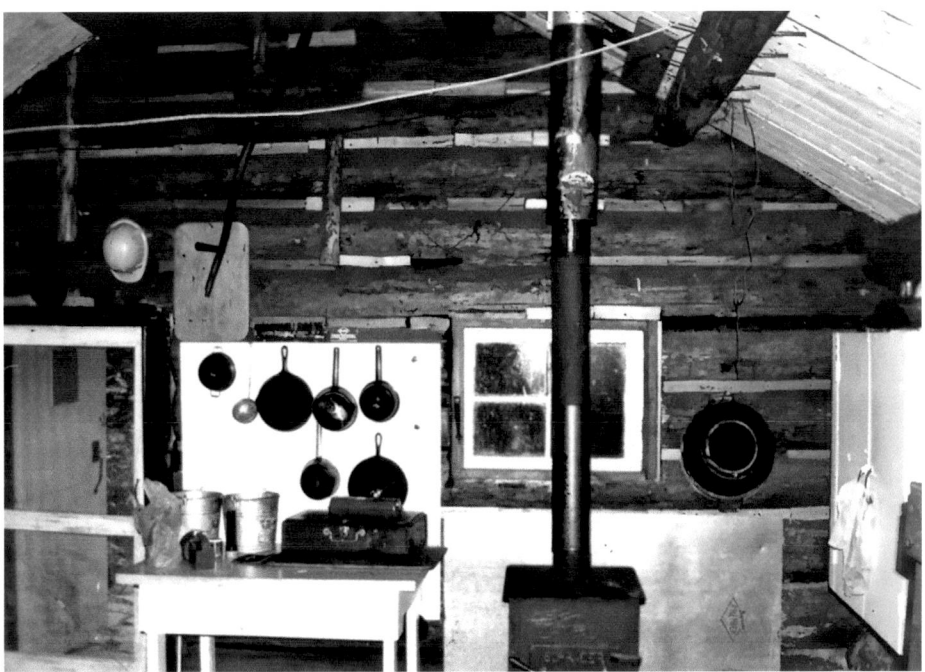

The tidy interior of the Pass Creek patrol cabin, photographed in August 1982. (*Photo by Historical Research Associates for GNP*)

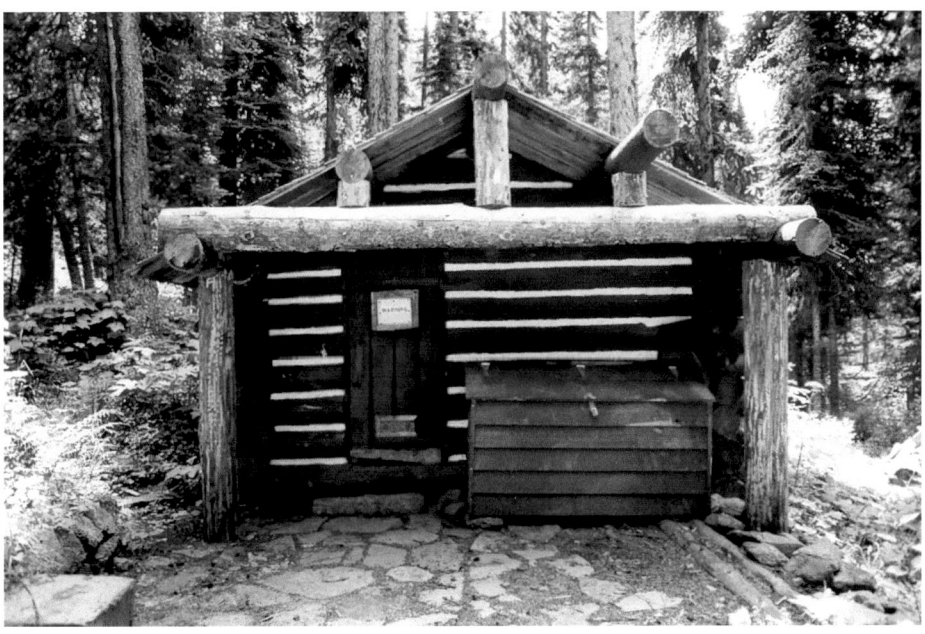

The Kootenai Creek patrol cabin, labeled as "Little Kootenai" on Leslie Lee's 1913 map of ranger stations and backcountry patrol/snowshoe cabins. (*Photo by Leroy Dudley for GNP, photo taken July 14, 1998*)

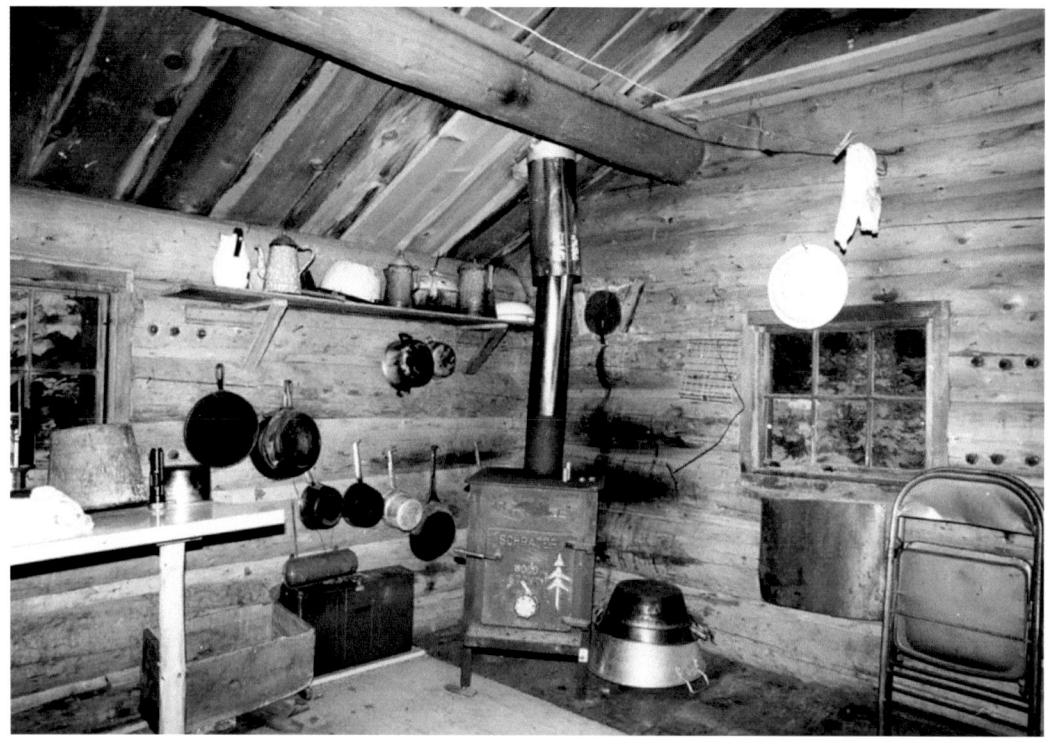

The interior of the Kootenai Creek patrol cabin reveals a well-kept, almost cozy environment. (*Photo by Leroy Dudley for GNP, photo taken July 14, 1998*)

Patrol Cabins West of the Continental Divide and North of the McDonald Valley

The Cattle Queen patrol cabin is one of the oldest currently standing cabins in the park, having been constructed in 1926. It may or may not be the structure labeled as "Ahern Pass" on Leslie Lee's map. The cabin has been damaged by trees falling onto the roof, and it is located on an obscure trail that has minimal maintenance. It is still used by Park Service and U.S. Geological Survey personnel conducting winter snow course surveys.[6]

Moving into the drainages of the North Fork of the Flathead River, the Upper Kintla Lake snowshoe cabin sits at the very head of Upper Kintla Lake. It allowed backcountry patrolling of the Boundary Mountains region along the Canadian border which was occasionally crossed by poachers from the north. Built in 1931, the cabin remains in good condition. Its barred rear window attests to the necessity for keeping bears, both grizzlies and black, from entering the cabin in search of food.[7]

The Ford Creek patrol cabin was constructed in 1928. Located along the Inside North Fork Road south of the turn to Kintla Lake, it was a useful stopping spot for rangers operating out of the Kishenehn Ranger Station to the north. Unfortunately, an arsonist destroyed the cabin completely in a fire set in July 2020. As of this writing in April 2024, the arsonist remains at large.[8,9]

Glacier's Backcountry Patrol/Snowshoe Cabins

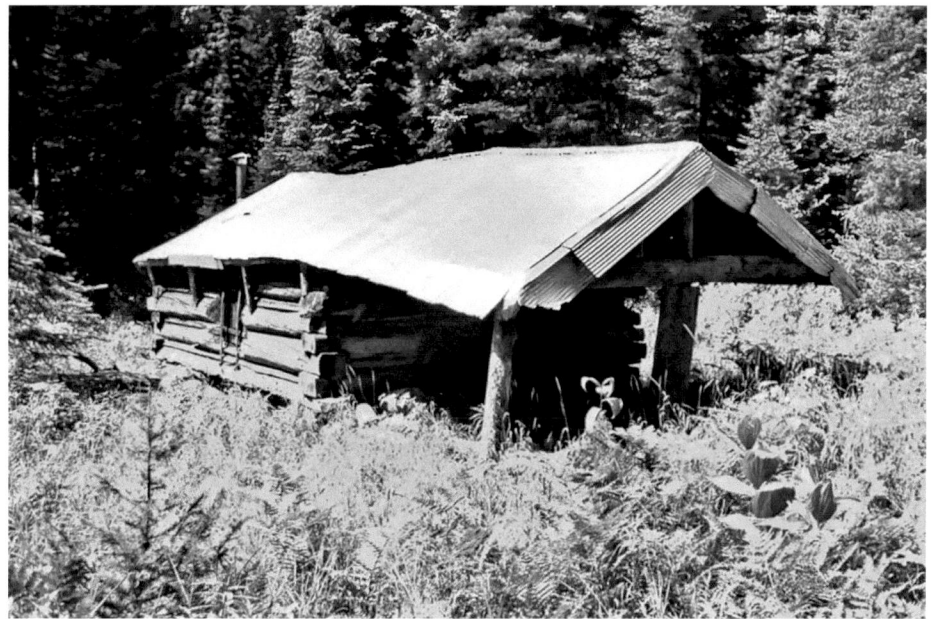

The rather run-down Cattle Queen patrol cabin, labeled as "Ahern Pass" on Leslie Lee's 1913 map. The cabin is adjacent to Cattle Queen Creek, a tributary (not shown) to Mineral Creek on Lee's map. (*Photo by Leroy Dudley for GNP, taken on an unspecified date in 1998*)

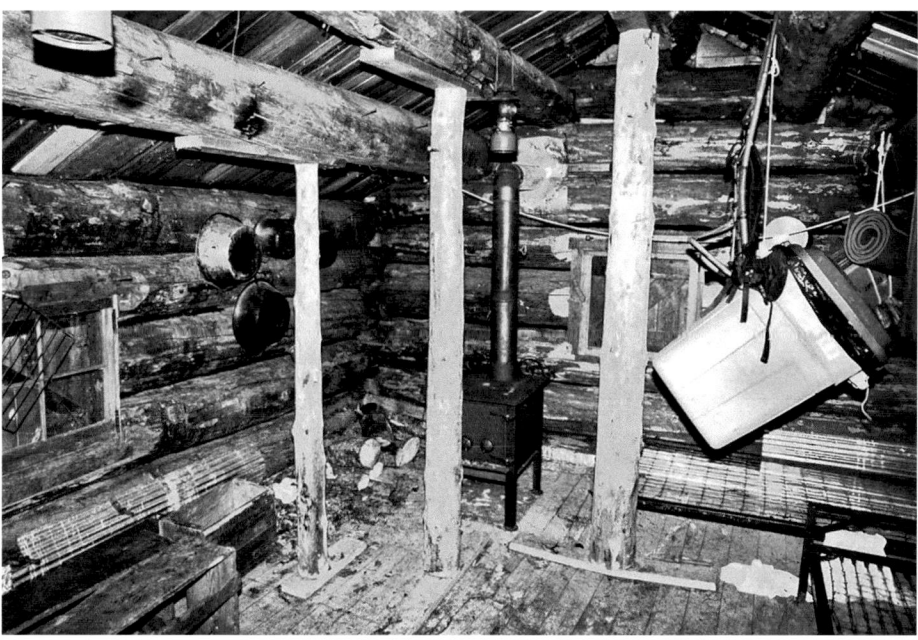

The interior of the Cattle Queen patrol cabin looks like a haven for mice and packrats, as photographed on an unspecified date in 1998. (*Photo by Leroy Dudley for GNP*)

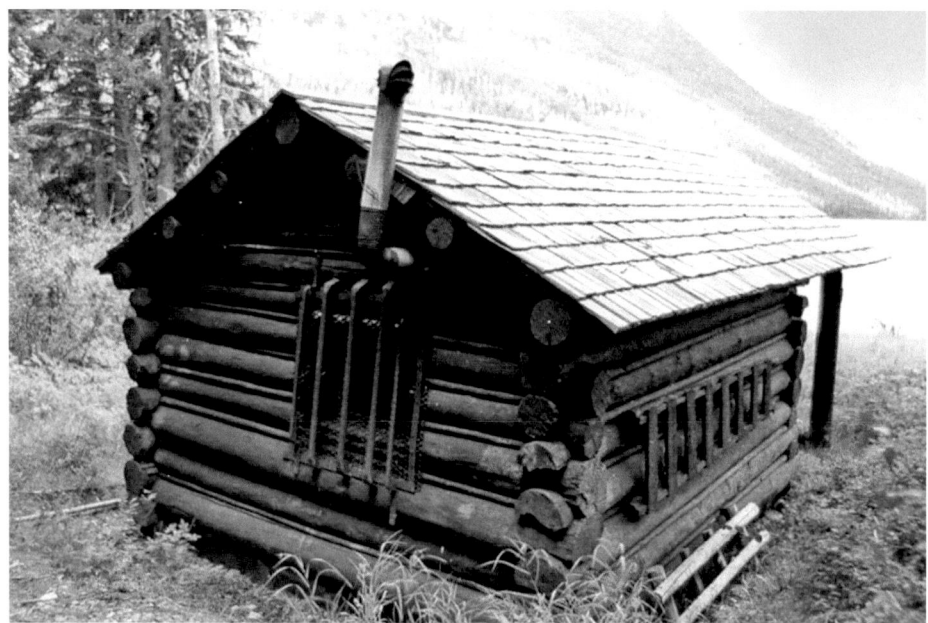

The Upper Kintla Lake patrol cabin, at the head of Upper Kintla Lake (visible in background). Note the heavily barred window, designed to discourage marauding bears from entering the cabin. (*Photo taken in August 1982, by Historical Research Associates for GNP*)

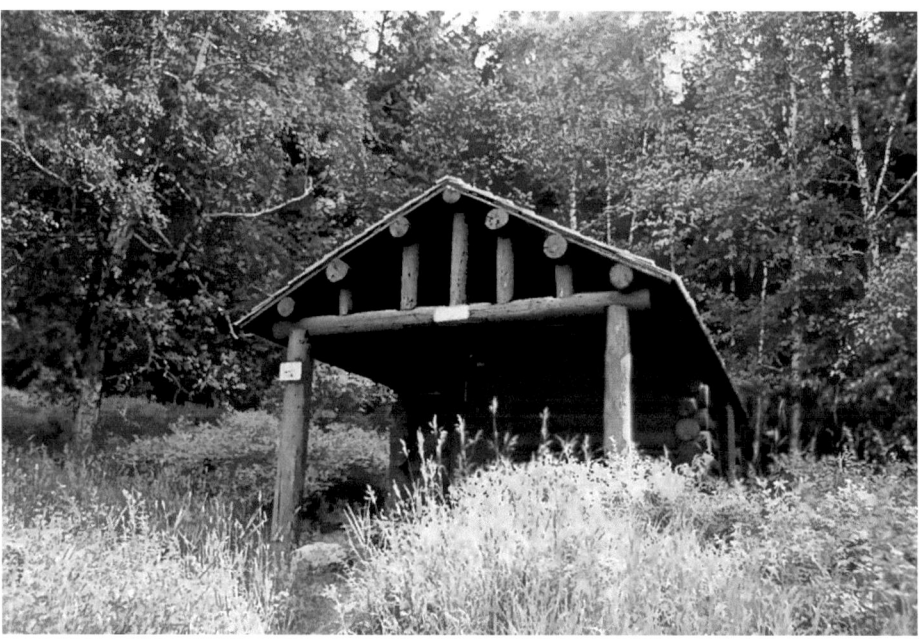

View of the front of the Upper Kintla Lake patrol cabin, taken from the adjacent lakeshore. (*Photo taken in August 1982, by Historical Research Associates for GNP*)

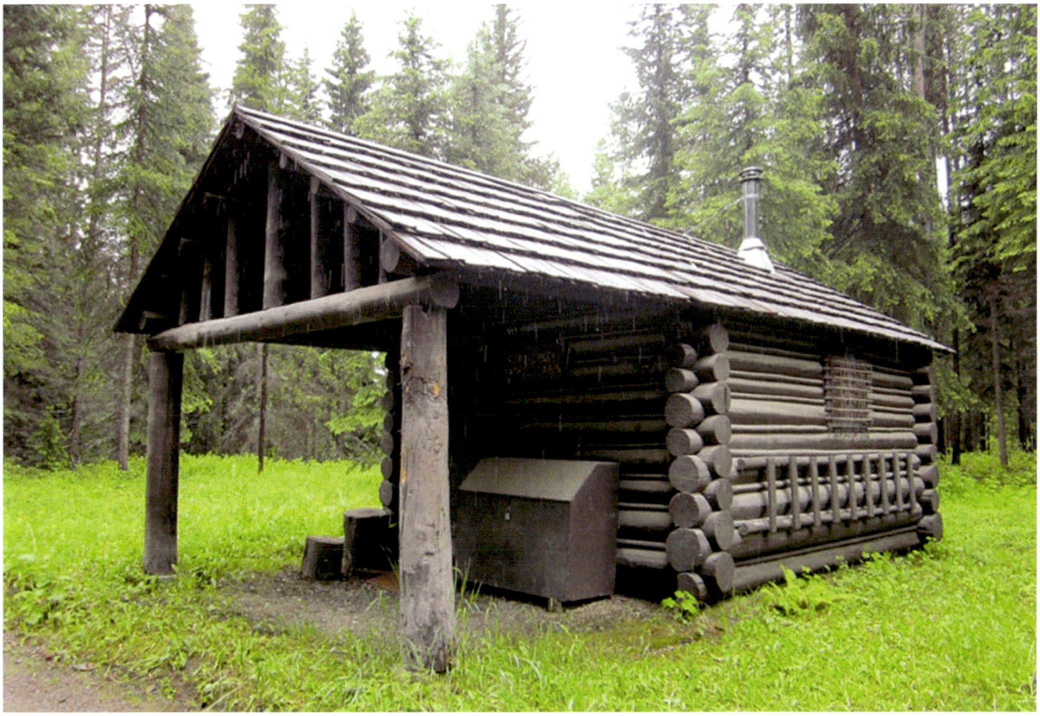

Glacier's Backcountry Patrol/Snowshoe Cabins

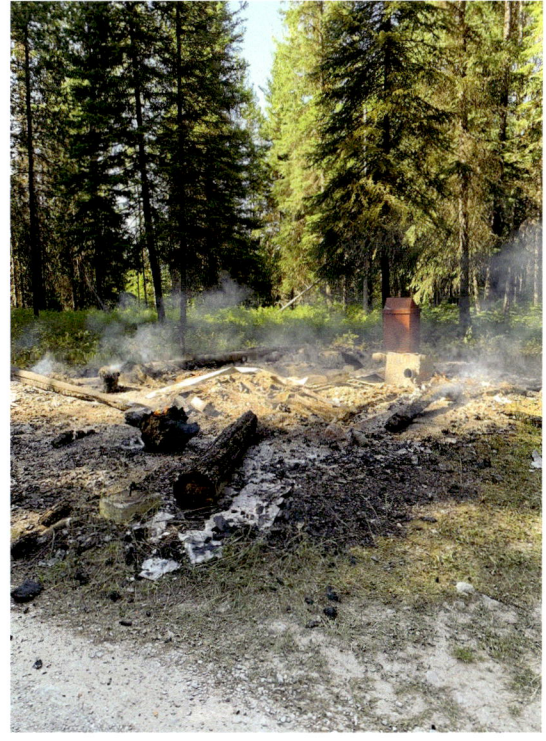

Above: The Ford Creek patrol cabin was located along the Inside North Fork Road (Glacier Route 7) roughly halfway between Bowman and Kintla Lakes. It was primarily used as a snowshoe cabin during winter. It was destroyed in an arson fire set on July 23, 2020. (*NPS photo, unattributed*)

Right: The remains of the Ford Creek patrol cabin, burned in an arson fire on July 23, 2020, as photographed on July 26, 2020. (*GNP, photographer unattributed*)

The Bowman Lake patrol cabin is not located in an isolated location compared to most of the patrol cabins, it is located only about a half mile east of the Bowman Lake Ranger Station. Recall, however, that the Bowman Lake Ranger Station was not converted from the Culver Military Academy until 1940, so prior to that the patrol cabin was the only Park Service presence at Bowman Lake. The cabin was constructed in 1934 and is located near the Bowman Lake boathouse.[10]

The Quartz Lake patrol cabin is located at the mouth of Quartz Lake. Constructed in 1930, it is quite similar to most of the patrol cabins in the North Fork area. One major valley to the southeast, the Upper and Lower Logging Lake patrol/snowshoe cabins are similar in appearance except that the Upper Logging Lake cabin has an additional support column for the porch roof extension. The Upper cabin was constructed in 1925, whereas the Lower Lake cabin dates from 1933.[11, 12, 13]

The former Camas Creek patrol cabin was located near the junction of the Inside North Fork Road where it is crossed by Camas Creek. A version of the cabin appears on Leslie Lee's map, but the photograph here of the cabin being removed by the Glacier National Park Volunteer Associates shows a much more modern-looking structure. The cabin was removed in 2019 because of a long period of inactivity.[14]

Up the valley of Camas Creek, Leslie Lee's map shows a patrol cabin at Arrow Lake. The cabin was a standard log-style snowshoe cabin, as shown in an accompanying photograph here. Unfortunately, massive snow avalanches are common in this valley, and apparently it was deemed by the Park Service to be too dangerous to maintain the cabin as a snowshoe patrol location. The cabin was, therefore, removed by the park sometime in the 1970s according to a longtime local individual who also provided the accompanying photos of the massive snow avalanche damage common at this site.

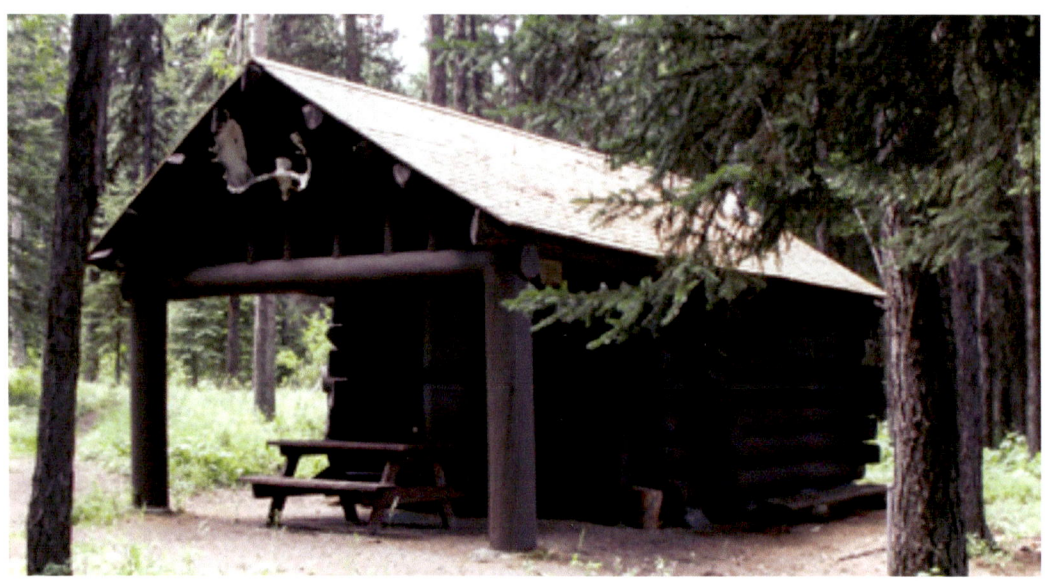

The Bowman Lake patrol cabin was located approximately a half mile east of the Bowman Lake Ranger Station. Note the large set of moose antlers above the picnic table. (*Undated and unattributed public domain photo*)

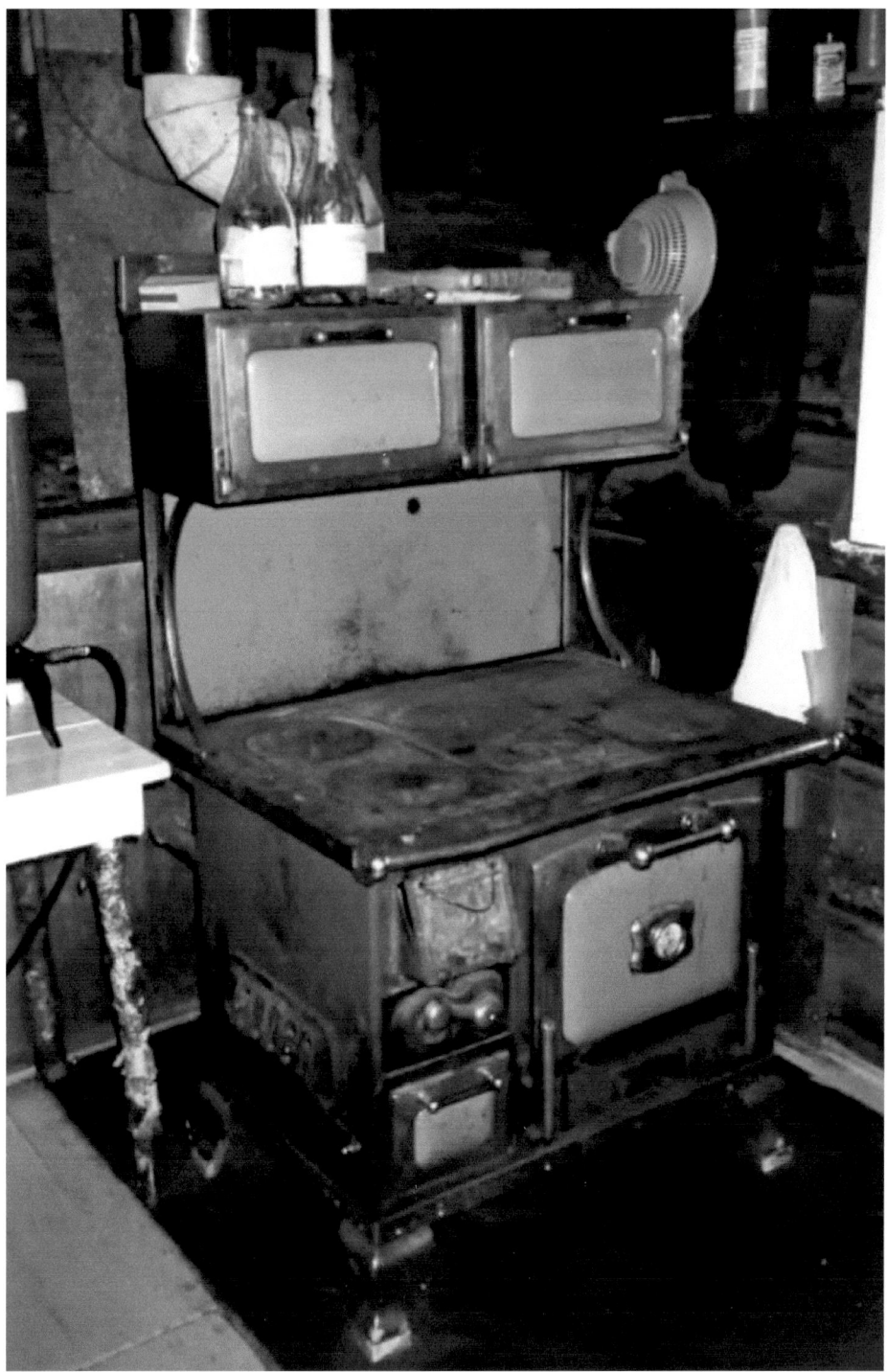

The interior of the Bowman Lake patrol cabin, focused on its large, wood-fed stove. (*GNP, photo unattributed, taken in 1981*)

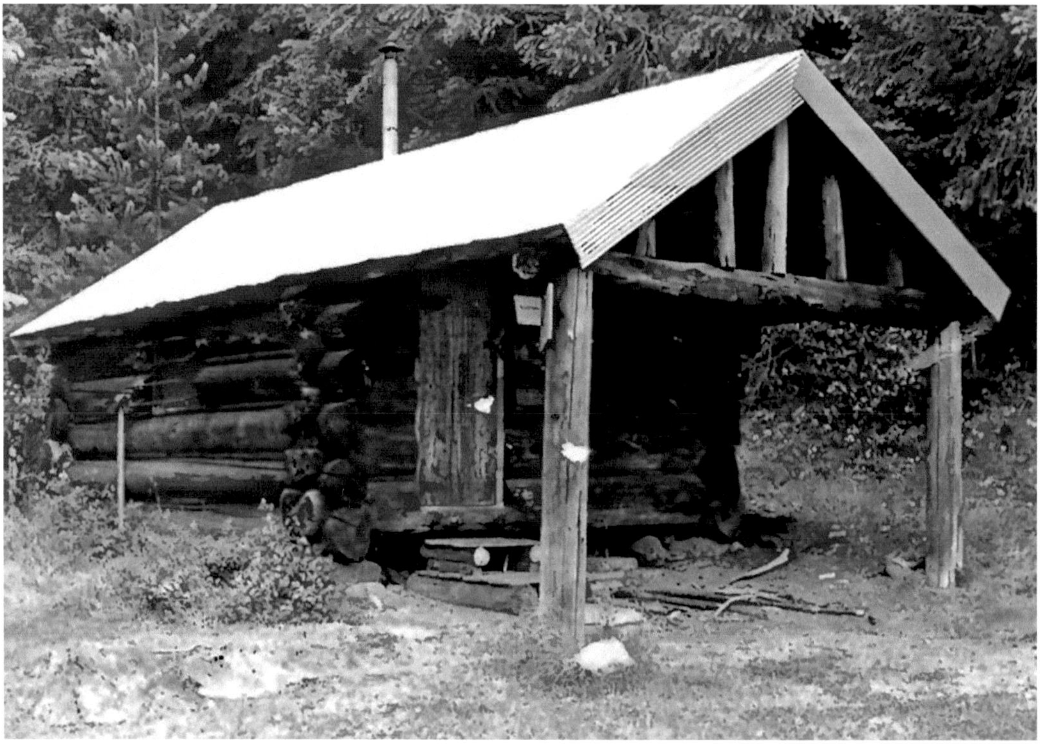

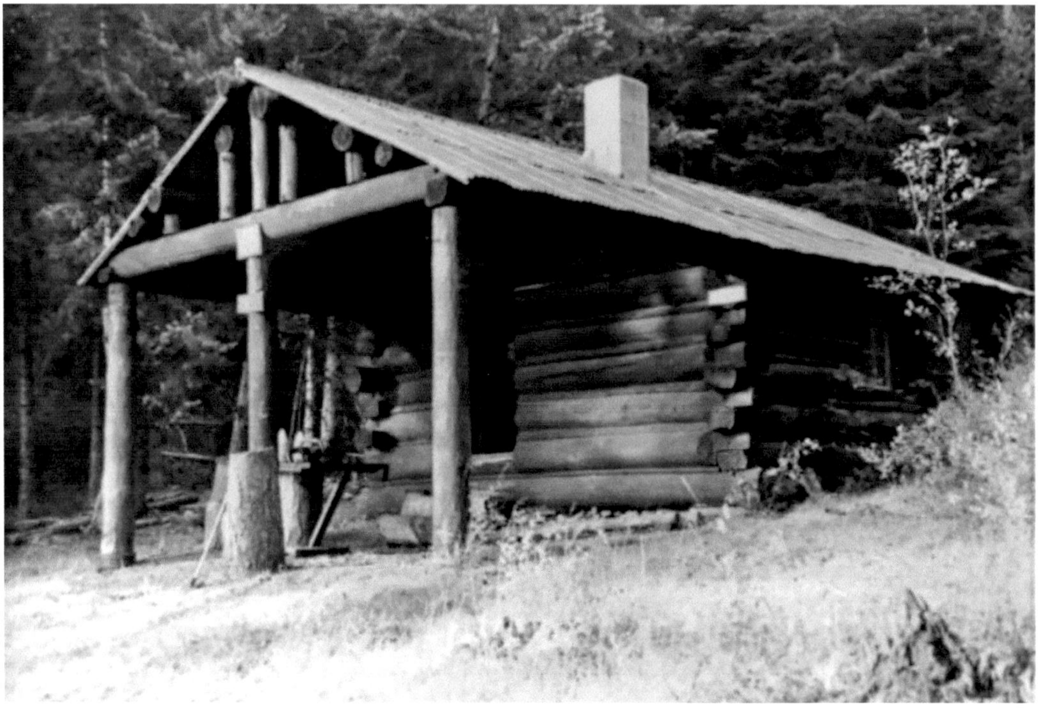

Glacier's Backcountry Patrol/Snowshoe Cabins

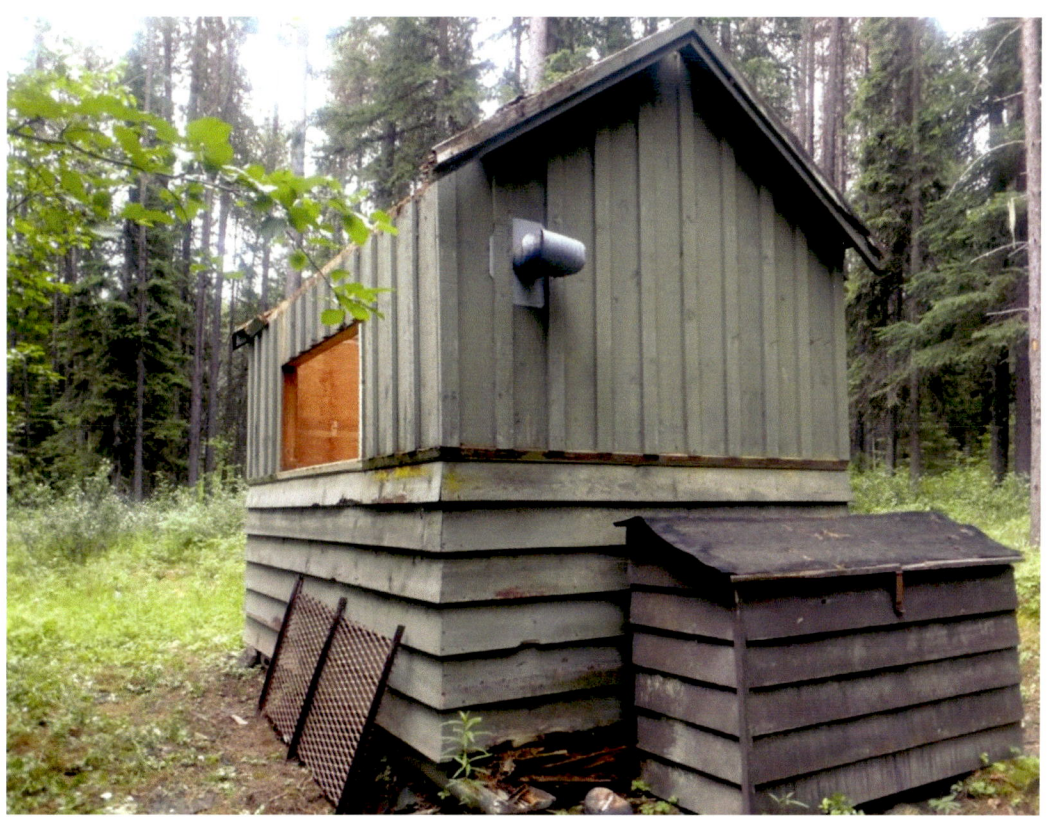

The Camas Creek patrol cabin, located adjacent to the Inside North Fork Road where it crosses Camas Creek, was removed in July 2019, by GNP in association with the Glacier National Park Volunteer Associates. (*GNP, unattributed*)

Opposite above: The Quartz Lake patrol cabin, similar in appearance to the nearby Bowman Lake and Ford Creek patrol cabins. (*Photo by Historical Research Associates for GNP, photo taken in August 1982*)

Opposite below: The Upper Logging Lake patrol cabin, located at the up-valley end of Logging Lake. Note the third support pole for the porch roof extension. (*Photo taken in 1981 by unattributed photographer for GNP*)

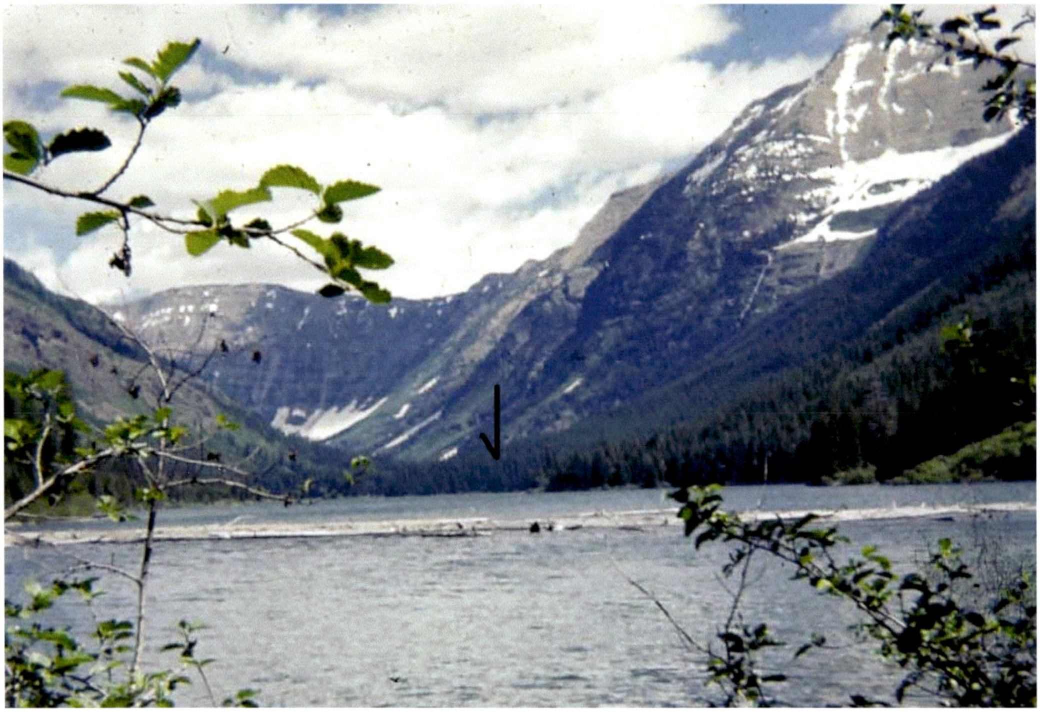

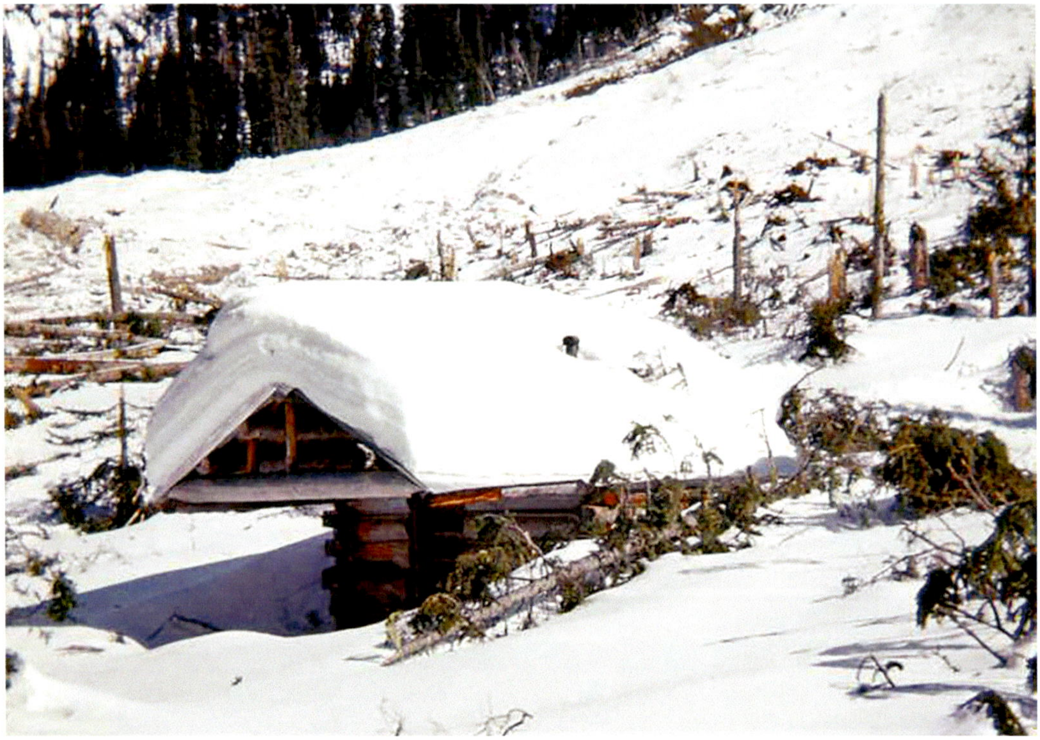

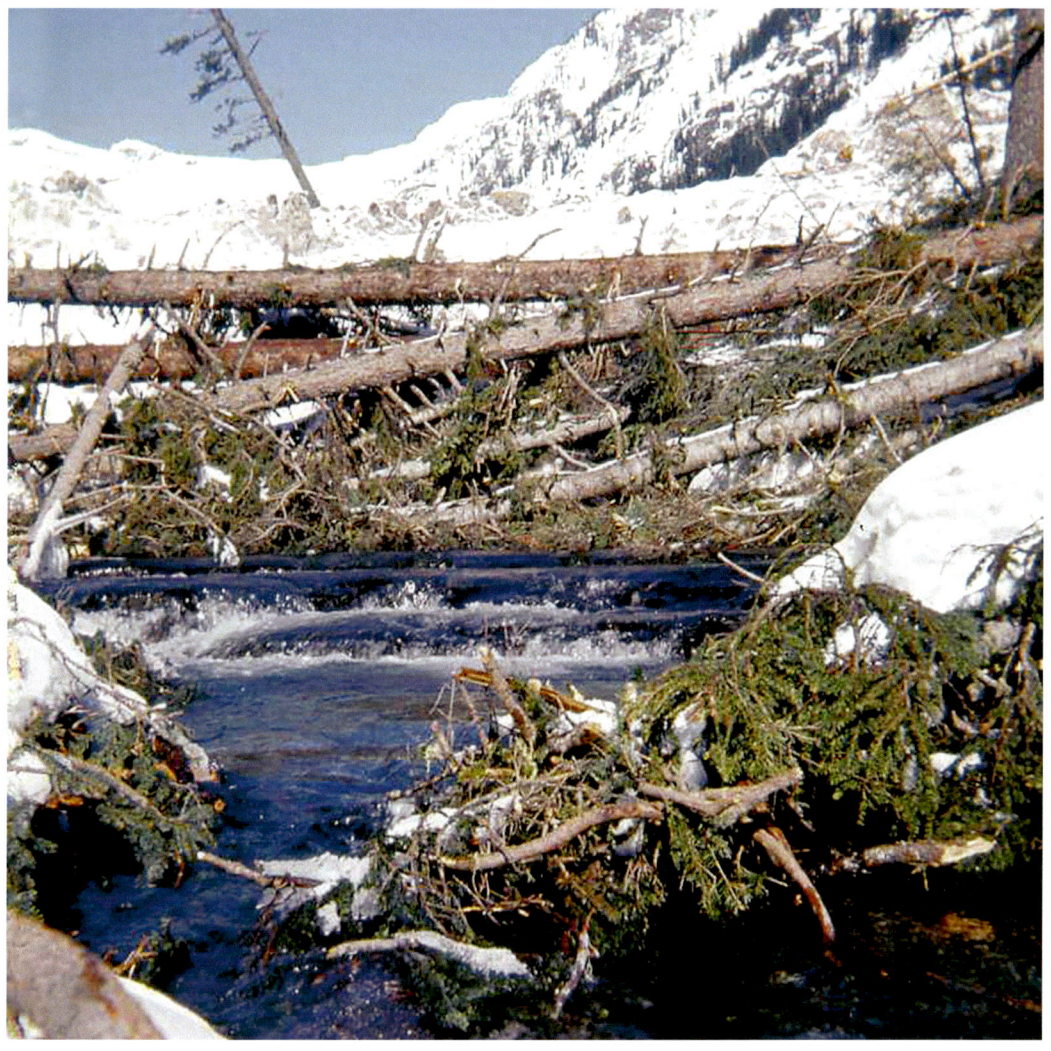

The massive snow avalanche debris that barely missed destroying the Arrow Lake patrol cabin. *(Jerry Stolte photo provided by Don Stolte, used with permission)*

Opposite above: View in the Camas Creek valley, looking upstream from Trout Lake to the approximate location of Arrow Lake and the Arrow Lake patrol cabin shown by the black arrow. The valley is renowned for severe snow avalanches. *(Photo by author, taken in June 1974)*

Opposite below: The Arrow Lake patrol cabin in the winter of 1964 or 1965, soon after a major snow avalanche descended off adjacent Heavens Peak on the right and nearly demolished the cabin. *(Jerry Stolte photo provided by Don Stolte, used with permission)*

Patrol Cabins of the Middle Fork Drainages

Visitors on the floor of the McDonald Creek valley above Lake McDonald whiz past Logan Creek and typically never realize that they are passing one of the park's snowshoe cabins. The cabin's location allows for winter patrols of the McDonald Creek valley and serves as a jumping-off point for an extended backcountry patrol from there eventually to Waterton Lake. The structure was built in 1925.[15]

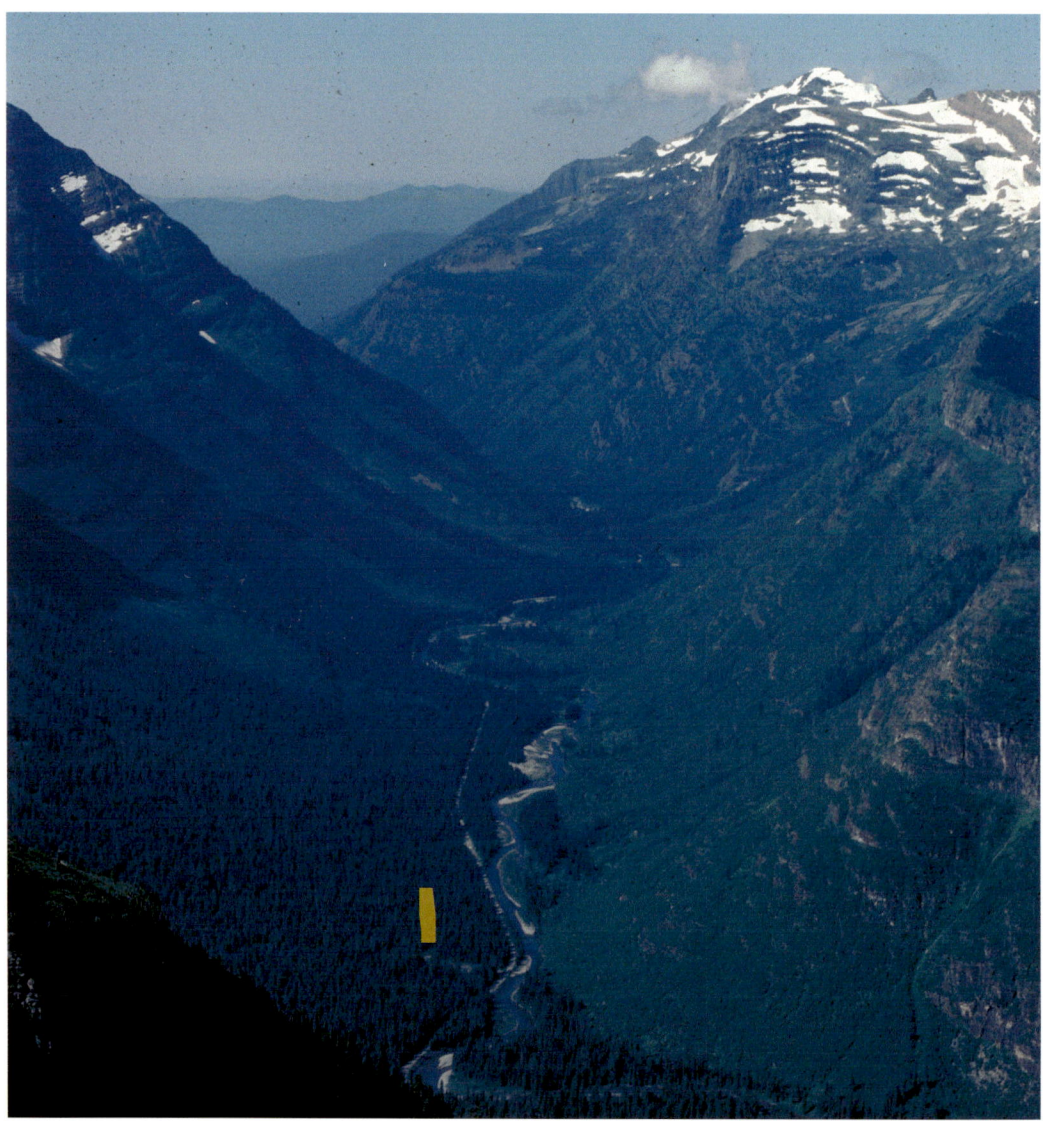

View down the McDonald Creek valley from the Highline Trail. McDonald Creek and Going-to-the-Sun Road to the left of the creek are visible. The vertical yellow line points down to the location of the Logan Creek patrol cabin. (*Photo by author, photo taken July 1990*)

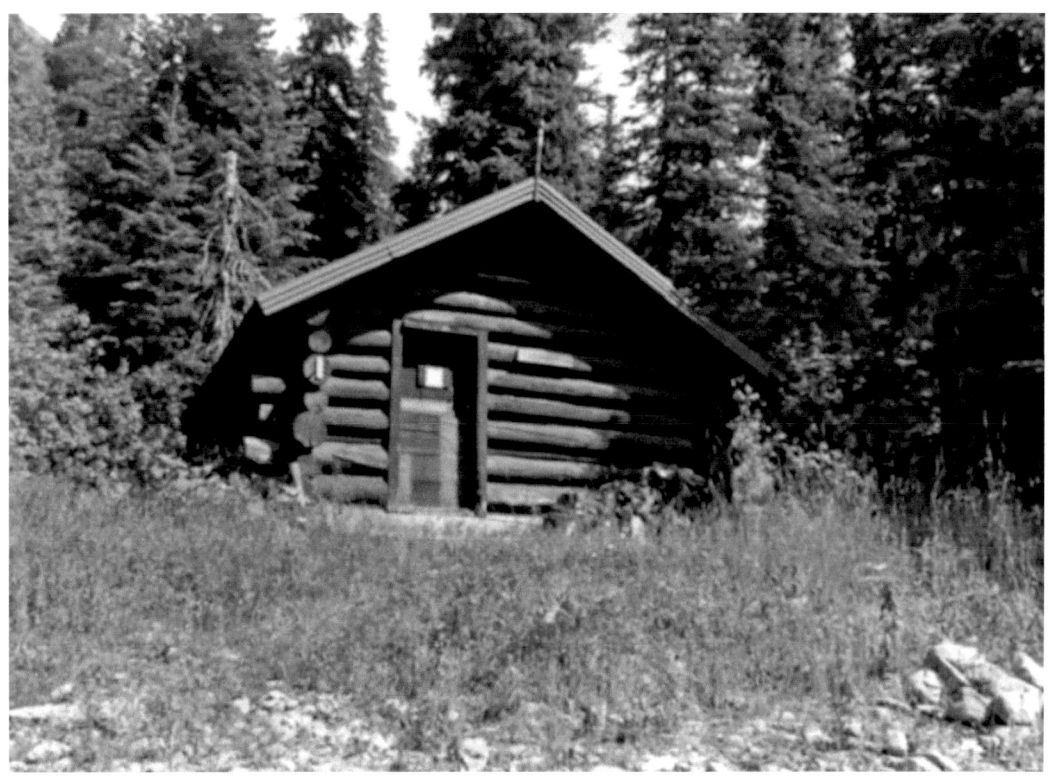

The Logan Creek patrol cabin in August 1982. (*Photo by Historical Research Associates for GNP*)

South of the McDonald Creek valley, every major drainage has a snowshoe patrol cabin, and some of the longer valleys (Nyack and Park Creeks) have two. The cabin for Ole Creek is actually not in that valley, but only about a mile south of it at the easily accessible Fielding Patrol Cabin, reached easily from a spur road off of U.S. Highway 2 a few miles southwest of Marias Pass. Dates of construction for the patrol cabins, from north to south are Lincoln Creek, 1925; Harrison Lake, 1925; Lower Nyack Creek, 1927; Upper Nyack Creek, 1926; Lower Park Creek, 1925; Upper Park Creek, 1928; and Fielding, 1936. Fielding's later date and unusual construction style (compared to all the other Middle Fork cabins) result from its original construction as a fire cache (of firefighting equipment) rather than a snowshoe cabin.[16, 17, 18, 19, 20, 21, 22]

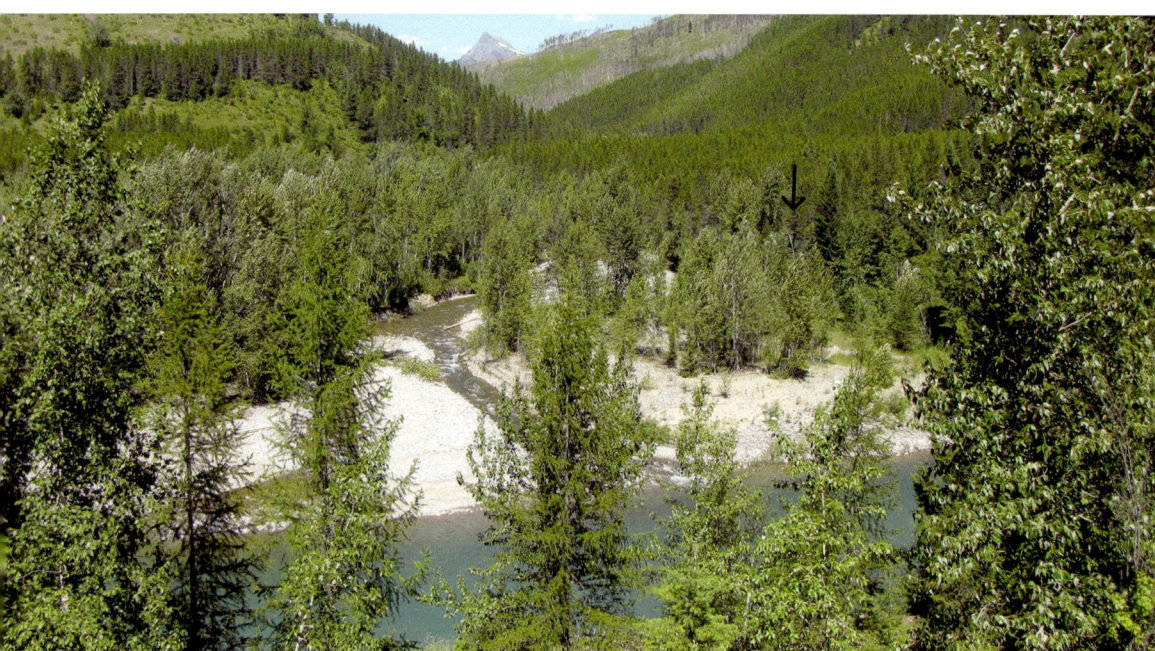

View of the Lincoln Creek delta where it flows into the Middle Fork of the Flathead River, and the location of the Lincoln Creek patrol cabin (arrow). (*Photo by author, taken July 23, 2012*)

Opposite above: The Lincoln Creek patrol cabin. (*Photo by Corey Shea for GNP, May 1999*)

Opposite below: The rustic interior of the Lincoln Creek patrol cabin. (*Photo by Corey Shea for GNP, May 1999*)

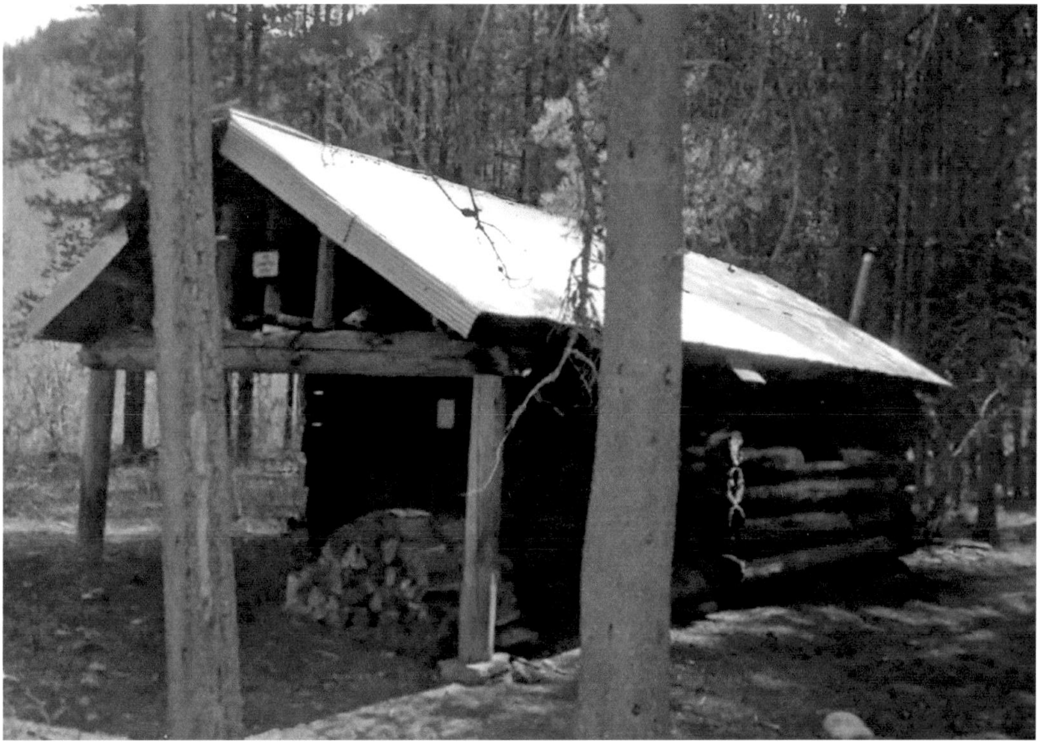

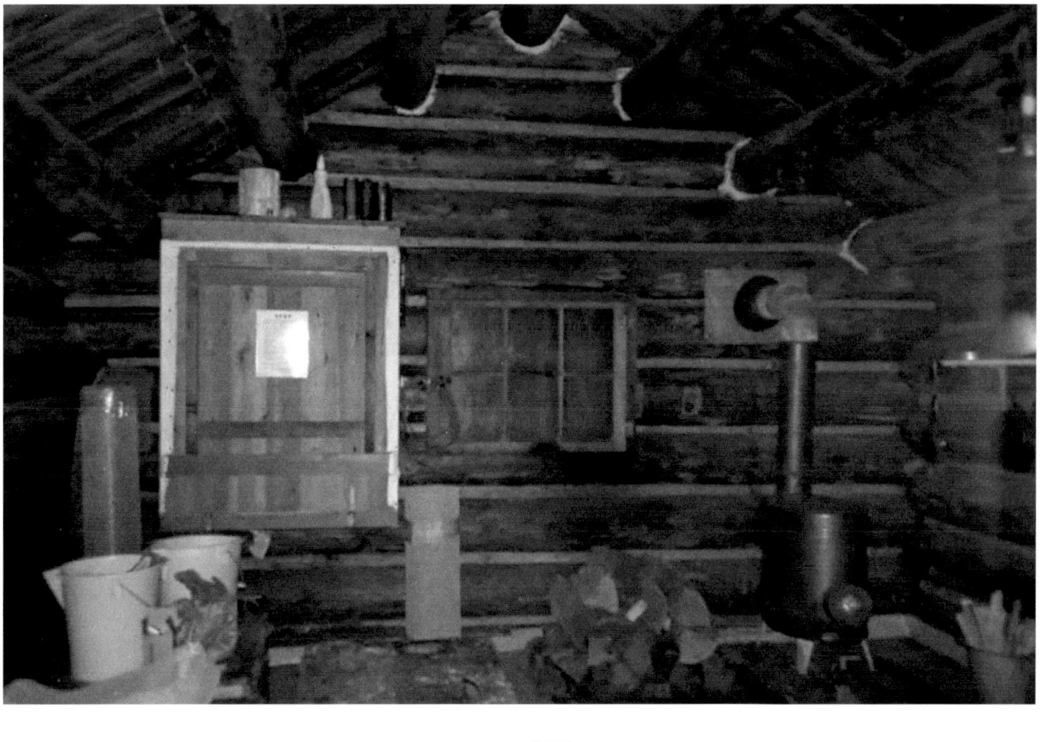

Glacier's Backcountry Patrol/Snowshoe Cabins

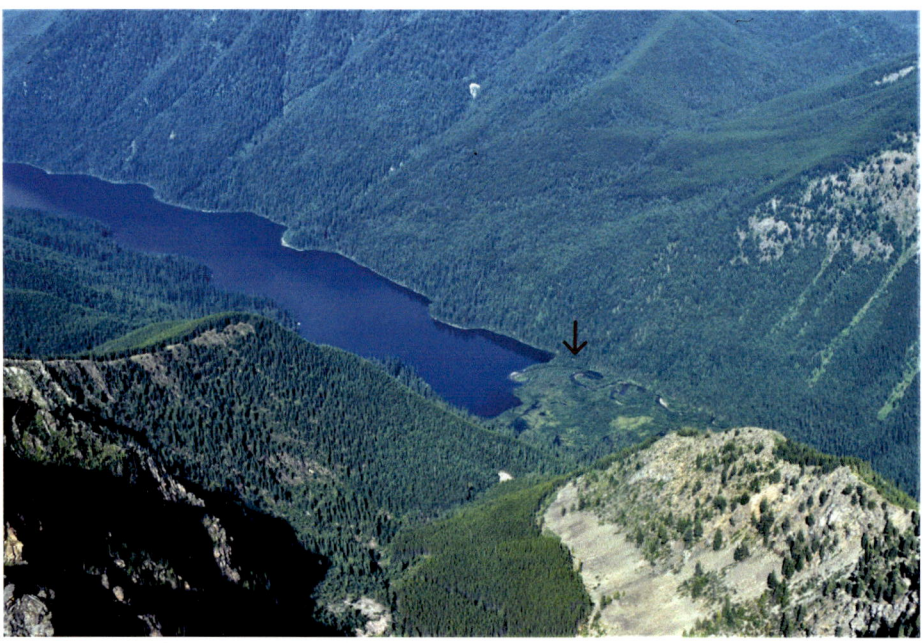

Location of the Harrison Lake patrol cabin (arrow), just beyond the head of Harrison Lake. Photo taken from a helicopter. (*Photo by author, photo taken July 26, 1994*)

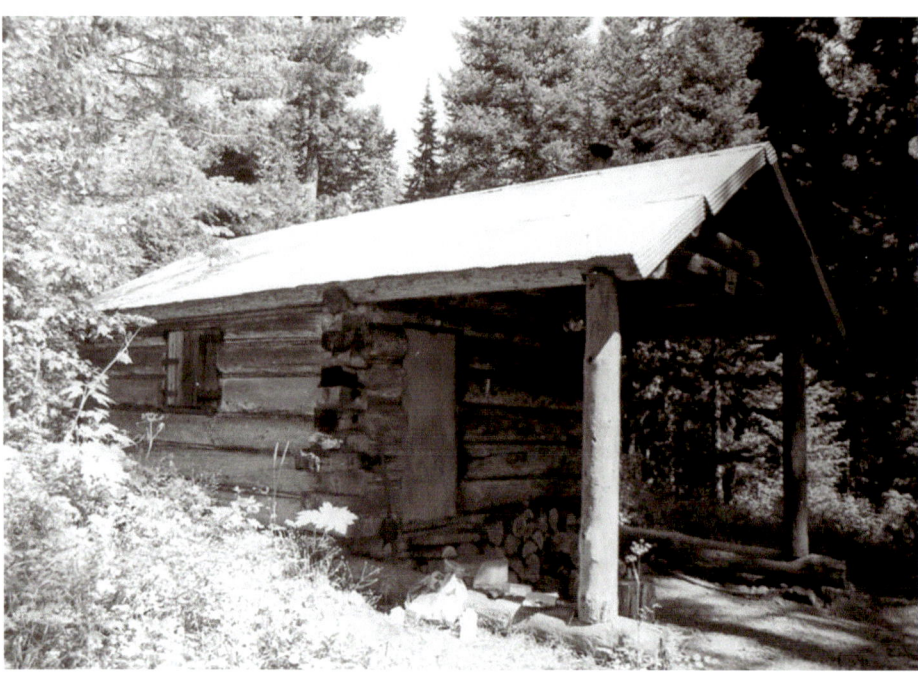

The Harrison Lake patrol cabin, located about 100 feet from the shore of Harrison Lake. (*Public domain photo, undated and unattributed*)

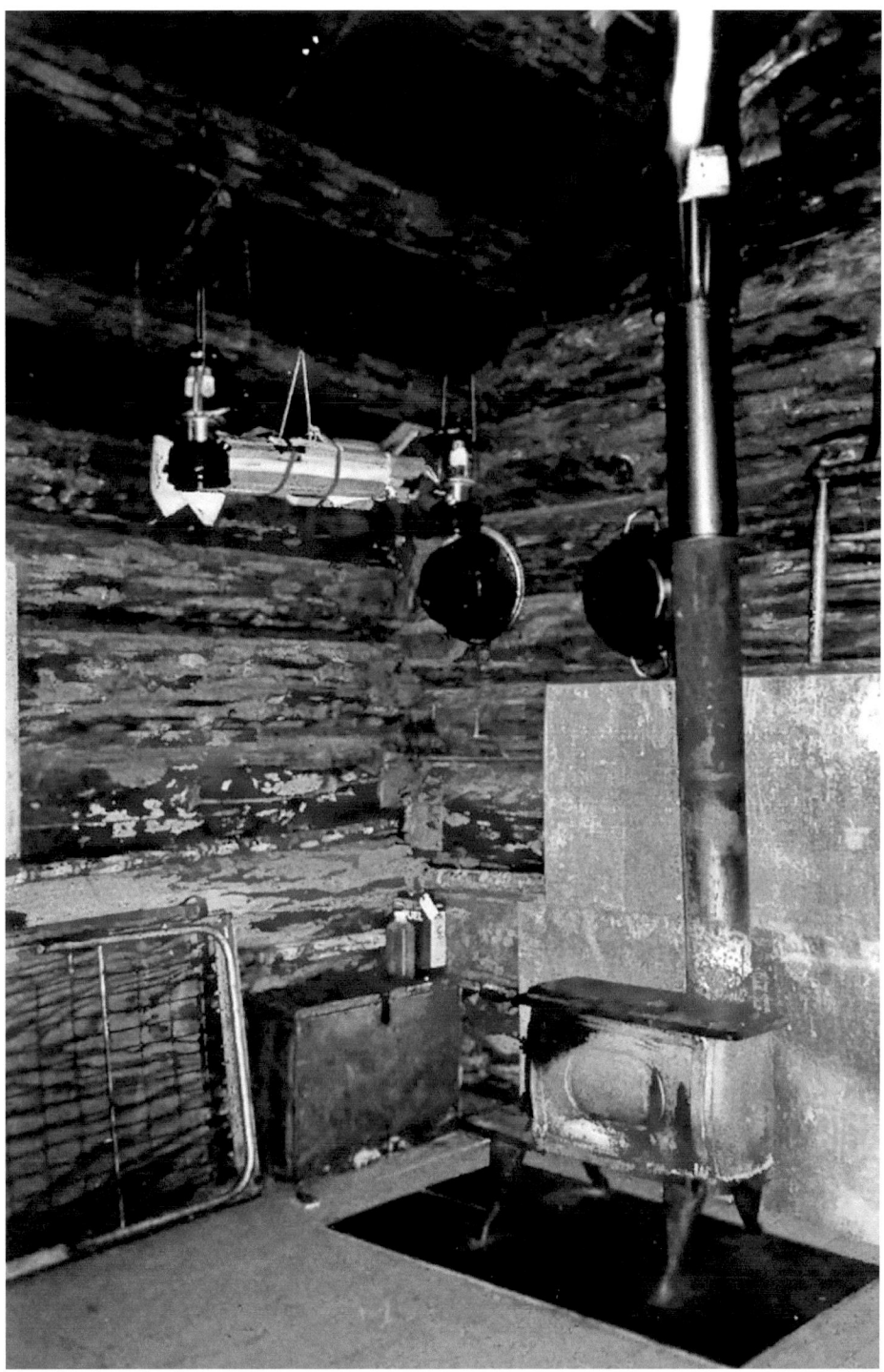

The rustic interior of the Harrison Lake patrol cabin, photographed in August 1999. (*GNP, unattributed photographer*)

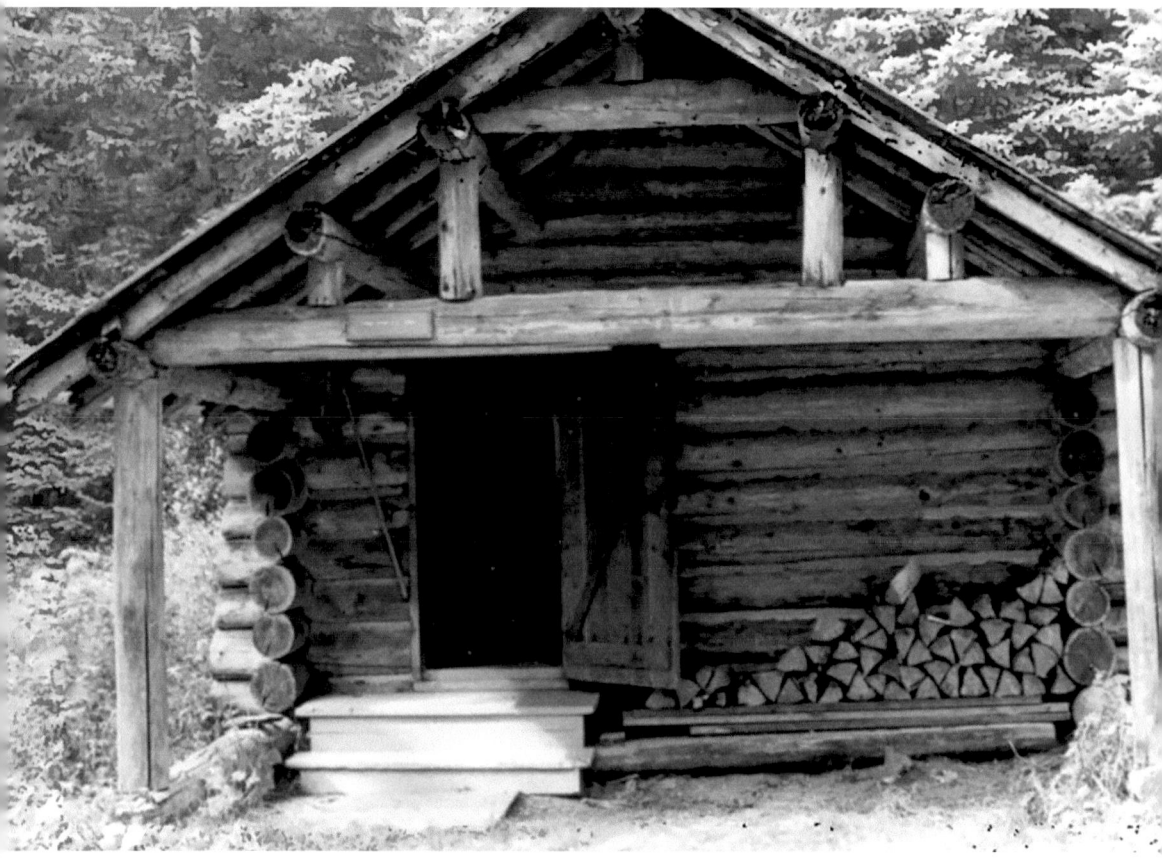

The welcoming front porch of the Lower Nyack Creek patrol cabin. (*GNP, unattributed photographer, 1982*)

Opposite page: The well-maintained interior of the Lower Nyack Creek patrol cabin. (*GNP, unattributed photographer, 1982*)

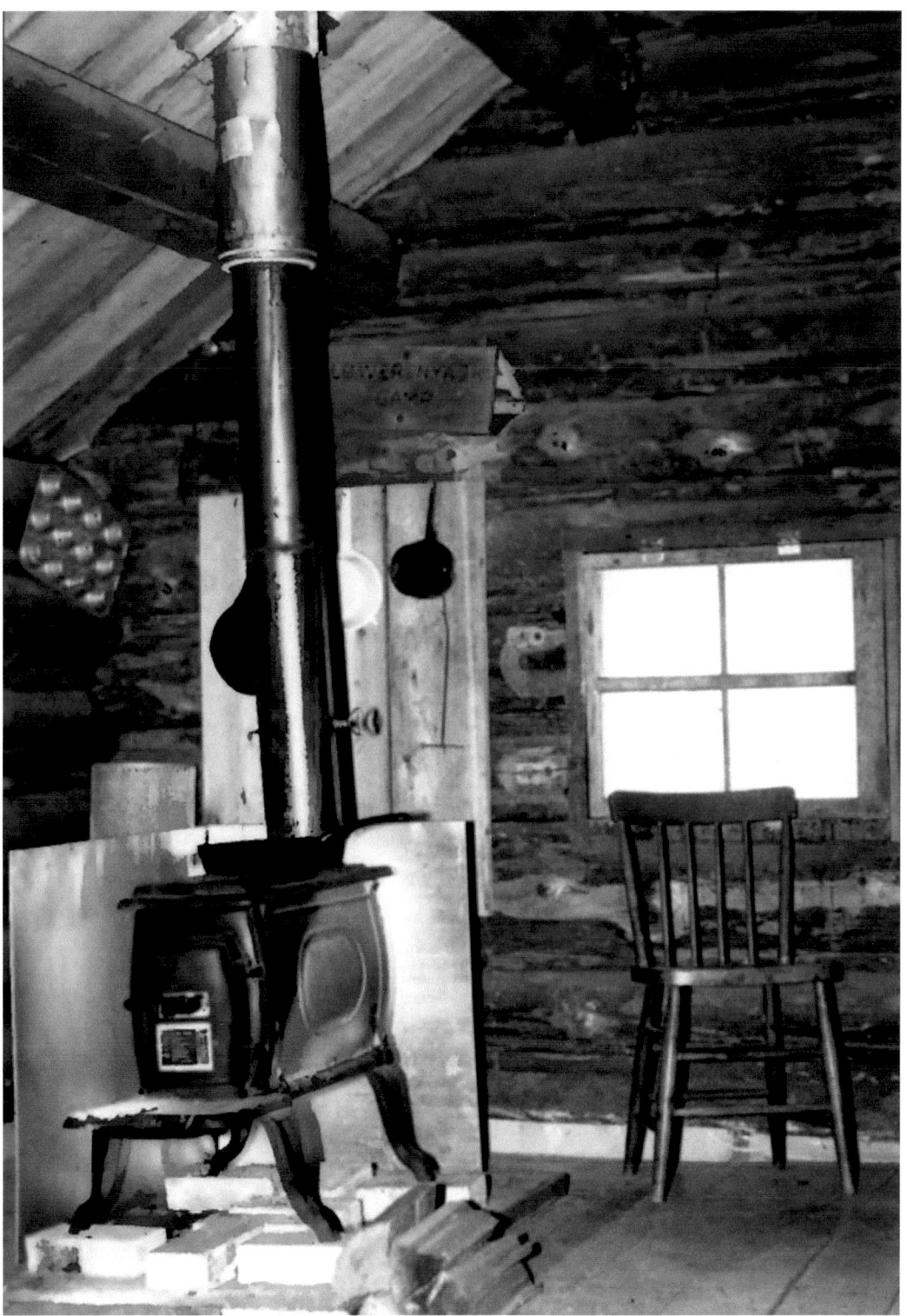

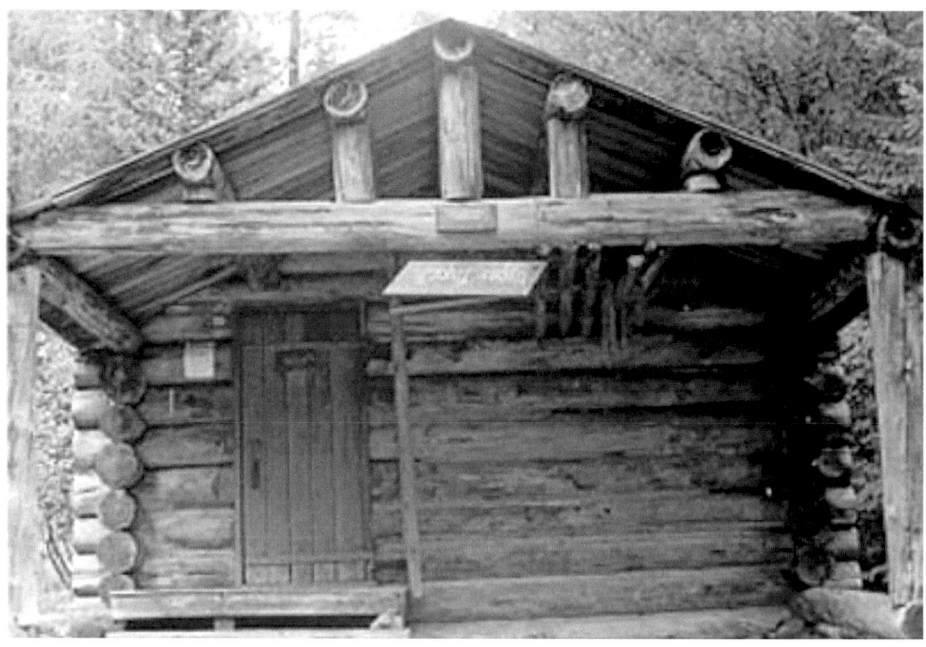

The Upper Nyack Creek patrol cabin. (*Public domain photo, undated and unattributed*)

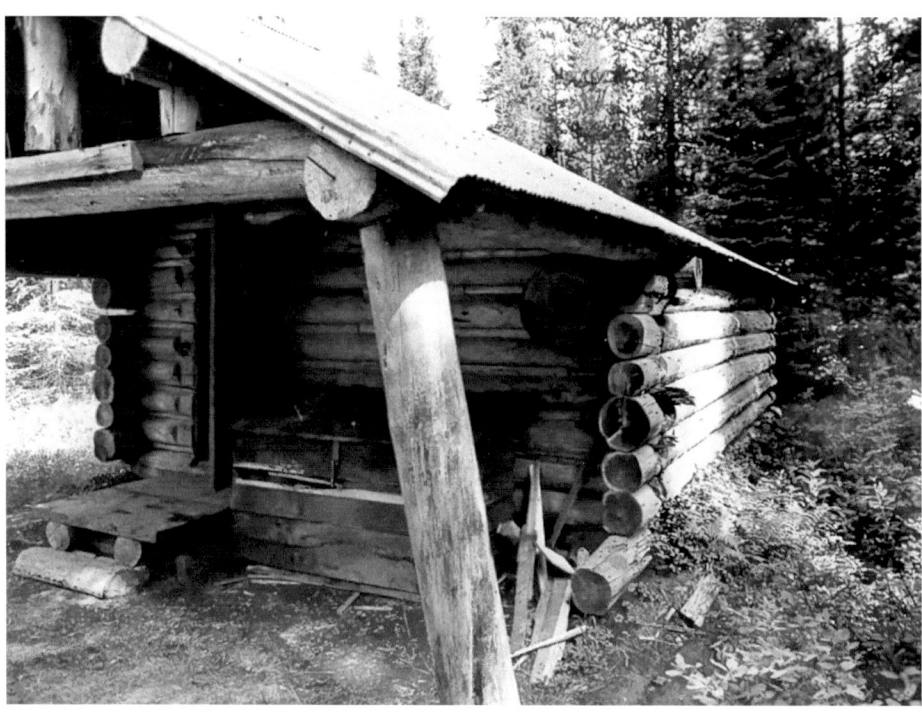

The Coal Creek patrol cabin, seen obliquely from the front. (*Photo taken by Leroy Dudley for GNP, July 1998*)

Glacier's Backcountry Patrol/Snowshoe Cabins

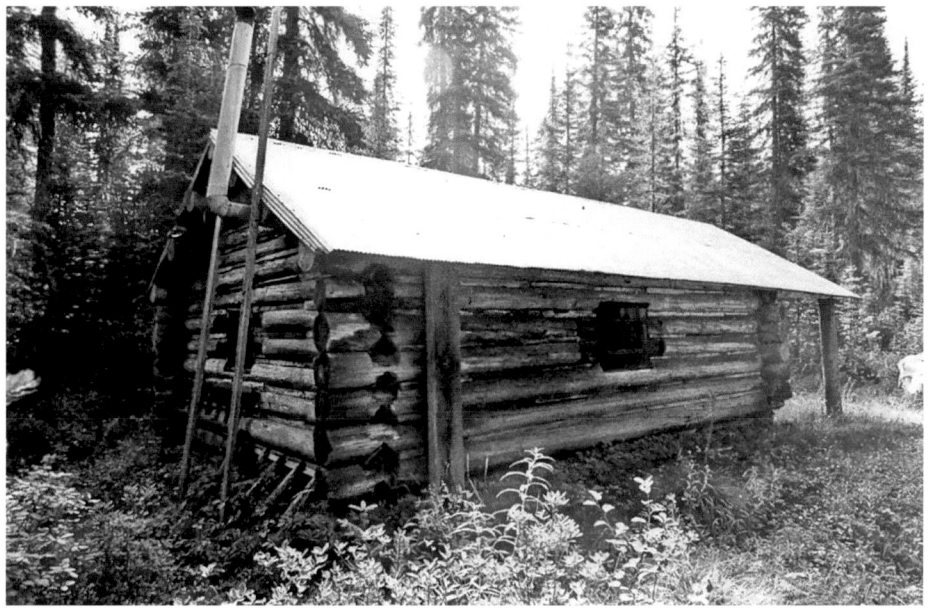

The rear and one side of the Coal Creek patrol cabin, with small windows with bars designed to keep marauding bears from entering the cabin. (*Photo taken by Leroy Dudley for GNP, July 1998*)

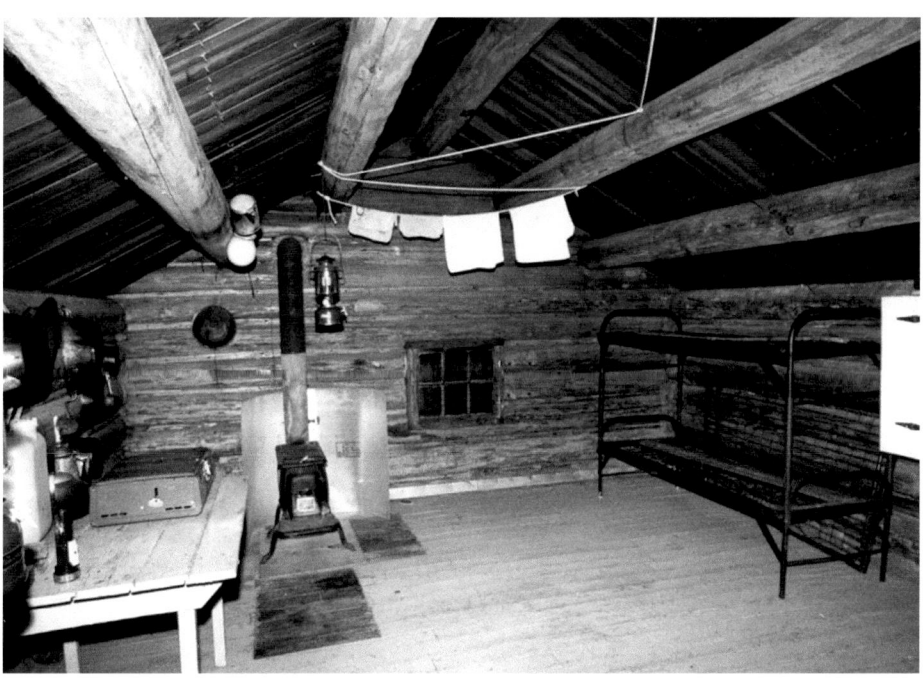

The tidy interior of the Coal Creek patrol cabin. (*Photo taken by Leroy Dudley for GNP, July 1998*)

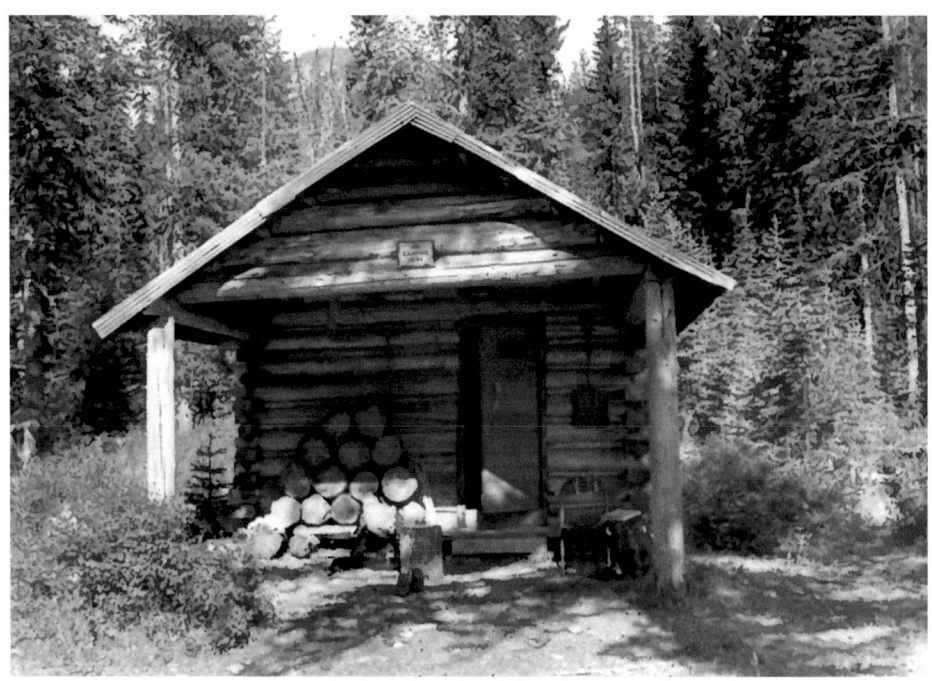

The front of the Lower Park Creek patrol cabin, photographed in July 1985. (*Photo by Park Ranger Charlie Logan for GNP*)

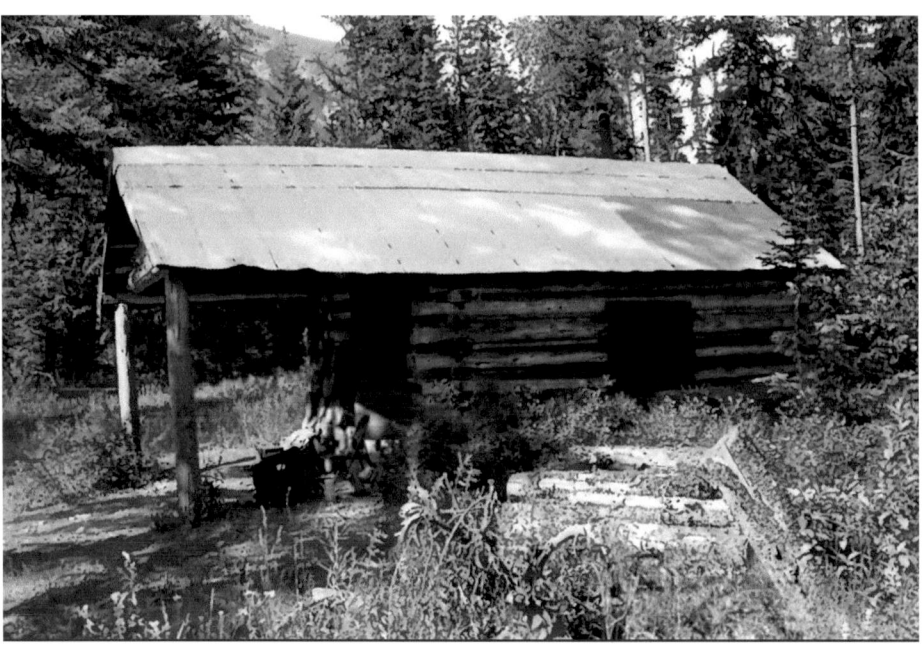

An atypical side view of the Lower Park Creek patrol cabin. (*Photo by Park Ranger Charlie Logan for GNP, taken in July 1985*)

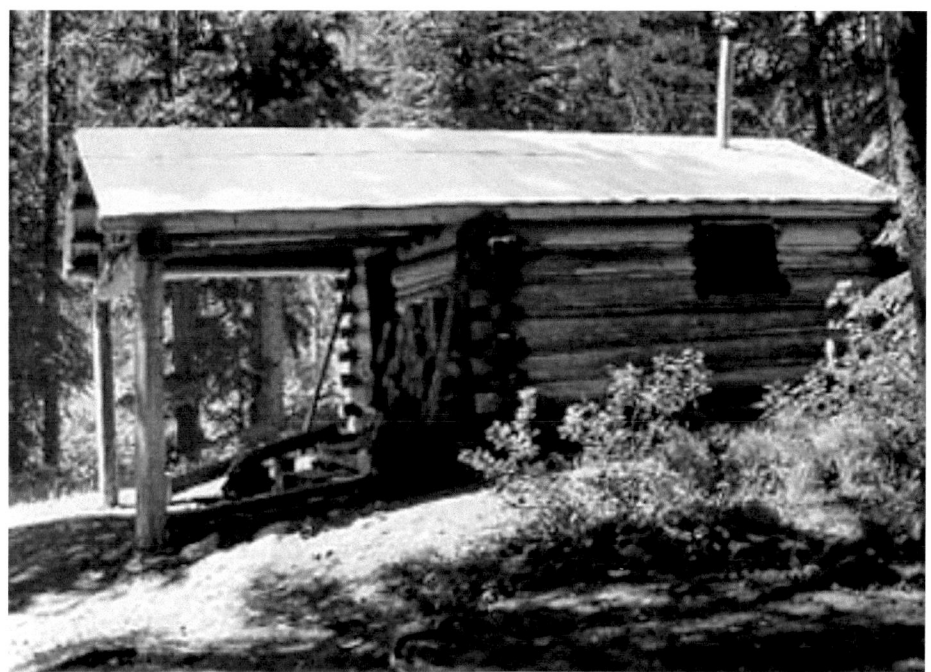

The Upper Park Creek patrol cabin, similar in appearance to the Lower Park Creek cabin. (*Public domain photo, undated and unattributed*)

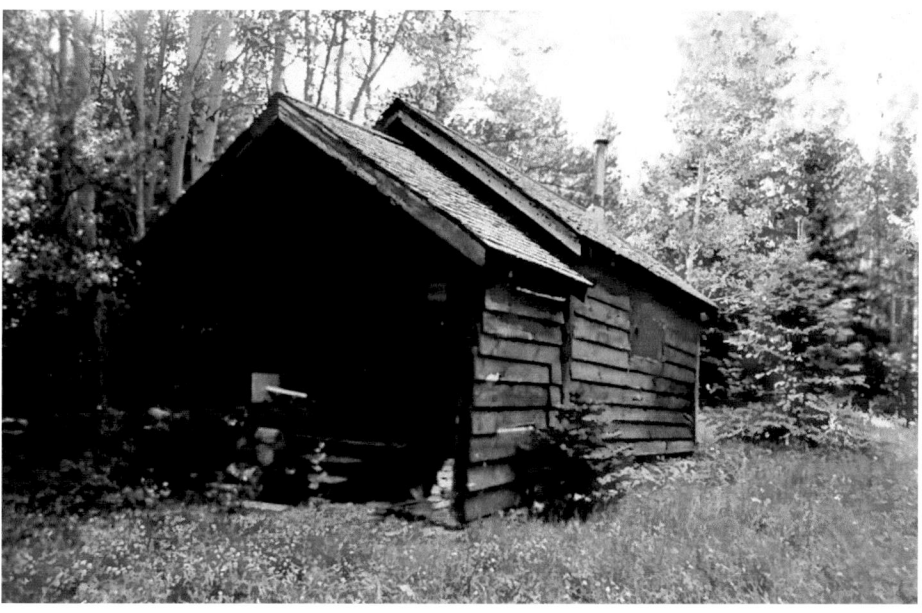

The atypical, board-construction Fielding patrol cabin just inside the southern boundary of Glacier Park near the mainline of the BNSF railway. (*Photo taken in 1982 by Historical Research Associates for GNP*)

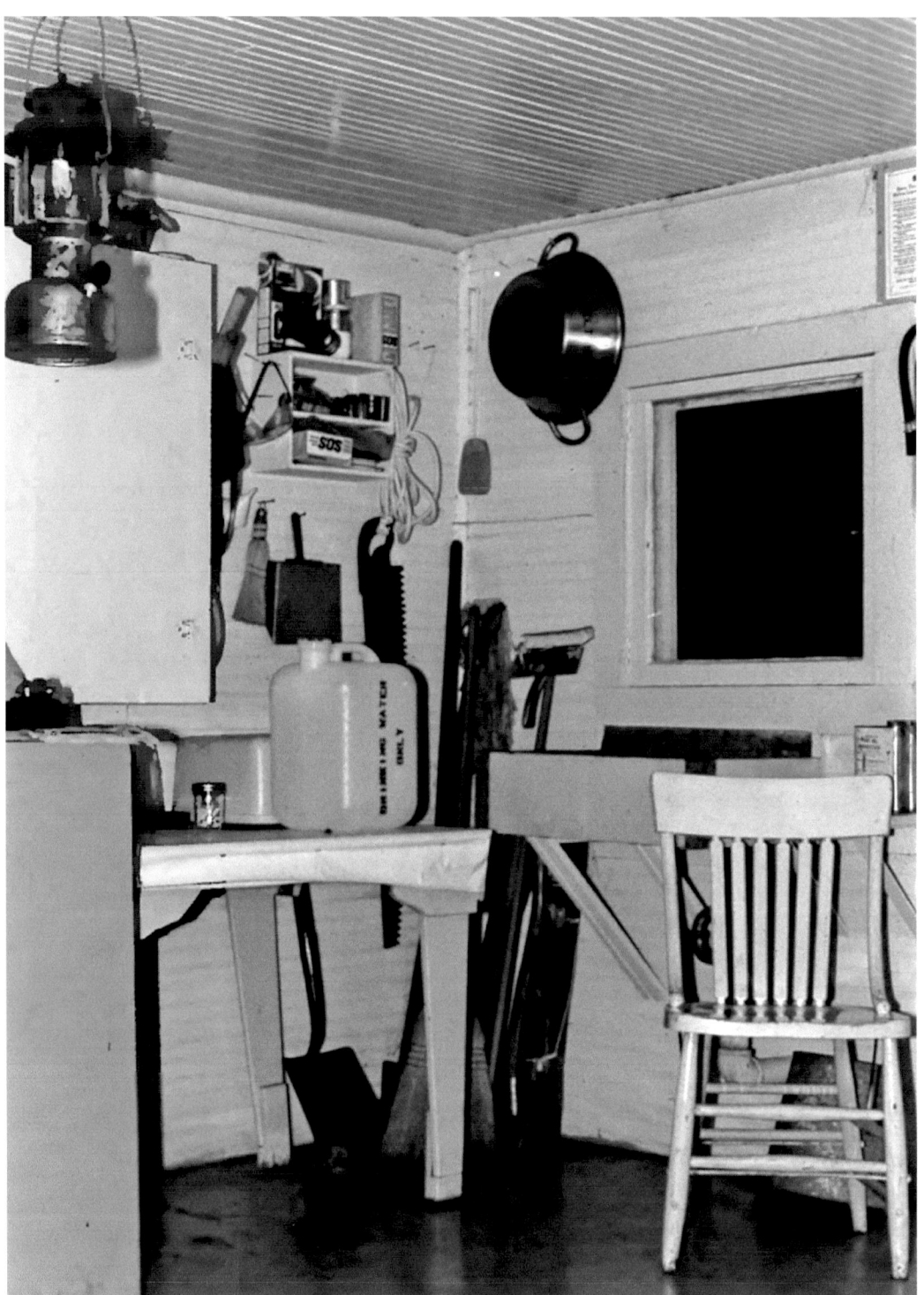

The interior of the Fielding patrol cabin. (*GNP, undated photo*)

Endnotes

Introduction

1. Workman, R. B., *National Park Service Uniforms—In Search of an Identity 1872–1920* (Harpers Ferry, WV: National Park Service History Collection, Office of Library, Archives and Graphic Research, No. 2, 1994), various pages.

Chapter 1

1. Howell, C. T., "Charged by a Bull Elk," *Nature Notes from Glacier Park* (West Glacier, MT: Glacier National Park, 1930, Vol. 3 No. 3), p. 26.
2. Fauley, C., "An Encounter with an Elk," *Glacial Drift Notes from Glacier National Park* (West Glacier, MT: Glacier National Park, 1931, Vol. 4 No. 11), p. 80.
3. Miller, B. C., "Backwoods Sport," *Glacial Drift Notes from Glacier National Park* (West Glacier, MT: Glacier National Park, 1932a, Vol. 5 No. 2), p. 11.
4. Buchanan, H. W., "Masters of the Trail," *Nature Notes from Glacier National Park* (West Glacier, MT: Glacier National Park, 1930, Vol. 3 No. 7), p. 63.
5. Miller, B. C., "Pugnacious Mother," *Glacial Drift Notes from Glacier National Park* (West Glacier, MT: Glacier National Park, 1932c, Vol. 5 No. 6), p. 55.
6. Gildart, R. C., *Montana's Early-Day Rangers* (Helena, MT: Montana Magazine, Inc., 1985), p. 80-81.
7. Lee, L. (ed.), *Backcountry Ranger—The Diaries and Photographs of Norton Pearl in Glacier National Park 1910–1913* (Elk Rapids, MI: Fen's Rim Publications, 1994), various pages.
8. Miller, B. C., "Buried in the Snow", *Glacial Drift—Notes from Glacier National Park* (West Glacier, MT: Glacier National Park, 1933, Vol. 6, No. 2), p. 10.
9. *Ibid*.
10. Fauley, C. C., "An Elk Fatality", *Nature Notes from Glacier National Park* (West Glacier, MT: Glacier National Park, 1930, Vol. 3 No. 1), p. 9.
11. Miller, B. C., "The Destruction of the Pole Bridge," *Glacial Drift—Notes from Glacier National Park* (West Glacier, MT: Glacier National Park, 1932b, Vol. 5, No. 2), p. 20.

12 Ruhle, G. C., "Grim Duty", *Glacial Drift—Notes from Glacier National Park* (West Glacier, MT: Glacier National Park, 1934, Vol. 7, No. 1), p. 14.
13 Hufstetler, M., "The Lonesome Life in Glacier National Park—Kishenehn Ranger Station, 1910–1940", *Montana, The Magazine of Western History* (Helena, MT: Montana Historical Society, 2010, Vol. 60, No. 4), p. 70.

Chapter 2

1 Harrington, L., *History of Apgar* (Apgar, MT: Apgar School and Teacher, Mrs. Leona Harrington, 1950, updated through 1957), p. 38.
2 Gildart, R. C., *Montana's Early-Day Rangers* (Helena, MT: Montana Magazine, Inc., 1985), p. 36-37.
3 Guthrie, C. W., *The First Ranger: Adventures of a Pioneer Forest Ranger, Glacier Country 1902–1910* (Huson, MT: Redwing Publishing, 1995), p. 117.
4 Guthrie, C. W., *First Rangers: The Life and Times of Frank Liebig and Fred Herrig, Glacier Country 1902–1910* (Helena, MT: Farcountry Press, 2019), p. 94.
5 Ibid.
6 *Ibid*, pp. 18-28.
7 *Ibid.*, pp. 47-48, 86.

Chapter 3

1 Djuff, R., and Morrison, C., *Waterton and Glacier in a Snap! Fast Facts & Titillating Trivia* (Surrey, BC: Rocky Mountain Books, 2005), p. 38.
2 Hagen, J., "Ranger Tales—An Anthology of Park Service Stories", *The Inside Trail—Voice of the Glacier Park Foundation* (Minneapolis, MN: Glacier Park Foundation, 2016, Vol. 31, No. 2), pp. 4-5.
3 MacDonald, G.A., *Where the Mountains Meet the Prairies—A History of Waterton Country* (Calgary, Alberta: University of Calgary Press, 2000), p. 51.
4 Djuff and Morrison, *op. cit.*, p. 38.
5 Hagen, *op. cit.*, p. 5.
6 MacDonald, *op. cit.*, pp. 51, 53.
7 Rodney, W., *Kootenai Brown, His Life and Times 1839–1916* (Sidney, BC: Gray's Publishing Ltd., 1969), p. 201.
8 MacDonald, *op. cit.*, p. 53.
9 Lee, L. (ed.), *Backcountry Ranger—The Diaries and Photographs of Norton Pearl in Glacier National Park 1910–1913* (Elk Rapids, MI: Fen's Rim Publications, 1994), pp. 1-51.
10 *Ibid.*, pp. 51-245.
11 *Ibid.*, various pages.
12 Ober, M., "The Diary of Norton Pearl," *Montana Outlaw*, Winter Issue (Big Sky, MT: Mountain Outlaw, 2024), pp. 160-164.
13 Lee, *op. cit.*, various pages.
14 Minetor, R., *Historic Glacier National Park—The Stories Behind one of America's Great Treasures* (Guilford, CT: Rowan and Littlefield, 2016), pp. 100-108.

Endnotes

15 McClung, B., *Belly River's Famous Joe Cosley* (Kalispell, MT: Life Preservers, 1998a), various pages.
16 DeSanto, J., "The Legendary Joe Cosley," in Stanley, D. (ed.), *The Glacier Park Reader* (Salt Lake City, UT: University of Utah Press, 2017), p. 141.
17 McClung, *op. cit.*, pp. 24-26.
18 Cosley, J., *The Meeting of Kootenai Brown* (publisher location and publisher unattributed, undated pamphlet), 12 pp.
19 McClung, *op. cit.*, pp. 41-50.
20 Butler, D. R., *Pioneering Women of Glacier National Park* (Charleston, SC: America Through Time, 2023), pp. 43-46.
21 *Ibid.*
22 *Ibid.*
23 McKay, K. L., *Trails of the Past: Historical Overview of the Flathead National Forest, Montana, 1800–1960* (Kalispell, MT: U.S. Forest Service, 1994), p. 256.
24 Gildart, R.C., *Montana's Early-Day Rangers* (Helena, MT: Montana Magazine, Inc., 1985), pp. 39-42.
25 Butler, 2023 *op. cit.*, p. 46-49.
26 *Ibid.*
27 *Ibid.*

Chapter 4

1 Butler, D. R., *The Civilian Conservation Corps in Glacier National Park, Montana* (Charleston, SC: America Through Time, 2022), pp. 71-78.
2 Butler, D. R., *Pioneering Women of Glacier National Park* (Charleston, SC: America Through Time, 2023), pp. 52-53.
3 *Ibid.*
4 Fraley, J., *Rangers, Trappers, and Trailblazers—Early Adventures in Montana's Bob Marshall Wilderness and Glacier National Park* (Helena, MT: Farcountry Press, 2018), pp. 48-49
5 Fraley, J., *Wild River Pioneers—Adventures in the Middle Fork of the Flathead, Great Bear Wilderness and Glacier National Park* (Whitefish, MT: Big Mountain Publishing, 2008), p. 127.
6 Fraley, J., *A Woman's Way West—In and Around Glacier National Park from 1925 to 1990* (Whitefish, MT: Big Mountain Publishing, 1998), pp. 71-101.
7 Reece, M., "The First Native American Ranger," *Flathead Living* (Kalispell, MT: Flathead Beacon, 2016), various pages.
8 Butler, D. R.,2023, *op. cit.*, p. 54.
9 Reece, *op. cit.*, pages unnumbered.
10 Green, C., *Montana Memories Vol. IV* (Great Falls, MT: Blue Print and Letter Co., 1972), pp. 27-28.
11 Butler, 2023, *op. cit.*, p. 54.
12 *Ibid.*
13 Parratt, M.W., *Fate is a Mountain* (Whitefish, MT: Sun Point Press, 2009), p. 87.
14 Gildart, R. C., *Montana's Early-Day Rangers* (Helena, MT: Montana Magazine, Inc., 1985), p. 49.

15 McClung, B., *Hooked for Good, Hooked for Life: The Passion for Fishing Belly River* (Kalispell, MT: Life Preservers, 1998b), p. 128.
16 DeSanto, J., "The Legendary Joe Cosley," in Stanley, D. (ed.), *The Glacier Park Reader* (Salt Lake City, UT: University of Utah Press, 2017), pp. 150-151.
17 *Ibid.*
18 Gildart, *op. cit.*, pp. 48-49.
19 Djuff, R., and Morrison, C., *Waterton and Glacier in a Snap! Fast Facts & Titillating Trivia* (Surrey, BC: Rocky Mountain Books, 2005), p. 41.
20 Guthrie, C. W., Fagre, D., and Fagre, A., *Death & Survival in Glacier National Park—True Tales of Tragedy, Courage, & Misadventure* (Helena, MT: Farcountry Press, 2017), pp. 221-222.
21 *Ibid.*
22 Geoghegan, H., *Historic Structure Report: Old St. Mary Ranger District* (West Glacier, MT: Glacier National Park, 1978), p. 34.
23 Fraley, 2008, *op. cit.*, p. 125.

Chapter 5

1 Gildart, R. C., *Montana's Early-Day Rangers* (Helena, MT: Montana Magazine, Inc., 1985), pp. 77-78.
2 Historical Research Associates, *National Register of Historic Places Nomination, East Glacier Ranger Station Historic District, Residence/Office* (Missoula, MT: Historical Research Associates, 1984a), various pages.
3 Butler, D. R., *The Civilian Conservation Corps in Glacier National Park, Montana* (Charleston, SC: America Through Time, 2022), p. 105.
4 Historical Research Associates, *National Register of Historic Places Nomination, St. Mary Ranger Station* (Missoula, MT: Historical Research Associates, 1984b), various pages.
5 Glacier National Park, *Dedication of the Old St. Mary Ranger Station* (West Glacier, MT: Glacier National Park, 1976), 4 pp.
6 Historical Research Associates, *National Register of Historic Places Nomination, Sherburne Ranger Station Historic District* (Missoula, MT: Historical Research Associates, 1984c), various pages.
7 Historical Research Associates, *National Register of Historic Places Nomination, Swiftcurrent Ranger Station Historic District* (Missoula, MT: Historical Research Associates, 1984d), various pages.
8 Historical Research Associates, *National Register of Historic Places Nomination, Belly River Ranger Station* (Missoula, MT: Historical Research Associates, 1984a), various pages.
9 Historical Research Associates, *National Register of Historic Places Nomination, Kishenehn Ranger Station Cabin* (Missoula, MT: Historical Research Associates, 1984a), various pages.
10 Historical Research Associates, *National Register of Historic Places Nomination, Kintla Lake Ranger Station* (Missoula, MT: Historical Research Associates, 1984x), various pages.
11 *Ibid.*
12 Historical Research Associates, *National Register of Historic Places Nomination, Skyland Camp/Bowman Lake Ranger Station* (Missoula, MT: Historical Research Associates, 1984x), various pages.

Endnotes

13 Historical Research Associates, *National Register of Historic Places Nomination, Polebridge Ranger Station Historic District* (Missoula, MT: Historical Research Associates, 1984x), various pages.
14 Walker, L. E., *History of the Polebridge Mercantile* (Polebridge, MT: L. E. Walker, self-published, 2023), various pages.
15 National Park Service, *A "New" First Permanent Woman Ranger* (Washington, DC: National Park Service, 2022), online pages at www.nps.gov/articles/000/a-new-first-permanent-woman-ranger.htm.
16 Historical Research Associates, *National Register of Historic Places Nomination, Logging Creek Ranger Station Historic District* (Missoula, MT: Historical Research Associates, 1984x), various pages.
17 Historical Research Associates, *National Register of Historic Places Nomination, Upper Lake McDonald Ranger Station Historic District* (Missoula, MT: Historical Research Associates, 1984x), various pages.
18 Peterson, C., "Howe Sadness: As Cabins Lost, Inholders Frustrated by Response to Fire," *Hungry Horse News* (Columbia Falls, MT: Hungry Horse News, August 14, 2018), online version, unpaginated.
19 Fraley, J., *Wild River Pioneers—Adventures in the Middle Fork of the Flathead, Great Bear Wilderness and Glacier National Park* (Whitefish, MT: Big Mountain Publishing, 2008), pp. 124-125.
20 Historical Research Associates, *National Register of Historic Places Nomination, Nyack Ranger Station* (Missoula, MT: Historical Research Associates, 1984x), various pages.
21 Fraley, J., *Rangers, Trappers, and Trailblazers—Early Adventures in Montana's Bob Marshall Wilderness and Glacier National Park* (Helena, MT: Farcountry Press, 2018), pp. 55-56.
22 Historical Research Associates, *National Register of Historic Places Nomination, Walton Ranger Station* (Missoula, MT: Historical Research Associates, 1984x), various pages.
23 Rocky Mountain Regional Office National Park Service, *Lubec Ranger Station* (Denver, CO: National Park Service, 1982), 7 pp.

Chapter 6

1 Glacier National Park, *National Register of Historic Places Registration Form, Sun Camp Fireguard Cabin* (West Glacier, MT: Glacier National Park, 1998), various pages.
2 Historical Research Associates, *National Register of Historic Places Nomination, Slide Lake (Otatso Creek) Patrol Cabin* (Missoula, MT: Historical Research Associates, 1984x), various pages.
3 Glacier National Park, *National Register of Historic Places Registration Form, Lee Creek Snowshoe Cabin* (West Glacier, MT: Glacier National Park, 2000), various pages.
4 Historical Research Associates, *National Register of Historic Places Nomination, Pass Creek Snowshoe Cabin* (Missoula, MT: Historical Research Associates, 1984x), various pages.
5 Glacier National Park, *National Register of Historic Places Registration Form, Kootenai Creek Snowshoe Cabin* (West Glacier, MT: Glacier National Park, 1999b), various pages.
6 Glacier National Park, *National Register of Historic Places Registration Form, Cattle Queen Snowshoe Cabin* (West Glacier, MT: Glacier National Park, 1999a), various pages.
7 Historical Research Associates, *National Register of Historic Places Nomination, Upper Kintla Lake Patrol Cabin* (Missoula, MT: Historical Research Associates, 1984x), various pages.

8   Historical Research Associates, *National Register of Historic Places Nomination, Ford Creek Patrol Cabin* (Missoula, MT: Historical Research Associates, 1984x), various pages.

9   Glacier National Park, *North Fork Fires in Glacier National Park Still Under Investigation* (West Glacier, MT: Glacier National Park, July 28, 2020), 1 p.

10   Historical Research Associates, *National Register of Historic Places Nomination, Bowman Lake Patrol Cabin* (Missoula, MT: Historical Research Associates, 1984x), various pages.

11   Historical Research Associates, *National Register of Historic Places Nomination, Quartz Lake Patrol Cabin* (Missoula, MT: Historical Research Associates, 1984x), various pages.

12   Historical Research Associates, *National Register of Historic Places Nomination, Upper Logging Lake Snowshoe Cabin* (Missoula, MT: Historical Research Associates, 1984x), various pages.

13   Historical Research Associates, *National Register of Historic Places Nomination, Lower Logging Lake Snowshoe Cabin* (Missoula, MT: Historical Research Associates, 1984x), various pages.

14   Glacier National Park Volunteer Associates, *2019 Removal of Camas Creek Cabin* (Kalispell, MT: Glacier National Park Volunteer Associates, 2019), online pages at gnpva.org/News/tabid/7132/ID/2079/2019-Removal-of-Camas-Creek-Cabin.aspx#.

15   Historical Research Associates, *National Register of Historic Places Nomination, Logan Creek Patrol Cabin* (Missoula, MT: Historical Research Associates, 1984x), various pages.

16   Historical Research Associates, *National Register of Historic Places Nomination, Lincoln Creek Patrol Cabin* (Missoula, MT: Historical Research Associates, 1984x), various pages.

17   Glacier National Park, *National Register of Historic Places Registration Form, Harrison Lake Snowshoe Cabin* (West Glacier, MT: Glacier National Park, 2000), various pages.

18   Historical Research Associates, *National Register of Historic Places Nomination, Lower Nyack Snowshoe Cabin* (Missoula, MT: Historical Research Associates, 1984x), various pages.

19   Historical Research Associates, *National Register of Historic Places Nomination, Upper Nyack Snowshoe Cabin* (Missoula, MT: Historical Research Associates, 1984x), various pages.

20   Historical Research Associates, *National Register of Historic Places Nomination, Lower Park Creek Snowshoe Cabin* (Missoula, MT: Historical Research Associates, 1984x), various pages.

21   Historical Research Associates, *National Register of Historic Places Nomination, Upper Park Creek Snowshoe Cabin* (Missoula, MT: Historical Research Associates, 1984x), various pages.

22   Historical Research Associates, *National Register of Historic Places Nomination, Fielding Snowshoe Patrol Cabin* (Missoula, MT: Historical Research Associates, 1984x), various pages.

Bibliography

Buchanan, H. W., "Masters of the Trail," *Nature Notes from Glacier National Park*, Vol. 3, No. 7 (West Glacier, MT: Glacier National Park, 1930)

Butler, D. R., *The Civilian Conservation Corps in Glacier National Park, Montana* (Charleston, SC: America Through Time, 2022)

Butler, D. R., *Pioneering Women of Glacier National Park* (Charleston, SC: America Through Time, 2023)

Cosley, J., *The Meeting of Kootenai Brown* (publisher location and publisher unattributed, undated pamphlet)

DeSanto, J., "The Legendary Joe Cosley," in Stanley, D. (ed.), *The Glacier Park Reader* (Salt Lake City, UT: University of Utah Press, 2017).

Dillon, T., *Over the Trails of Glacier National Park* (St. Paul, MN: Great Northern Railway, 1911)

Djuff, R., and Morrison, C., *Waterton and Glacier in a Snap! Fast Facts & Titillating Trivia* (Surrey, BC: Rocky Mountain Books, 2005)

Fauley, C. C., "An Elk Fatality," *Nature Notes from Glacier National Park*, Vol. 3, No. 1 (West Glacier, MT: Glacier National Park, 1930)

Fauley, C., "An Encounter with an Elk," *Glacial Drift—Notes from Glacier National Park*, Vol. 4, No. 11 (West Glacier, MT: Glacier National Park, 1931)

Fraley, J., *A Woman's Way West—In and Around Glacier National Park from 1925 to 1990* (Whitefish, MT: Big Mountain Publishing, 1998)

Fraley, J., *Wild River Pioneers—Adventures in the Middle Fork of the Flathead, Great Bear Wilderness and Glacier National Park* (Whitefish, MT: Big Mountain Publishing, 2008)

Fraley, J., *Rangers, Trappers, and Trailblazers—Early Adventures in Montana's Bob Marshall Wilderness and Glacier National Park* (Helena, MT: Farcountry Press, 2018)

Geoghegan, H., *Historic Structure Report: Old St. Mary Ranger District* (West Glacier, MT: Glacier National Park, 1978)

Gildart, R. C., *Montana's Early-Day Rangers* (Helena, MT: Montana Magazine, Inc., 1985)

Glacier National Park, *Dedication of the Old St. Mary Ranger Station* (West Glacier, MT: Glacier National Park, 1976)

Glacier National Park, *National Register of Historic Places Registration Form, Cattle Queen Snowshoe Cabin* (West Glacier, MT: Glacier National Park, 1999a)

Glacier National Park, *National Register of Historic Places Registration Form, Kootenai Creek Snowshoe Cabin* (West Glacier, MT: Glacier National Park, 1999b)

Glacier National Park, *National Register of Historic Places Registration Form, Sun Camp Fireguard Cabin* (West Glacier, MT: Glacier National Park, 1998a)

Glacier National Park, *National Register of Historic Places Registration Form, Lee Creek Snowshoe Cabin* (West Glacier, MT: Glacier National Park, 2000)

Glacier National Park, *National Register of Historic Places Registration Form, Sun Camp Fireguard Cabin* (West Glacier, MT: Glacier National Park, 1998b)

Glacier National Park, *North Fork Fires in Glacier National Park Still Under Investigation* (West Glacier, MT: Glacier National Park, July 28, 2020)

Glacier National Park Volunteer Associates, *2019 Removal of Camas Creek Cabin* (Kalispell, MT: Glacier National Park Volunteer Associates, 2019)

Green, C., *Montana Memories Vol. IV* (Great Falls, MT: Blue Print and Letter Co., 1972)

Guthrie, C. W., *The First Ranger—Adventures of a Pioneer Forest Ranger, Glacier Country 1902–1910* (Huson, MT: Redwing Publishing, 1995)

Guthrie, C. W., *First Rangers—The Life and Times of Frank Liebig and Fred Herrig, Glacier Country 1902–1910* (Helena, MT: Farcountry Press, 2019)

Guthrie, C. W., Fagre, D., and Fagre, A., *Death & Survival in Glacier National Park—True Tales of Tragedy, Courage, & Misadventure* (Helena, MT: Farcountry Press, 2017)

Hagen, J., "Ranger Tales—An Anthology of Park Service Stories," *The Inside Trail—Voice of the Glacier Park Foundation*, Vol. 31, No. 2 (Minneapolis, MN: Glacier Park Foundation, 2016)

Harrington, L., *History of Apgar* (Apgar, MT: Apgar School and Teacher, Mrs. Leona Harrington, 1950, updated through 1957)

Historical Research Associates, *National Register of Historic Places Nomination, Belly River Ranger Station* (Missoula, MT: Historical Research Associates, 1984a)

Historical Research Associates, *National Register of Historic Places Nomination, Bowman Lake Patrol Cabin* (Missoula, MT: Historical Research Associates, 1984b)

Historical Research Associates, *National Register of Historic Places Nomination, East Glacier Ranger Station Historic District, Residence/Office* (Missoula, MT: Historical Research Associates, 1984c)

Historical Research Associates, *National Register of Historic Places Nomination, Fielding Snowshoe Patrol Cabin* (Missoula, MT: Historical Research Associates, 1984d)

Historical Research Associates, *National Register of Historic Places Nomination, Ford Creek Patrol Cabin* (Missoula, MT: Historical Research Associates, 1984e)

Historical Research Associates, *National Register of Historic Places Nomination, Kintla Lake Ranger Station* (Missoula, MT: Historical Research Associates, 1984f)

Historical Research Associates, *National Register of Historic Places Nomination, Kishenehn Ranger Station Cabin* (Missoula, MT: Historical Research Associates, 1984g)

Historical Research Associates, *National Register of Historic Places Nomination, Lincoln Creek Patrol Cabin* (Missoula, MT: Historical Research Associates, 1984h)

Historical Research Associates, *National Register of Historic Places Nomination, Logan Creek Patrol Cabin* (Missoula, MT: Historical Research Associates, 1984i)

Historical Research Associates, *National Register of Historic Places Nomination, Logging Creek Ranger Station Historic District* (Missoula, MT: Historical Research Associates, 1984j)

Historical Research Associates, *National Register of Historic Places Nomination, Lower Logging Lake Snowshoe Cabin* (Missoula, MT: Historical Research Associates, 1984k)

Bibliography

Historical Research Associates, *National Register of Historic Places Nomination, Lower Nyack Snowshoe Cabin* (Missoula, MT: Historical Research Associates, 1984l)

Historical Research Associates, *National Register of Historic Places Nomination, Lower Park Creek Snowshoe Cabin* (Missoula, MT: Historical Research Associates, 1984m)

Historical Research Associates, *National Register of Historic Places Nomination, Nyack Ranger Station* (Missoula, MT: Historical Research Associates, 1984n)

Historical Research Associates, *National Register of Historic Places Nomination, Pass Creek Snowshoe Cabin* (Missoula, MT: Historical Research Associates, 1984o)

Historical Research Associates, *National Register of Historic Places Nomination, Polebridge Ranger Station Historic District* (Missoula, MT: Historical Research Associates, 1984p)

Historical Research Associates, *National Register of Historic Places Nomination, Quartz Lake Patrol Cabin* (Missoula, MT: Historical Research Associates, 1984q)

Historical Research Associates, *National Register of Historic Places Nomination, St. Mary Ranger Station* (Missoula, MT: Historical Research Associates, 1984r)

Historical Research Associates, *National Register of Historic Places Nomination, Sherburne Ranger Station Historic District* (Missoula, MT: Historical Research Associates, 1984s)

Historical Research Associates, *National Register of Historic Places Nomination, Skyland Camp/ Bowman Lake Ranger Station* (Missoula, MT: Historical Research Associates, 1984t)

Historical Research Associates, *National Register of Historic Places Nomination, Slide Lake (Otatso Creek) Patrol Cabin* (Missoula, MT: Historical Research Associates, 1984u)

Historical Research Associates, *National Register of Historic Places Nomination, Swiftcurrent Ranger Station Historic District* (Missoula, MT: Historical Research Associates, 1984v)

Historical Research Associates, *National Register of Historic Places Nomination, Upper Kintla Lake Patrol Cabin* (Missoula, MT: Historical Research Associates, 1984w)

Historical Research Associates, *National Register of Historic Places Nomination, Upper Lake McDonald Ranger Station Historic District* (Missoula, MT: Historical Research Associates, 1984x)

Historical Research Associates, *National Register of Historic Places Nomination, Upper Logging Lake Snowshoe Cabin* (Missoula, MT: Historical Research Associates, 1984y)

Historical Research Associates, *National Register of Historic Places Nomination, Upper Nyack Snowshoe Cabin* (Missoula, MT: Historical Research Associates, 1984z)

Historical Research Associates, *National Register of Historic Places Nomination, Walton Ranger Station* (Missoula, MT: Historical Research Associates, 1984aa)

Howell, C. T., "Charged by a Bull Elk," *Nature Notes from Glacier National Park*, Vol. 3, No. 3 (West Glacier, MT: Glacier National Park, 1930)

Hufstetler, M., "The Lonesome Life in Glacier National Park—Kishenehn Ranger Station, 1910–1940," *Montana, The Magazine of Western History*, Vol. 60, No. 4 (Helena, MT: Montana Historical Society, 2010)

Lee, L. (ed.), *Backcountry Ranger—The Diaries and Photographs of Norton Pearl in Glacier National Park 1910–1913* (Elk Rapids, MI: Fen's Rim Publications, 1994)

MacDonald, G. A., *Where the Mountains Meet the Prairies—A History of Waterton Country* (Calgary, Alberta: University of Calgary Press, 2000)

McClung, B., *Belly River's Famous Joe Cosley* (Kalispell, MT: Life Preservers, 1998a)

McClung, B., *Hooked for Good, Hooked for Life: The Passion for Fishing Belly River* (Kalispell, MT: Life Preservers, 1998b)

McKay, K. L., *Trails of the Past: Historical Overview of the Flathead National Forest, Montana, 1800–1960* (Kalispell, MT: U.S. Forest Service, 1994)

Miller, B. C., "Backwoods Sport," *Glacial Drift—Notes from Glacier National Park*, Vol. 5, No. 2 (West Glacier, MT: Glacier National Park, 1932a)

Miller, B. C., "The Destruction of the Pole Bridge," *Glacial Drift—Notes from Glacier National Park*, Vol. 5, No. 2 (West Glacier, MT: Glacier National Park, 1932b)

Miller, B. C., "Pugnacious Mother," *Glacial Drift—Notes from Glacier National Park*, Vol. 5, No. 6 (West Glacier, MT: Glacier National Park, 1932c)

Miller, B. C., "Buried in the Snow," *Glacial Drift—Notes from Glacier National Park*, Vol. 6, No. 2 (West Glacier, MT: Glacier National Park, 1933)

Minetor, R., *Historic Glacier National Park—The Stories Behind one of America's Great Treasures* (Guilford, CT: Rowan and Littlefield, 2016)

Moravek, V., *It Happened in Glacier National Park* (Guilford, CT: The Globe Pequot Press, 2005)

National Park Service, *A "New" First Permanent Woman Ranger* (Washington, DC: National Park Service, 2022)

Ober, M., "The Diary of Norton Pearl," *Montana Outlaw*, Winter Issue (Big Sky, MT: Mountain Outlaw, 2024)

Parratt, M. W., *Fate is a Mountain* (Whitefish, MT: Sun Point Press, 2009)

Peterson, C., "Howe Sadness: As Cabins Lost, Inholders Frustrated by Response to Fire," *Hungry Horse News* (Columbia Falls, MT: Hungry Horse News, August 14, 2018)

Reece, M., "The First Native American Ranger," *Flathead Living* (Kalispell, MT: Flathead Beacon, 2016)

Rocky Mountain Regional Office National Park Service, *Lubec Ranger Station* (Denver, CO: National Park Service, 1982)

Rodney, W., *Kootenai Brown, His Life and Times 1839–1916* (Sidney, BC: Gray's Publishing Ltd., 1969)

Ruhle, G. C., "Grim Duty," *Glacial Drift—Notes from Glacier National Park*, Vol. 7, No. 1 (West Glacier, MT: Glacier National Park, 1934)

Walker, L. E., *History of the Polebridge Mercantile* (Polebridge, MT: L. E. Walker, self-published, 2023)

Workman, R. B., *National Park Service Uniforms—In Search of an Identity 1872–1920* (Harpers Ferry, WV: National Park Service Office of Library, Archives and Graphic Research, No. 2, 1994)